AF505983

Roy Martin

For Marvie Patterson —
with my thanks
for your insightful
questions.
All good wishes,
Roy Martin
3/12/98 Salem, VA

TRYON PUBLISHING COMPANY, INC.
CHAPEL HILL

Pen & ink illustrations by
Julie Barham

Copyright © 1997 Roy Martin
All rights reserved. No part of this book may be reproduced
in any form or by any electronic, mechanical or other means,
except for brief quotes for reviews, without express written
permission from the publisher.

Printed in the United States of America
Published by
Tryon Publishing Company, Inc.
P.O. Box 1138
Chapel Hill, North Carolina

Jacket Design by Julia Calhoun Williams & Wallace Kuralt
Book Design by Julia Calhoun Williams

ISBN 1-884824-10-2

DEDICATION

For my wife, Sylvia

For my friends, Ovid Williams Pierce and Geoffrey Chapman

To the memories of my parents, Lillian and Roy.

Whisper
My
Name

PART I

Chapter 1

Across the gray, swiftly running river, a few crows complained from a large, vine-entangled oak. Chattering women, men, and some children walked where they pleased, pulled at the police tape, peered over at the men in the hole, and drifted away as if it didn't matter that a skeleton had been found not three feet from the War Memorial Fountain.

A serious young man in pressed blue, a large pistol belted to his waist, motioned with hands and head to make the crowd understand they shouldn't come too close.

"Move along," he said in exaggerated gruffness, his voice even and automatic like a rehearsing radio announcer, testing his microphone.

Nobody listened.

An aluminum boat carrying two men—one at the outboard motor and the other near the front with a TV news camera in hand — plied up and down before the breakwater.

Grace Lynn Rose, pretty, young, and Ransom's only female newspaper reporter, gave the scene a final glance, pushed a notebook into her purse and headed on up the street toward *The Telegraph*'s car. One detective whistled low and used his hands to describe her form in tight-fitting jeans and sweater. Police Chief Toby Pugh frowned. The detective winked and walked toward the street.

Chief Pugh, who had arrived with siren blasting, stood inside the tape and sweated in the midday sun of early September.

"How much you got intact?"

"Still digging." The voice from the hole sounded distant, muffled and impatient.

"Hurry up, Mr. Rule. We got people milling around here, state investigators on the way, the FBI calling and the Mayor coming back from Raleigh."

"Chief, you can't dig up something in half a day that's been buried a million years."

Toby Pugh stepped to the ragged edge of the hole. He touched one cheek with a white handkerchief and bent over. His eyes quickly worked the mostly square pattern of the digging, then settled on the man who had spoken.

"Prehistoric Indian, you say?"

"Of course. Down here a long time."

The courthouse chime sounded one o'clock. Chief Pugh, in tan suit and white shirt, maroon tie knotted tightly, straightened and turned to watch the crowd move away, back to their work in the courthouse, post office and law offices. Some dropped balled-up lunch bags and aluminum pop cans in green trash barrels with Town of Ransom seals.

I watched and listened a few minutes longer. Toby Pugh wanted to know about the broken water line to the fountain. The man in the hole, a retired junior high school science teacher, said they'd have to reroute the pipe because they couldn't chance damaging the specimen. Then he got Toby to agree to call the funeral home for a tent to cover the hole and to assign a police guard while he worked.

"How do you know it's an Indian?"

The man in the hole laughed. "Good teeth."

Toby blinked and looked around as if he couldn't believe what he'd heard.   "Evidence, Mr. Rule.   Found any beads or arrowheads?"

Silence.   A little dirt flew from the hole.

I walked closer to the tape. Toby Pugh noticed me and nodded. "Ever see Indian bones, Mr. Frost? You've been around Ransom a long time. Step over here."

He motioned me forward. A second later I stood looking down at white-haired, wild-eyed Anson Rule, a town workman I recognized, and next to him, a partially uncovered skeleton. I saw part of a bony hand, a dark, clay-caked eye socket, half a forehead and two rows of well-preserved teeth.

"It's grinning, Mr. Frost.   Do you think that's an Indian? What Indians lived around here, Mr. Frost?"

"Tuscarora," I said, looking at Anson Rule, expecting disagreement and remembering the archaeological nonsense I got the last time he spoke of his new hobby and pestered me about digging for Indians on my farm near the river narrows.

But Anson Rule didn't acknowledge me. He kept digging, picking at the dirt with a trowel and clearing bones with a small paint brush. The workman squatted on the other side of the hole, listening and watching the movement of trowel and brush.

"Good thing I walked by here after breakfast." Rule looked up at me and then back to the skeleton. "I heard this man yelling he'd found something.   This is a real discovery. I ran all the way home to get my tools."

I pulled my straw hat down over my eyes to escape the sun, and moved away from the hole and back to the other side of the tape. Chief Pugh kept looking down.

"Coroner's coming," I heard him say.

Old Anson got excited and insistent: "Don't you let him in this hole unless I say so." he shouted, pointing at Toby Pugh with the trowel. "This is rare, rare and significant.   Very significant."

"Sure, sure," the chief muttered, pulling at his tie.

I headed for my car, wondering if I should have mentioned the gold, front tooth filling on Anson Rule's prehistoric Indian.

Finally, somebody had found Bobby Crawford. Even the coroner's and Army's identification reports issued two weeks later, gushed about his tell-tale, immortal teeth. All seemed enthralled, affected much the same way Kennedy teeth excited politics, sending Republicans to dentists and driving voting-age women pink-cheeked to the polls.

There's magnetism in teeth, they say. But just seeing so much smiling on television that fall made me vote for Mr. Nixon. Smiling doesn't mean substance and that's what I tried to tell Augusta that night in front of her house in the Spring of 1951.

Of course, she wouldn't listen. She refused to focus on me, speaking as though I had no feelings or tangible presence. "Wiley, exactly where is Korea? Can you imagine our boys having to trudge up and down those bleak hills? How frightened they must be!"

How little that mattered to me! I tried to say that life and breath had narrowed to us—two struggling souls, absorbed in loving each other and undisturbed except for the crackle of wind-stirred magnolia leaves in the old tree next to the porch.

But Augusta's voice cut me off.

"Don't grieve so," she said, her face nearly invisible in the darkness. "It doesn't matter. I'm not worth your grief. Really, I'm not."

On the sidewalk, I toed the bottom wooden step and looked up at her, a form on the porch. "Mourning," I said, trying to sound intelligent and keep my voice from cracking.

She came back quickly: "Maybe it's the war. Maybe we all have too much mourning in us. So many pictures in the paper. So many people dying."

How kind. How noble. After more than forty years, I still wonder about that instant—about where her mind had gone. Could it have been flitting through the shrubbery, nervously pitching, branch to branch, like some witless bird? And where had my mind gone?   How could I not care about people dying?

"I don't think it's the war," I said, my voice restraining impatience.   I wanted to shout, to awaken her, to make her remember that I had just held her and softly kissed her, felt her tremble and heard her whispers at my ear.   Where had those feelings gone?

Then we talked about Bobby Crawford.   Our words droned on, tones rising and falling.   Painful conversation pushed his smile into my mind like a flickering, alien intrusion.   His grin even settled into the glow of the porch light, the scuffed, gray planks of the porch, and I wondered if God branded his teeth into the dangling, pale quarter-moon above us.

No. But it seemed so.

"I'm his wife," Augusta said, her tone cold.   "He'll be here tomorrow and welcomed like the hero he is.   I don't know what happened to me. I let myself go. Forget about tonight. Forget about me."

I put one foot on the last step.

"No," she said.   "Go home now." It sounded like scolding.

"I don't want to go home," I whispered, wondering if I should try to take her hand.   Perhaps then she would change back to my Augusta, the girl who wasn't Bobby Crawford's wife.

"It's late now," she said.   "I have the parade tomorrow."

Perhaps I should have left then—to argue Truman-MacArthur politics in the den with my father.   But I couldn't.

"You don't have to do anything," I said, a tremble in my voice. How could I save the moment? "Come with me now. You won't have to go to the parade.   You won't have to be his wife."

"Too late." Her words hung in the night air and I imagined myself as one who had just seen the glimmer of the headsman's blade.

"We'll leave Ransom," I said.

"I have to be with him tomorrow."   After she spoke, she lifted her head as if she had shifted her eyes beyond me—to the nothingness of the dark mass of the Franklin house beyond the far curb.

Then my tears: "I love you."

"Bobby loves me," she said, unmoved.

"Not like me."

Silence.

Suddenly, rage snatched at me. My voice spilled like involuntary, bitter overflow from a churning stomach.

"You think he's going to stay home? He left you stranded at Virginia Beach. Got back to Ransom and hid from you. Showed up at the train. Remember how he marched up Richmond Street with the rest of the Guard, got on the train and left for the war? Never said goodbye, did he?"

Shrill?

"Augusta, I saw you standing alone on the platform, waving. Why did you even go?"

More silence.

"He's different now," she insisted, her voice quick and breathless, wavering in and out of falsetto. Little girl voice, little girl mind. "He wrote to me—about the mud and the cold and the death all around him. Don't you think men who see death so closely can have new awakenings?"

Sweet Jehovah. I'd embalmed bodies with more new thought than Bobby Crawford. His awakenings likely occurred in scented Tokyo whorehouses, not the heroic grime of foxholes caught in the glow and rumble of shellfire.

I backed away a couple of steps but kept my eyes on her. Her long hair rippled in a breeze that began as an easy, cool current and spread about me like an enclosing cloud.

"I don't want you to sleep with him," I said suddenly.

In a quick vision, I saw hands, Bobby Crawford's hands, reaching for Augusta.

She looked toward the edge of the porch. I glanced that way and back at her. Had she heard something? Did it matter?

"I can't live like a thief," she said. "I'm not going to sneak about and jump at every sound and be afraid of eyes, speculations, and opinions." I heard an edge on the last sentence. Did I hear it or hope it? Anger? For Bobby Crawford?"

Of course not. I couldn't have been that lucky.

"I'm not asking that," I said. "I want you to leave with me."

She folded her arms. I could have held her and kept her from being cold. "I'd rather be Bobby Crawford's wife than worry about what people say." She took a breath. "My parents are dead and I've no brothers and sisters. I do have a decent reputation, this house and a few friends. Unfortunately, I also have all of Ransom wanting a daily report on me and their hero, Bobby Crawford. What's he doing today? Can she cook squash like his mother?"

I interjected: "When is he going to run away again?" But she didn't want my opinion.

"I understand how you must feel," she said, softer. "But in the state I'm in and the situation I'm in, I'd be wasting your time. We can be friends."

How nice.

"I've been your lover."

"I made a mistake."

Nothing more? "Then being in your bed meant nothing? Why did you do it? You felt something. People have to feel something, don't they?"

"I don't know," she said.

I turned toward the street, walked a way then stopped and looked back. She stood by the door, her face partially illuminated by the hall light. Shadow-figure. Grown-up games.

"Go home," she said.

I wanted to die.

"Find a girl," she said.

"He's good at finding girls," I said, my voice sarcastic and totally without warmth. "Why can't he find a girl?

She should have slammed the door. Then it would have ended quickly—like a shot through the brain. But she answered me when she quietly closed the door, turned off the light, and left me in the dark.

Chapter 2

The speculation about Augusta Morefield Crawford has neither died nor left the minds of the townsfolk. Most of the people who saw the parade that next day talk about it and probably remember it as I do—in moving gray and fragmentary frames. Flags lined old Richmond Street and the high school band, with majorettes prancing and horns blaring, turned heads and drowned out conversations. Small children struggled to the shoulders of anyone taller for a look at Sergeant Crawford, in khaki uniform, blond and waving from the open back of a white Buick convertible.

"I see him. Can you see him?" I remember the small, excited voices and Bobby Crawford's wife beside him, smiling and waving.

Time has dulled much of the pain of that day and Augusta and I—in our separate ways—have held on to pieces of life and memory. People discuss her as the mysterious recluse, "Miss Augusta," and I am the old and strange "Mr. Wiley" Frost. She lives alone in her father's house on Pickett Street. I sold my funeral home and automobile businesses to look after farms, wait for Social Security checks, watch liver spots spread on my hands, often preoccupied with white and thinning hair and the pain of poor teeth.

No one cares about that.

The people of Ransom, North Carolina hurry about, working and laughing and breathing and dying and living high, if they can find a way.   Most are too young to remember the days of Augusta and Bobby Crawford, but have heard the stories.   Finding the skeleton naturally generated questions for older people like me.

Certainly, I provided no answers, remaining content to be the tight-lipped old man who drives too slowly to breakfast on the boulevard every morning.   Indeed, my routine at the Sheraton has given me "character" status.   Babbling young waitresses pretend to mother me and quickly remedy complaints of dust on silverware and spots on glasses.   Sometimes, they snicker because I give the same order each day: Bran cereal, sausage and gravy, grits, two scrambled eggs, one biscuit with margarine and grape jelly.   I also read two newspapers at the table and leave large tips.

But I don't answer questions about Augusta and Bobby.

Pattern, of course.   But I have long been behaving deliberately.   At 64, I keep all senses attuned to the slightest or newest pain.   Twinges make me suspicious, even paranoid.   Frequently, I have found my hand at my chest, pressing for the regularity of heartbeat, worrying and wondering when the thumping, in whatever final cadence, will end.

Living has been, at best, tedious and exacting.   I can't forget the lieutenant at the Ransom Armory who smiled at me in the summer of 1950, amused that even with a heart murmur I wanted to enlist in the National Guard.   Young and fit and full of spirit, he laughed at me.

"You can't qualify, Frost," he said, pushing papers on his desk. "Hell, Frost, we got to kill gooks and you'd probably fall out and die before you ever got close enough to shoot one."

The Guard took Bobby Crawford.   I stayed home.

But remember: Wiley Frost, the one with the sputtering, shifting heart, remains.   Alive.   Adrian Tyndall enlisted that year and died of cancer in the Veterans Hospital in Durham.   Petey Clark never made it to the ships on the West Coast; he got sent home with paralysis after a syphilis stroke and passed away within a year. Others got killed on Korean hilltops or in rice paddies and those who lost toes to frostbite came home limping as if they'd been shot in their feet.   They hobbled up and down Richmond Street until nobody paid attention.   Then they got jobs or shot pool all day and drank beer.   When they married they still got together and talked about the war and about Korean women and Japanese women and California women.

Proud veterans.   Most who came back joined the American Legion and the VFW and, with those who came to Ransom College after the war, remained ready to fight again or talk about the pain of distance, the girl or wife who didn't wait, or damp weather that made old wounds ache.   From time to time, they drifted together—in the veterans hut at the college, at the bridge tables in the student union, on the athletic fields or in the Syrian's restaurant on Richmond Street.   They argued about MacArthur, not using the A-bomb or how they should have carried their attack into China.

Most of them—from Ransom and Raleigh, New Bern and Greensboro, Kinston, Creswell and Manteo—became Democrats like nearly everybody else and griped about Truman, communists in the Washington government, and how we should have dealt with the Red menace in 1945.   Some just wore their uniforms to July 4th celebrations, clapped at the fireworks, danced to the country bands and became Republicans.

But not Bobby Crawford.

The truth is Bobby Crawford had been missing since the parade.   But you would think from the way many people talked that he lived all that time right in Ransom—and still drove his red rocket Oldsmobile on Richmond Street and snapped orders during the weekend Guard drills.

He stayed everybody's hero and the mystery endured: Where did he go?   Did he become a mercenary in Africa?   Join the CIA?   Run guns in Northern Ireland?

But the real sadness of it all has been Augusta.   She remained Bobby Crawford's wife and stayed in her house, waiting for him to come home.

Why?

Some say she's a natural-born recluse, one who felt better withdrawing, hoping sturdy walls could hold back the hurt that flows from living too close to people. Others believe she's simply embarrassed, that a man like Bobby Crawford, winner of the Silver Star, vanished when he could have easily gone on to become a general or a congressman.

Theories, however, don't amount to much. For years, I thought I could break through, but stopped because she wouldn't answer the door and had no telephone. All I do now is pass her house every day for any reason I can offer myself and hope to see her only in distant, accidental glimpses.

Curiously, she has always seemed a calculated step ahead of me some mornings, standing at the front window, looking out at the yard and the street. When I've caught sight of Augusta—if I've been early enough—I've seen her, well-groomed and nicely dressed.

But when I slowed the car and waved, she dropped the curtain and pulled the shade, acting more like I'd left her, not Bobby Crawford. Always alone. Wrapped in silence. As far as I know, she's never had a television and doesn't take a newspaper.

As for visitors, Augusta Crawford has only opened the door for the Reverend Philip I. Rayner of Pettigrew Memorial. Their meetings lasted hours, and since Augusta hasn't been to church since the fifties, I always thought Mr. Rayner took the message to her—as he would the sick or homebound.

Sometimes, I have followed his old blue Plymouth and eased by in time to catch the door opening and a sight of her. In the evenings, I have driven by just after dinner, watching for signs: A form at a window, a shadow? I convinced myself that was the equivalent of seeing her.

On a good, dry morning, the Reverend Mr. Rayner arrived about 10:15. They might stand at the door for a minute, then go inside. When he left, Augusta watched only briefly as he stepped down the root-cracked cement walk to his car. Even on clear days, he brought his umbrella. He always called to her to secure her doors.

What did they talk about?

I don't know. God?

Money?

Bobby Crawford?

Over the years, I've been amused at Philip Rayner's big-footed, dainty lope and envious of his place with Augusta and the quick smiles she gave his animated arrivals and departures. Often, I've wondered what they've said about Bobby or poor, dead Blithe Tanner. But mostly, for the brief time I've had to glance at them and still manage the car, I've looked to Augusta's face. If I focused quickly, I could see lines and creases and short, curled, sand-brown hair. All things considered, she ought to be white-headed, like me.

Avery's Food Store delivers to her back porch once a week. She waits until the truck has left to take the bags inside. Larry Gross, the real estate broker, handles yard work and repairs to the house. Sometimes, people say, Augusta comes to a window and watches the mowing and trimming. I've heard when children stray close to the house—after a ball or a kitten, perhaps—she peeks at the edge of curtains, raps on the window and motions toward the front or back gates.

At the library, I've heard some of the children who have seen her question their mothers about why "Miss Augusta" stays in the house. "Why doesn't she sit on her front porch on nice evenings?" one tiny girl asked.

I 've wondered, too, child.

Some afternoons, I've read out-of-town newspapers at the library and discovered children looking at me and touching their mothers' hands. Perhaps they had noticed me driving on Pickett Street, trying to behave like anything other than an evil old cruiser with a penchant for odd, older women, who live alone in big houses.

I have missed her. Time and hard work have not removed the ache. My mind continues to return to those long ago days—to the joy and feel of Augusta, the crush and pain of Bobby Crawford's homecoming and the door that closed at the house on Pickett Street. Even now, I feel the terrible weight of loss and often my mind wanders through those hard days, trying to measure the pain of one day against another.

Often, I have felt guilt—that I should have had the sense to withdraw long before we found our way to her bed. Perhaps then I might have spared her whatever shame or regret she might still feel.

Perhaps, too, I might have spared myself the pain of this telling.

But I could not. That last night, control never mattered until we stood outside in the dark with Augusta telling me what my heart has never accepted. In the long days and nights since, I have found no fault, believing strongly that we guided each other into a blameless, sweet accord that sought nothing but the blending of two souls.

Why did Bobby Crawford come home that Spring in 1951? I have often wished he had died in some forgotten, faraway field or become the anonymous victim in a street fight in San Francisco or Oakland—anywhere far from Ransom. If that had happened, there would have been no skeleton on the common, no revival of old stories—or pesky people across the street from Augusta's house, laughing and wagering on which window she might pass next.

At night, waiting for sleep, I have seen the faces: Augusta, Bobby, young Blithe. I've prayed for all of them.

And me.

Chapter 3

If I'd been handed an unfinished script before that night at the pavilion, I surely would have completed story and characters without including Bobby Crawford.

The crowd overflowed into the parking lot. Townspeople mixed with farm hands and paving crews and nearly all the men had whisky in paper cups or held beer bottles. River water sloshed against pilings in regular rhythm and the air felt heavy and the skin sticky. Dancing too close meant prying yourself loose from a girl's cheek and suddenly finding yourself alone when she scurried to the rest room to repair makeup.

Everyone talked about the heat.

Some of the women held cardboard church fans and stood grim-faced, enduring and fanning as if waiting for William Jennings Bryan to appear and shout again against the monkey theory. During pauses in the music, the few who danced to fast numbers circulated the floor, going from one knot of people to another, patting cheeks with Kleenex or pulling dampened shirts or blouses away from damp skin. Pleasantly, they complained about being overheated as if they had just won a jitterbug contest.

Not me. I leaned against the railing next to the exit, not far from Augusta, who talked with a girl she'd known at Woman's

College and two boys from Davidson passing through on their way to the beach. Occasionally, Augusta turned to me and smiled. Then she looked back to her friends. But her eyes soon trailed away—roaming the pavilion, scanning the faces of people sitting on the railings, standing by the jukebox or dancing.

Right there, I hoped Bobby Crawford had gone to his car to commune with more beer and some pagan darling from downriver who only knew what she'd heard about him and wanted to confirm (never deny) the rumors.

On nights like that, Bobby played to his audience. After finishing with a girl, he found one of the pavilion's darker, less crowded corners and pretended to brood. Could he be in love? What happened in the car? Did everyone want to know? Sure.

As if cued, his admirers drifted over to offer companionship or consolation or encouragement and soon he had a group of men and boys around him and he would transform (when the gathering grew large enough) into a spirited story teller. Some listeners snickered or clapped when Bobby pretended to squeal like the girl he had in the car. "She went crazy," he'd say, twirling a pair of white panties he'd taken from his pocket. "When I yanked them off, she lost her mind."

For a moment, silence. Then they all laughed again and or coughed. Others wiped their faces with hands or handkerchiefs.

If he felt especially inspired, he'd describe the action with hand motions and body language. He'd start with one hand before his chest at an angle and move it downward in a sliding motion. That meant he had no trouble going down the girl's blouse. The quick snap of his fingers signaled loosening buttons and the slow, careful extension of his arms—imitating lifting a woman's wrap from her shoulders—told of easing the blouse to the seatback.

"Smooth." He'd stop talking and let his eyes walk the faces. His voice, by now, had drifted into a low purr.

At that point, he'd start up again, put thumbs and forefingers of both hands together, make a twisting motion, grit his teeth and grunt several times, no doubt to dramatize degree of difficulty, to simulate unsnapping the brassiere.

The finale of extending his tongue and shaking his head—

looking and sounding like a mule at a trough—always delighted his audience. Had he indeed buried his head in the girl's breasts?

"I thought I'd smother," he said, delighted.

Curtain.

Usually, the last lines generated loud laughter, more clapping and much head-turning. All wanted to see the girl and silently speculate on their chances of miraculously losing breath the same way. Where could she be, this wild and erotic bare-bottomed night creature?

Gone. Any girl who left the pavilion with Bobby Crawford knew he'd talk, but that must have been part of the thrill: To be a point of heated discussion. In a week or so, one of Bobby's girls usually trickled back and got a rush from men who'd heard a story. If you watched carefully, you'd see her headed for the parking lot with somebody else. Then later, you might hear of the same girl pregnant, married or both. Most just vanished. Bobby wouldn't have touched the same one twice anyway.

The pavilion, music, people, the odors of beer and whiskey, perfume and Wildroot Cream Oil, clouds of cigarette smoke, the laughing and coughing, tires squalling in the parking lot and the curiosity about who had just left with whom amounted to real entertainment in Ransom in those days. Except for some of the traveling tobacco buyers and auctioneers, most people had never seen television. You could dance and drink beer or see Bogart on the corner at The Ransom Theater. Lash Larue, Hoppy, the Durango Kid and all the villains appeared across the street at The North Carolina.

Boring?

Never. Nobody knew any better.

Besides, something always happened. Nearly every Saturday night, somebody rolled a car and either lived to describe it or died broken in a cornfield. On mornings after, people gathered at my father's body shop lot to view wreckage and speculate on speed or how much they'd had to drink. Some even came to the back of our funeral home next door to ask if we'd counted the broken bones of the dead.

"Eighty-six," I'd say, poking fun with a serious face.

"How many bones a body got?"

"Near that many," I'd say.

"Honest?"

I never saw such wide eyes. Always, at that point, I'd shake my head and look to the floor and mumble that I needed help moving a body and they'd be gone, not even waiting to hear my pitch about the wonders of embalming fluid on facial tissue and our guarantees on leak-proof vaults.

Some Saturday nights decided entire lives. Women became widows, small fortunes moved from one heir to another, romances blossomed or died. Sometimes, people on the fringes got sucked in and if those boys from Davidson have lived to be old men, they haven't forgotten what happened that steamy night in Ransom. Certainly they don't realize that chance helped me lose Augusta.

Bobby Crawford's football game started it and that couldn't have surprised anybody in the Pavilion. That time of year, most thought—reasonable or otherwise—concentrated on the Ransom High Warriors. A mid-week walk through nearly any neighborhood offered sights of grandstand cushions and coats and sweaters airing on grass or hanging from clotheslines. The Warrior band practiced late, wheeling up and down the stadium field, trumpet players red-faced and blasting, woodwinds squeaking. Drummers pounded out sounds only a wild war party could have thought rhythmic.

On Friday game nights, frenzy traveled the air. Cars and trucks appeared on Richmond Street by seven, all headed impatiently to the stadium. Along the way, policemen stood by their cars, waving at people they liked; throwing hard glances at those they had greeted with citation books.

State Troopers, gray, crisp and authoritarian in campaign hats, stood near the stadium gate, signaling—flashlights in hand—arms snapping like Fort Bragg MPs. They watched the moving line, sensing perhaps that one breach in the parking process could mean a stampede of moving metal, all competing in a real-life bumper car arena.

By eight, the stadium had filled, the National Anthem had played and the screaming started. In a rush of color and arm-waving and pad-thumping, the teams ran on the field. Sometimes noise blessedly drowned out the band. Sometimes people from the stands rushed onto the field to protest a referee's call and got escorted back to the seats or out of the stadium. When a Warrior scored, young boys slapped each other's backs and danced on the seats or in the dust near the playing field. Men smashed at the air with their fists. Girls hugged each other and women closed their eyes.

"Thank you, Lord. One more, Lord."

When the other team scored, a cloud of muttered curses rose from the crowd and drifted ominously about the stadium until the next play began a new round of screaming.

If the Warriors won, the players ran off the field, waving helmets, and the faithful Ransom horde from the grandstands pushed toward the parking lot, eager for a spot in the race for the exit—so they'd be on time for celebrations.

But if the Warriors lost, pure surliness: People shoving people, people punching other people and policemen moving between cars to settle arguments.

The same kind of thing started the trouble at the pavilion that night. But why did Augusta stand and watch? Why didn't she let me take her home?

When anybody talks about that night now, it's because some older person, somebody who saw it, told them. No doubt the story's been embellished, exaggerated, forgotten and resurrected so many times, the truth doesn't matter. The essence of it has become a small town epic—with Bobby Crawford as hero—and it still appeals, no matter that the pavilion's gone for a rowboat dock, Senator Ervin's dead, and we've had Republican governors.

Augusta's friend, the girl from Woman's College, stood between the two boys from Davidson. I didn't think her beautiful but she attracted attention. She wore a pink cotton dress and some of the men whistled softly and shook their heads as they walked behind her.   The dress clung in the heat.

Titus Ramsey moved in next to me and whispered: "Bobby's watching that one." His voice combined whisper and nasal whine. He nodded toward the girl from Woman's College. "He'll get that one to the parking lot first and then he'll come back for Augusta Morefield."

Never.   Not Augusta.   Besides, everybody knew about Augusta and me. I faced Titus, quickly calculating a direct angle to his chin but dropped the idea when I considered Augusta might not care for me to brawl. Either way, Titus didn't care. He paid me no more attention but leaned over to the person on the other side of him at the railing, probably to make the same prediction.

Bobby Crawford stood against the railing across the floor from me, drinking a bottle of High Life and watching Augusta and her friend. Some of the men who worked for him at his brother's sawmill gathered around Bobby, talking in whispers, obviously feeding him close-up descriptions of the girl in the tight, pink dress. Bobby grimaced and chuckled, sipped beer and smiled.

About then you could smell trouble. Augusta and the girl and the two Davidson boys didn't seem to notice anything. But I sensed blood. Sweaty hair and sour breath and noises suddenly descended on me. In my mind, I heard cursing and screaming and thumping and bone cracking bone. I remember thinking no fight I ever saw resembled those among screen cowboys at the North Carolina Theater. Sometimes a white-hatted star bled a little at the corner of his mouth but he always wiped it away with a gloved fist, then pounded his enemy into a lump. The bad guy didn't bleed much either.

Thinking about blood made me move. With a couple of steps, I got next to Augusta, across from the girl in pink and next to one of the Davidson boys. I started to tell them to leave but Augusta thought I'd come to chat.

"Wiley, these are my friends, Marylou Ayers, Skip Smith and Webster Tuttle. I think I told you Marylou is in her last year at WC and Skip and Webster go to Davidson."

My. My. I nodded like I had good sense if not admirable

breeding and tried to speak again but Augusta and Marylou fell into conversation about a friend staying at Atlantic Beach for the summer.   The poor girl had caught cold and couldn't go anywhere. Webster Tuttle and the boy named Skip talked reverently about Carolina's football team.

Finally, I raised my voice and pulled at Augusta's elbow. "Listen. We need to leave. Let's go this way."

They kept talking.   They didn't even look at me.

"Augusta?"

Too late.

Bobby Crawford sprinted across the floor, swept around the five of us, and jogged off to the middle of the floor with Marylou's small, white handbag. He yelled, "Set!" and two football formations unfolded before him.

Marylou started out onto the floor. "How about my purse?" she said, her mouth grim, her eyes fearless. I remember her as a small girl with shoulder-length brown hair.   "I got my glasses in that purse."

So childish.   Bobby played quarterback and called the signals.   He passed to Robbie Wood who'd buttonhooked and waited, panting, near the jukebox. The white purse zipped through gray air, skimming just below unpainted rafters and hit Robbie in the stomach. But he dropped it and it took three or four hard bounces on the plank floor.   Marylou Ayers called out: "I can't see without my glasses. I need my bag."

Augusta didn't move. I didn't move. Robbie picked up the purse and flipped it back to Bobby. Then somebody pulled the plug on the jukebox and everything got real quiet.

By this time, Marylou had gotten in front of Bobby, the formations had disintegrated, and a circle grew around the two of them.

"What's your name, sugar?"

"I want my purse."

People squeezed closer. Augusta and I got pushed up in front and I twisted and turned until I could see tiny Marylou between bunched bodies. She stood in the center of the ragged circle, quite unafraid, facing Bobby Crawford.

"That's my bag," she said.

"I'll give it to you," Bobby said, playfulness edging his lips. His eyes moved over the surrounding faces.

"We'll go to my car. I'll give it to you at the car."

The pink dress did cling.

That's when Marylou Ayers slapped Bobby Crawford. The pop and the collective breath going out of people sounded like a lightning hit on a power line.

Bobby didn't hesitate. He stepped forward and put his hand in Marylou's face and for a moment he pulled her around the floor like a human yo-yo. He pulled and she screamed and people watched, excited eyes following, darting, mouths open.

Then he shoved her to the floor.

About the time she hit the floor, the two boys from Davidson jumped at him and the swinging started. I looked around for Augusta. She stood behind me, chewing her lip, trembling, eyes fixed on the confusion of flailing arms. Frankly, she looked excited but I didn't have time to talk about it so I pushed her toward the exit and started back for Marylou. But I stumbled over somebody on the floor and landed on my side in spilled beer. In the tangle of feet and legs—people trying to get out and people maneuvering to hit some-body—I sighted Marylou. She lay just ahead of me, face down, head covered with her arms.

I raised up, called to her, took a kick in the head and blacked out.

When I came to, Aubrey Winslow, the late-shift policeman, had me propped against a post fanning me with a folded newspaper. He chuckled about me smelling like beer. I gathered myself slowly, first pushing up with my arms, then sitting up straight.

"Did you get a lick in?" Aubrey had more curiosity than sense. "Does your head hurt?."

"Hell, yes," I said. "Did those boys and that girl get hurt? Where's Augusta?" Suddenly, I felt dizzy. I'd asked too many questions at once.

Aubrey pointed across to the far railing.   I saw Marylou Ayers using a handkerchief on Skip Smith's bloody mouth. Webster Tuttle lay curled up on the floor, eyes closed, lips contorted and moving but soundless.   Both hands clutched his groin.

But I didn't see Augusta anywhere.

Chapter 4

At one a.m., I ordered coffee at the counter of the Carolina Cafe and listened to Aubrey Winslow talk about the Lindburgh kidnapping, one of his favorite crimes. "Police acted like gobblers: All noise and strut. Poor child just vanished, and killing Hauptmann satisfied national blood lust. It's still a mystery, dark and sinister, unsolved."

I felt the same way about Augusta's disappearance.

"I think Augusta's been kidnapped," I said. To me, it seemed a perfectly reasonable conclusion.

Early thirties, balding and bulging at all parts of his uniform, Aubrey pushed his fork into a thick slice of pecan pie and looked at me. "I'm never surprised at anything," he said. His usually steady voice descended into a weary, philosophical tone. "There's so damn much meanness in this world. Did you see it out there tonight? Did you see that boy down on the floor? For God's sake, it hurts to get kicked in the balls."

I ached. I nodded. I agreed.

"But you got to figure. Why would somebody want to kidnap Augusta Morefield?"

She's beautiful, I thought. "Money," I said. "She's got money. "They could call the bank. The bank's got the trust from her father."

Aubrey chewed and scanned the stacked glasses and little Kellogg's cereal boxes on the shelf behind the counter. With the fork, he pointed at the bowl of butter squares next to the corn flakes. "See those ice cubes there? On top of the butter?"

I nodded, expecting the profundity I got.

"What happens when the ice melts? What you got in the bowl?"

"Butter soup," I said, faintly amused despite my worry about Augusta and curiosity about Aubrey's thinking.

"Exactly what I'm talking about," Aubrey said, his expression very serious. "Just sitting here looking at the bowl, you know what's going to happen. But women aren't like ice cubes on butter. You got to ask a lot of questions to figure one out. Men got simple insides; meat and potatoes thinking, raw instincts."

My father told me that once but not the same way. I still didn't understand. "This doesn't take a lot of figuring, Aubrey. I always take her home. I need to find her," I said. "Then I'll find out her mind."

Aubrey raised a hand toward the waitress, signaling for more coffee. Waiting, he stabbed another chunk of pie. "I think she left with somebody."

I preferred kidnapped.

"I don't believe she'd do that."

"That's just a hopeful guess and it doesn't make any difference, Wiley. Don't get your heart set on finding her alone."

Since Aubrey had been married three times and had five children by two of his wives, I decided he understood a few things. But I couldn't grasp that Augusta walked out of the pavilion, in the middle of the uproar, got into a car and rode off with somebody she barely knew.

Most of all, I couldn't believe she might have left with Bobby Crawford. My head throbbed and I burned my mouth on the coffee, but I had sense enough to know that's what Aubrey meant.

"You're wrong," I said, trying to balance the too-hot cup in my right hand and mop up the overflow in the saucer with my left. "I'm reporting her missing. You can take my report, Aubrey."

He looked at me and I remember his blue eyes swam just a little. Had he retreated to an unpleasant moment with one of his wives, to a time when fear and hurt began to converge, to tear at reason?

Aubrey put down his fork. "You don't need to file a report, Wiley. Go home now and call Augusta Morefield in the morning."

"Augusta and I belong to each other, Aubrey." I didn't like the sound of my own voice. I heard whimpering.

"You might think so, Wiley. Let her get home by herself. Get some sleep. Call her early. She'll be there."

I pushed the coffee away.

"You going to take a report or not?" My voice sounded loud and angry.

Aubrey's face glowed red and he swung around on the stool and stood. He leaned over and picked up the checks for both of us. "I'll get this," he said. "Least I can do is buy the coffee. How's your head, anyway?"

At the cash register, we talked for a minute with Andros, the Greek. He said some in the fight at the pavilion had gone to the emergency room for patches and band-aids.

Aubrey Winslow took his change. "We'll go out there, Wiley," he said, slipping a toothpick between his lips. "That's a good place to start looking." He even seemed enthusiastic about the idea— like we'd probably find Augusta in the emergency room or patiently sitting with someone who'd been hurt.

But once we got outside, he stopped and in the blinking red and yellow glow of the Carolina Cafe's neon, he faced me and made himself clear. "You're going to get your feelings hurt tonight and it's going to ache worse than your head. God knows, I'm willing to take you to the hospital but that's not where we're going to find Augusta Morefield. I promise you, if we look hard enough we're going to find her in somebody's bed or the back seat of a car. She's been to college, Wiley. You've been here in Ransom, selling cars and burying people."

I ignored him.

"I'll ride out there with you, Aubrey."

He tugged his pistol belt higher on his middle, took a deep breath and headed for the police car. I followed, feeling like I'd been thrown into a pit of rats and somebody had closed off the last sliver of light.

The crowd in the emergency room didn't pay much attention to me. Most kept their eyes on Aubrey Winslow. Who might get charged? Did he plan to drag somebody out the door and off to jail? Who? Who?

"Stay close, Wiley. I'm going to circulate a little." Aubrey moved down the hall where the wounded had collected. Young men and women—patches over eyes, across foreheads, over knuckles—sat in the line of straight-backed wooden chairs along the wall in the hall. Some stood, smoking or sipping Cokes. Webster Tuttle sat, hunched over, still grasping his groin.

Grim?

Comical maybe. It looked like a small natural disaster but I recognized people who had been swinging and kicking and biting and heard them chatter with excited camararaderie about events at the pavilion. In fact, nurses kept coming from the treatment rooms to quiet people who laughed and talked too loudly.

"If you've seen the doctor, go on and leave. Go on home." Agnes Noble, the stout, fire-eyed night nurse, stepped out and began a finger-waving tirade.

But nobody moved.

"I swear I'm going to get Officer Aubrey Winslow to take you all to Judge Waters. Am I going to have to do that? Officer Winslow? Where are you? Come on over here please. You got to clear my emergency room."

Talking to a girl with her arm in a sling, Aubrey looked up when he heard his name. "Yes, you're right," he said, giving Agnes Noble a half-wave. "Move on outside now. If you've been fixed up, move on outside."

Six or eight people grumbled, stirred and strolled toward the exit. Webster Tuttle stayed, rocking back and forth in his seat. Aubrey followed the exodus and I fell in behind him just as he passed through the double doors leading to the parking lot.

"What did you hear, Aubrey? Anybody seen Augusta?" Every word seemed to bounce off his broad back and I thought my voice sounded like a parrot's squawking. He didn't speak or turn around until we got to the bottom of the steps. I glanced up at the clear sky and marked in my mind the clarity of the stars and the warmth that had made Aubrey sweat through his pale blue shirt.

"Aunt Sarah's," he said.

"No. She wouldn't go there."

"I'm telling you, Wiley, Augusta's out there snuggled up with Bobby Crawford. Two or three people told me. One of them heard him ask her to go. She said yes and got in his car."

No.

I looked away, to the grill of an old Mercury somebody had backed into a nearby space and thought suddenly how all the meshed chrome resembled a broken smile. "She wouldn't go there," I said. "I've never taken her there, why should she go with somebody else?"

"Bobby Crawford talks sweet, Wiley. Augusta ain't a damn sight different from any other woman. With him, they grab life, not just live it." Aubrey said, looking around at the knots of people in the parking lot. "Maybe you should have taken her there."

What did he mean? I always took her home.

"If Augusta's already got money, sooner or later she's going to want a man to brag on. Mountain of muscle and hair. Hot breath."

"Bobby Crawford's mindless," I said, trying to decide if I wanted to keep my temper or not. Could I hit a policeman and get by with it?

"Don't take a mind to do what she wants, Wiley." Aubrey rattled coins in his pocket and came out with the keys to the police car. "Why do you think I've been married so many times, Wiley? I've had so many wives, most of my children stay confused about who their mother is.   I get one settled and she starts looking for somebody else.   I don't know if it's human nature or evil.   I quit thinking about it.   I can't pay child support and think, too."

"Bobby Crawford's got nothing but that car," I said.

"What you got? Farms and pens full of pigs and chicken shit and big tobacco fields? Think hard about yourself, Wiley. You're just in your twenties and you got short legs, a face like a serious uncle, your hair's already turning gray and you're looking thick in the jaws. The most exciting thing you do is go to Raleigh twice a year to buy shoes on Fayetteville Street."

How did he know?

Aubrey moved around to the driver's side of the police car. "Get in, Wiley.   Let's you and me go settle this.   I'll bet you ten dollars Bobby Crawford's got Augusta's pants hanging on his radio aerial right now."

"No!" I yelled at Aubrey and snatched open the door.

He got in and started the car.   I slammed my door.

"Get mad, but it's not going to help this any. Under the skin, one woman acts like another."

"No," I said. "I'll take the bet."

Aubrey turned on the inside light, took off his hat and put it on the seat between us.   He ran one hand down his face, using thumb and forefinger to massage the bridge of his nose like he had a headache, too.   Sweat stood on his heavy, pink cheeks.

"I'm not trying to force this on you, Wiley," he said, his voice kinder, less piercing. "I got to do it anyway. Miss Sarah Wingo don't like young love in her pine woods.   Want me to take you home instead?"

"I'll go with you," I said.   I didn't see much choice.

Anyway, we had a bet.

All the way there, I thought about my last sight of Augusta and silently pleaded with the merciful God to make her be somewhere else.   I even imagined a scene at the pavilion when she might have been pulled along in a crowd, through the exit and into the parking lot. Did someone push her into a car? Had anybody hurt her? With that, I longed for my father's old boot pistol in the desk drawer at the funeral home.

Aubrey Winslow lit a cigarette. The tip glowed and smoke filled the car. I coughed and waved smoke toward the open window, hoping it would catch a rush of warm night air.

"These pines are far enough apart you can drive around them and they're all so thick at the top that even the moonlight can't get through," he said, blowing smoke again. "Makes everything pitch black."

Poor Augusta. Frightened in the dark.

"Do you blow your horn?"

Busy with the cigarette, Aubrey didn't answer right away.

"Siren? I asked. "Or do you just thump on hoods to roust people down in the seats?"

"Spotlight," Aubrey said, blowing smoke. "I ride through and flip my light on the windows. I do the same thing every night and they're back in five minutes."

"Take them to the jail," I said, trying to sound tough and wishing Bobby Crawford behind bars forever. But I heard fear in my voice. A chill—a spreading, cutting cold—edged through my stomach and crawled toward my throat.

"You want Augusta in jail, her name in the paper? What charge? Stepping out on you?" Aubrey grunted and glanced to his left—to avoid the bright lights of another car. He shook his head.

"Wiley, you ever had any other girl? I mean, you ever had any other girl but Augusta Morefield?" In the faint, greenish light from the dashboard, I saw a shift in the creases and lines and jowls of Aubrey Winslow's face. He had something else to say. I sensed determination, even aggravation.

"No," I said,

Looking out my window, I waited for Aubrey to speak and aimlessly tried to count the few farmhouse lights at that hour. Did he want me to thump my chest and claim I kept a stream of women moving through my apartment in my father's house?

"How come just Augusta Morefield?"

Pour out feelings? In the heat? In a police car? I didn't answer. None of your business.

"Planning on getting married?"

"That's the plan," I said.

"Your plan or her plan, Wiley?"

"Our plan."

"Did you ask her yet?"

"Yes. Oh, yes. Long ago."

He drummed fingers on the steering wheel. Worn out? Probably. But mostly, he'd gotten tired of hearing about Augusta and wanted to go back to the Carolina Cafe and drink coffee and toy with a slice of pie.

"When long ago? How long ago?"

Why didn't he know? Everybody knew.

"I asked her before she left for school. At the beach. I took her to dinner at Tony's. I asked her at the table."

"Four years ago? That long? What did she say?"

"She kissed me."

"No kidding?" Aubrey smiled and I grinned, recalling the sound of water against fishing boats and piers, a bright yellow moon over Bogue Sound, salt smell in the air and how I took that kiss as bond.

"Then what happened?"

"We walked on the beach all night."

For a minute or so, we didn't talk. I lost myself in the memory of moonlight, sand and sea and thoughts of barefoot Augusta, carrying her loafers in one hand and holding my arm. I remembered the brilliant orange sunrise, trailing plumes and wisps of purple and gold. I remembered we stopped walking and kissed.

Aubrey flipped his cigarette out the window and slowed the car. He picked up the microphone and radioed the desk sergeant in Ransom, saying he planned to rout the lovers in Wingo's woods.

Through flickers of static, the desk sergeant chuckled. "Copy." The radio crackled again and the whole scene suddenly reminded me of a poor Hollywood attempt to animate doom — with the commander of a shot-up sub laughing at periscope images of a

Japenese fleet headed his way.

The police car picked up speed. "The turn is about a quarter-mile down," he said. "I always go in fast. Shock value. Makes them hurry to get their clothes on. Some sight."

At that juncture, I preferred to think of Augusta fully clothed—in the tan cotton dress she'd worn to the pavilion and the white socks and brown and white oxfords I bought her in Raleigh on the way back to Ransom from her graduation.

Aubrey whipped the car to the left and it seemed forever that we bumped and wallowed in the hard cart ruts of the dirt lane. I kept my eyes ahead, watching the police car's headlights cut the darkness. When we got into the trees, he cut on the spotlight and you could hear engines start. Parking lights came on, then full beams.

"See how they run," Aubrey said, laughing and bouncing the spot off windshields and truck cabs. He caught one bare-chested fellow standing by a white pickup, stopped the car and held the light steady while the man hurriedly pulled up and zipped his pants.

Aubrey laughed, gunned the car to the right between two small trees and swept the spotlight left to right.

Then he stopped, cut the engine and lights, reached over and patted the white handle of the spotlight on my side. "If Bobby Crawford's here, he'd be there—in a clear spot. He don't like scratches on his paint job. Flip on the light if you want to. Just flip it on."

I couldn't. My hands shook and I felt moisture on my face. Sweat? Tears? In the jumble of thoughts—of fear and hatred and pain—I begged the shadows to spare me what I almost certainly would see.

But what if she'd gotten home and even now sat in her father's library—reading the blue and gold volume on the Dutch museums? Yes. I needed to believe that.

I turned on the spotlight and swept the beam over the bright chrome bumpers and fender line of Bobby Crawford's red Oldsmobile. I saw white panties hanging limp and motionless on the outside mirror. I heard Aubrey Winslow breathing.

"On the ground," he whispered. "On the ground."

Hot. Yes. And in their own heat they lay naked on a ragged, multi-colored quilt spread on the pine straw. I saw a prone whiskey bottle, two paper cups, a ginger ale and an empty beer can.

"Damn," Aubrey said.

Augusta Morefield, wild-haired, wide-eyed and bare, stirred and sat up. She looked directly into the light and froze—like a light-stunned doe just before buckshot ripped away hide and flesh. She tried to cover eyes and breasts and reached out to the blonde-haired man on his side next to her. He didn't move and I turned off the spotlight.

Aubrey started the engine, turned on the headlights and the red, twisting roof lights. "Do you suppose she learned that in college?" he asked, his voice nearly a whisper.

"I don't know," I said, pulling a ten-dollar bill from my wallet. I dropped it on his hat.

Chapter 5

Enchantment with Bobby Crawford might have died that night if everybody in Ransom saw what I saw in Aubrey's headlights.

Short, thick arms. Puffed chest, protruding breastbone and ribs. No body hair. Thin legs—like sorry, warped molding.

Suddenly, he got to his feet, tried to cover himself with a shirt and pointed and swore and reminded me of a beaten, tattered rooster, defenseless but still squawking. Augusta edged across the quilt, kept her face from the light and worked desperately to pull herself and her clothes under the Oldsmobile. I watched her round, pale buttocks wiggle, twist, and disappear under the car.

Aubrey shoved the police car into reverse, pulled on the headlights, whipped around, and headed for the dirt lane to the highway. He turned on his roof lights, sending spots of red bouncing off trees and fenders and windshields.

"Now they'll know it's me and come like a funeral procession, sad and slow," he said, glancing to the side mirror and the rear window. "Right now, they think we spoiled everything. But they'll have so much to talk about tomorrow." He chuckled. The car rocked through a deep rut.

I couldn't think of anything but Augusta; a curious array of questions dashed through my mind. Could she dress under the car? Would Bobby forget her and crush her in a tire-spinning temper fit?

Then I couldn't think at all.

"Hard blow. Sorry for you, Wiley. Sorry. Here, take back your ten."

I refused. "Keep the money, Aubrey," I said. "We had a bet. Besides, sympathy's worth nothing."

At the highway, he cut the red lights and whipped left onto the pavement, accelerating and throwing off a shower of mud and rocks that thumped under the car like a barrage of hailstones.

"Sympathy's everything." Aubrey patted my shoulder. "I remember when my first wife left me for a snuff salesman. I sat in my house with three squalling children for a week until I realized I needed sympathy."

In the greenish glow of the dash lights, he seemed amused, even heartened by the thought of people feeling sorry. I turned back to the window and the darkness, picturing unshaven, red-eyed Aubrey Winslow slouched in an easy chair, floor littered with beer cans, children crawling at his feet, all with runny noses, all bawling like poor, abandoned calves.

Sympathy, he said. Works like a dose of salts.

Aubrey pulled up to the stop sign at the crossroads, looked to his left and turned right on Washington Road.

"In about five minutes, I'm going to show you sympathy," he said, enthusiastically thumping the steering wheel with a knuckle. "She don't care if you're slope-headed or big-eared, one-balled or got arthritis. She's got sympathy in her heart and she jangles when she walks."

"Who?"

Aubrey sighed and dimmed his lights for an approaching car. "Wiley? Where've you been, boy?"

I didn't answer. I didn't know.

Sound reasoning doesn't play a role in my mindset about Augusta Morefield Crawford. Had my head not remained so full of her, perhaps I could have lived with more sense of purpose. Persistent, tender, idealized thoughts of her cost me fatherhood and heirs, peace and the settling security of a home with some other woman. I might have joined Rotary or Lions or even become a tithing, saved and smiling member of Pettigrew Memorial.

Instead, I remained alone.

Always.

Always.

Not even recollections of that long ago warm autumn night with Madame Fatima, the fake Gypsy palm reader on Washington Road, have stirred me beyond the realization that most of my adult life has been spent in conversation with myself.

Even then, Aubrey Winslow knew.

"You talk to her," he said, reaching across to open my door. I made no move, preferring to wallow in images of Augusta and Bobby on Sarah Wingo's pine straw.

"Take me home, Aubrey."

"Even if you say nothing, Wiley, she'll listen."

"I have to go get Augusta and take her home."

"Augusta don't want you to take her home, Wiley."

"Oh," I said.

A screened door slapped and we looked toward the single light bulb at the door of the dim, unpainted frame house. Aubrey took a short breath. I saw a small woman, dressed in a thin, white and flowing gown step toward the edge of the porch.

"See that?"

"Yes."

We sounded like two small boys, whispering.

"She must be beautiful," I said, watching the dark, exotic form on the porch. Suddenly, I felt a curious, stirring kinship to Madame Fatima.

"God's sakes, Wiley, her face don't matter," Aubrey said. "Pay attention to what we're doing here."

At that point, Madame Fatima, the whispered joke of Ransom, motioned with one hand. "That means go on up there," Aubrey said. "Go on, Wiley."

I didn't move.

The driver's side door slammed. I heard Aubrey clumping around behind the car and then he had me by the arm. Firmly, he pulled. "Look here, Wiley," he said. "Do you see what she's got on? Damn near nothing. Come on. She'll give you chills. I swear."

He pulled again and I got out and stood beside him.

Madame Fatima, silhouetted against the porch light, struck a match and lit a cigarette. She blew out a cloud of smoke, moved over and sat on the top step.

"Come here," she said in an easy, pleasant tone. Aubrey took my arm and with a few steps we stood before her, watching pinpoints of light play on finger rings and heavy bracelets. Shadows edged across her face, to cover, to uncover, to define, to confuse. For a second, the mysterious Madame Fatima seemed like every man's dream of dark excitement, a brush with the Devil twisting carefully through the conscious mind.

Aubrey trembled.

Madame Fatima crossed her legs.

Jangle, jangle.

Madame Fatima flipped her cigarette into the yard.

Jangle, jangle.

Madame Fatima uncrossed her legs.

Jangle, jangle.

"Aubrey," I whispered, "it's past four in the morning. Take me home."

"No, Wiley. You need to talk to this good woman."

Madame Fatima stood. Early twenties, perhaps. Olive skin. Make believe foreign accent. Plump red lips. In the yellowish light, I saw black hair alive on her shoulders, cascading down her back, and earrings so big they looked like small brass barrel hoops. Bare feet. Ankle bracelets. Jangle, jangle.

"Aubrey? Where'd she come from? Emporia?"

"Arabia," he said, softly. He squeezed my elbow.

Madame Fatima stepped down into the dirt. She tugged at Aubrey's shirt sleeve, pulled him down and kissed his cheek. "Big policeman. You think I'm a good woman? I know you, Aubrey

Winslow. How you going to help me when they come to close up my house and run me away?"

"For telling fortunes?" Aubrey laughed. "Wiley Frost, this is Madame Fatima.   She tells fortunes."

The woman laughed. Then she took my hand. "Come into my little house, Wiley Frost. I'll tell your fortune. That's what I do here.   Officer Aubrey Winslow says so."

She guided me up the steps. At the door, I turned to Aubrey, who had almost reached the car. "You coming back?"

Madame Fatima laughed again. Bright, mischievous smile. White teeth. "You come back at six, Aubrey Winslow. If he doesn't come out in ten minutes, come back at seven thirty."

Aubrey nodded and got in the car.

I turned and stepped into the house and a smoky sea of blue light. Living room? No. Table and chairs. Tell fortunes. Read tea leaves. Flip cards. Smoke? Incense?

"Everything's floating," I said.

Madame Fatima laughed. "Sure," she said.

Then Augusta's face, blank, eyes fixed in a hard stare, bobbed in the blue and quickly faded away. Bobby Crawford's angry mouth jabbed at me, big teeth bared, curses rolling. Like leading a blind man, Madame Fatima took me to the table and a wooden chair.

I sat.

She left me alone.

The door lock snapped.

I felt the warmth of her mouth at my ear.

"I can tell your fortune, Wiley Frost. I can bathe you in oils and stroke your temples and kiss each of your fingertips."

Slowly, long fingers caressed my neck.

"What do you want?"

"I don't know," I said.

"Are you sad?"

"I don't know," I said.

Her hands crept through my hair and a chill rippled up my back. "I'm cold," I said. "Give me a whiskey."

She moved to my side and poured from a pint bottle into a small, shallow glass.   Then, back at my ear, she whispered: "We'll make her pay, Wiley Frost." Throaty, rasping voice. All business. No strain of sweetness.

"How do you know?" I mumbled the question, thinking of my mother and father, the stained glass window of the angry God at the Baptist church and the gleaming black horns of Satan.

Madame Fatima answered: She bit my ear.

I drank the whiskey.

Suddenly, flute music grew from a faint, curious intrusion to driving heat and I wondered if Madame Fatima had a snake in a basket or if we had somehow been transported to a dim back room in Algiers.

She stood before me.

Dark, commanding eyes.

"See me?"

"Yes," I said, wishing I had the whiskey bottle.

Madame Fatima said something else but I paid little attention because she knelt, and quickly became a glimmering light shadow, flickering in blue haze. She slithered toward me, laughing, long hair out of control. That's when I understood how to make Augusta pay.

PART II

Chapter 6

A week after Bobby Crawford's bones got identified, The *Telegraph* published Grace Lynn Rose's "Last Days of Sergeant Crawford" and I ran across Bobby's brother Champ in the Ransom Clinic waiting room.

The minute I sat down, he started talking: Shingles and kidney stones, he said. Closed up the saw mill. Living on nothing. Brother Bobby can't rest in his new grave because everybody wants to know what happened the last hour he lived.

"They all want me to tell how he got in that hole," he complained, dabbing at his nose with a wadded blue and white bandanna handkerchief. "Got no privacy. Policemen walk around my house all night, reporters knock on the door all day. Took out the phone to sleep."

In the late afternoon, we sat alone in the waiting room—across from each other in thinly padded arm chairs. A blonde receptionist in a white uniform doodled on a deskpad behind a sliding glass window at the far end of the room. Sunlight streamed through the blinds, bounced around on flowered wallpaper, adding a faint, golden glow to the frame of the Cape Hatteras lighthouse picture on the wall to my left.

Old Champ paused and looked away from the hunting magazine in his lap to a Billy Graham crusade poster near the door. Then he drifted back to the magazine, sniffed a couple of times and turned a page. "Going to get a big dog," he mumbled. "Keep traffic out of my yard."

Champ looked eighty or more. Short strands of hair dotted his freckled scalp like white field stubble. He had no teeth. That made his chin look like a piece of machinery out of control—a worn old grinder missing a screw.

"You sick?"

"Heart," I said, wishing I hadn't offered that much.

Champ dropped his eyes back to the magazine, holding for a moment on the picture of a setter with a dead partridge in its mouth.

"Still running ambulances, Wiley? How old are you? Older than Bobby? I can't remember. Did you go to Korea? No. Why didn't you go?"

"Heart," I said, silently pledging that I'd say nothing more, no matter what the question.

"Oh," Champ Crawford sniffed and angled his head to sweep a new page with his bifocals. "Wonder you're living, Wiley. I believe I'd rather have the kidney stones and shingles."

Old fool. Jaws flapping and pink gums flashing. Gray Big Yank pants and black, steel-toed shoes. Long-sleeved white shirt. Silly red suspenders. He kept a thumb under one side of the suspenders and popped the elastic while he read.

"I remember you driving your ambulance. Did you come to my mill? Find any loose fingers?"

He laughed and never looked at me. He kept his eyes on the magazine, snapped his suspenders and smacked his lips. I squirmed, looked around for the nurse and picked up an outdated National Geographic, quickly turning through a layout of Haitians making voodoo pilgrimages to trees and waterfalls.

Spirits.

All over Ransom, too.

Champ Crawford put down his magazine and looked at me.

"Do you know how famous Bobby is?" He started going

through his pockets, rummaging and pulling. He wasn't looking for a toothpick. "Grace Lynn Rose's writing a book with my help. Says she's starting with Bobby's childhood and going forward—to the war and the parade. Says she wants to show Bobby Crawford got past being a saw mill hand to became a war hero."

Hell. Now old dead Bobby's got Grace Lynn Rose panting and quivering.

"She going to tell us how he got in that hole?"

The remark didn't affect Champ's digging in his pockets. He smacked and fumbled until he pulled a wad of pressed and tattered newspaper from a hip pocket. Carefully and precisely, he unfolded the bits and taped strips. Then he held up a bottom half-page from the Norfolk newspaper. The headline used Grace Lynn Rose's favorite word, "macabre" and one old picture that showed Bobby Crawford in his uniform and another of police standing around the hole on the common.

"Reporter came all the way from Norfolk." Champ Crawford grinned, wide, pink and gummy. I looked away, down to my magazine to study the picture of a Haitian woman under a waterfall trying to rid herself of possession by a snake god.

"The day we finally got Bobby buried next to mama and papa, people handed me newspaper clippings from all over," Champ said. "Richmond, Raleigh, Charleston, Atlanta."

He paused and looked at me, eye to eye. "You know, Augusta Morefield didn't come out of her house for Bobby's funeral." His voice seemed to rise but I couldn't catch an inflection.

I nodded.

For a time, he didn't speak. His eyes ran over the clipping and he seemed completely self-absorbed. Sometimes he hummed an odd, mournful tune and pointed with a forefinger at something in the print. Then he just folded up the clipping and put it in his back pocket.

"I like Grace Lynn Rose's theory about Bobby."

I closed my magazine.

"She says somebody knows how he died. But that's just her theory, she says. She's got to work on it."

Wonderful. I could envision that young demon searching and questioning, terrorizing the whole town for years.

Champ Crawford pulled at his suspenders and rocked his head back and forth. "Me and Grace Lynn Rose got our eyes on Augusta Morefield. That woman's been in her house so long because she's afraid somebody's going to ask her how Bobby died. That's what I think."

I studied the magazine, glancing at another picture of more possessed voodooists bathing in a sanctified mud pond.

"Did you see what Grace Lynn Rose wrote? She told about how he got off the train, kissed his mother and marched up Richmond Street with a crowd, got on the convertible with his wife at Grimes Avenue and rode on from there—right up through the middle of town, bands playing. I just wish he'd had on sunglasses so he looked more like Douglas MacArthur."

Champ Crawford took a breath and smiled. He tilted his head back, slowly taking a blank, distant gaze to the ceiling. I wondered if he expected his brother to float gently down in a golden glow, robed in white, wings aflutter.

Then he straightened. He looked at me, folded his hands over the magazine and started talking about what Grace Lynn Rose's article said about the Korean War and how his brother won the Silver Star. I kept turning through the National Geographic.

"Threw grenades at North Koreans. She said he probably got fifteen. Then he pulled his buddies down a hill, one by one, bullets smashing all around him. Did you know he got hit two or three times? Gushing blood, she said. Gushing and pulling. Finally he just blacked out. That's how they found him. Unconscious. Wounded buddies all around him. Dead enemy everywhere."

Nothing new. Same old story. This time, however, Grace Lynn Rose doubled the numbers of enemy dead and emphasized gushing and pulling.

I said nothing.

Champ patted the open page of his magazine like he might try to get the attention of a day-dreaming child. "Bobby took his wife to her house and took off for the hotel to celebrate. Shame.

Somebody knows how he got in that hole. Ransom police moving too slow, scared to ask Augusta Morefield anything for fear they'll hurt her blue-blood feelings. Me and Grace Lynn Rose'll ask her."

I looked up and caught his eye. "Let everything that's dead rest." Country preacher talk. But it didn't work on Champ Crawford. He pushed himself to the edge of his chair.

"Me and Bobby can't rest." he said. "I hear his voice at night."

"What's the voice saying, Champ?" Inquiring about gas prices? I swallowed a laugh.

Champ Crawford dropped his eyes to the floor. "It's worse on cool nights. I feel like I need to go somewhere and put a blanket on him."

For a moment, I didn't speak and my thoughts drifted back to the dull, gray room at the Hotel Ransom. Blithe Tanner, mind wandering with fever, lips white, eyes half-open, frightened and pink with heat, lay on the bed, covered by a sheet.

"Give me a blanket," she whispered. "I'm cold."

I closed my magazine and looked at Champ. "Can you hear that girl's voice? Do you remember that girl Blithe you all left in the hotel room? Does she ever say anything to you, Champ?"

Suddenly, I felt an old anger. Her face and faint, pitiful voice crowded my mind. The old man's eyes snapped wide and he stood up, hitching up his pants and pulling at the suspenders.

"I don't remember a girl," he said, stepping toward the examining room door.

I stood up and pointed one finger straight at him.

"I saw you, Champ Crawford. I saw you and Bobby and Waverly Barnhill. One more, too. But I didn't see him."

He opened the door, paused and looked back at me.

"You didn't see nothing," he said.

Then he pushed past skinny Adelaide Hand, the nurse, who complained she hadn't called him yet.

All that evening, I expected a rock through the front window or the thump of a dead cat on the porch.

No matter.

Champ Crawford needed to know that, although Blithe Tanner lies beneath a tiny stone in Cobb's Graveyard, she could rise again, to walk and talk among us.

Oh yes.

She could describe her excitement when Bobby Crawford sat down beside her. The train shuddered and hissed and jerked and swayed and in an hour, destinations didn't matter. With him, she'd go anywhere.

Married? Sure. He said they'd get married when they got to Ransom. But then he sold her to Waverly Barnhill for a night for six dollars and a pint of gin.

She could tell about the bitter cold and wind of the Chicago spring how she got a fever and cried and coughed and nearly choked when Bobby got off the train in Washington and sent her on to Ransom with Waverly.

Taking another train, he said.

Why couldn't he stay with her? Passing through Alexandria, Waverly laughed and told her about Bobby having a wife.

Blithe Tanner said Champ Crawford came to the train in Ransom, took her to the old hotel and pushed her into a room. Waverly Barnhill took her clothes and they left her shivering and begging for a doctor.

"You wait for Bobby," somebody said. They grinned and laughed.

She told me everything.

After the eleven o'clock news, I turned out the porch light, checked the front door bolt and took a stack of magazines down the hall to the bedroom. I put the magazines on the night stand, turned back the bed and pulled down the window shade.

Then I opened the closet door.

Caught in the moment, I thought of Augusta, enigma behind heavy curtains, shadowy curiosity, Ransom's Greta Garbo. I pictured Blithe Tanner's pink-glowing, puffed face and heard the fevered, struggling effort of her voice. Champ Crawford's angry eyes burned across my mind.

The plastic clothes bag crackled as I stretched it on the bed and drew down the zipper. The polished brass insignia and the medal on the left breast gleamed, even in low light. My hands ran over fabric, quickly finding my starching and ironing had held.

The scene on the courthouse reviewing stand came back to me: "Sergeant Crawford?" The colonel from Fort Bragg stood straight as Ransom's hero stepped to center stage. Augusta moved behind the two men—like a President's wife on inauguration day. The colonel pinned the medal on Bobby Crawford, stepped back and saluted. Bobby saluted. The school band played the national anthem and the crowd got still, hands over hearts, eyes glued to the flag on the courthouse pole.

When the music ended, the crowd cheered, clapped, whistled and hooted. Bobby and Augusta waved and smiled. The Colonel waved and smiled. The band left and everybody headed away to celebrate.

Images. Faces. Movement. Colors. Sounds.

There in the bedroom, with my hands on Bobby Crawford's uniform, my mind suddenly drew blank. I stood still, listening for sounds outside my window. Fear? After so many years, how could I be afraid? Could Champ Crawford and his friends be there? I listened. But I heard nothing—except an occasional passing car or wind stirring a small pine against the bedroom window screen.

So I undressed, put my clothes on a chair, pulled the uniform pants from the hanger and stepped into them, pushing hard with each foot to penetrate the heavy starch. Fumbling in the bag, I found black socks and polished GI shoes and sat on the bed to pull them on. Then I put on the shirt, stood and buttoned it before the mirror on the closet door.

Stepping back and sitting on the bed again, I threaded the belt through the loops and fastened the gleaming brass buckle, tied the shoes and got the folding, cloth cap from the plastic bag. I put it on my head, stood and shuffled back to the mirror.

What poor parody! The sleeves flowed over my hands and the shirt buttoned so tightly I could hardly breathe. Zipped and belted, the pants made my stomach hurt while cuffless legs spilled over shoe tops.

Nevertheless, I snapped to attention and saluted the mirrored, comic image of old Wiley Frost, pretender. I thought of Chaplin or Keaton, wobbly legs and baggy pants, deadpan looks and wiggling, caught on the hands of a skyscraper clock.

Just dangling.

Chapter 7

Three days later, my car approached the man in the chair across the street from Augusta's house. I thought somebody might be trying to peddle late summer tomatoes or pictures of Jesus.

He wore bib overalls, long-sleeved white shirt and thick black work shoes. Short-haired, long and thin, he lay back in a folding lounge chair under a green and white Salem cigarettes beach umbrella.

Then I saw the signs near the curb. White poster paper tacked to sticks. Heavy black words, hand-printed.

"Tell the truth."

"Did somebody kill Bobby Crawford?"

"Fasting for Justice."

Then I saw -- it was Champ Crawford.

As my car eased by, he struggled out of his chair and grabbed a newspaper from the top of a white Styrofoam cooler. He came toward my passenger window, stretched the paper open and pushed it at me so I could see the headline on another Grace Lynn Rose story.

Suddenly, he recognized me and let go of one end of the paper, stepped back and snatched up a large sign which said, "Augusta Morefield, Show Your Face!" Grinning his gummy grin, Champ Crawford shook it at me.

I didn't smile, touch my hat brim or speak but kept driving, watching through the side mirror as he stood by the curb, raising one sign and then another, waving them at cars in the growing flow of early traffic.

At the corner, I pulled into the Stop Quick Market, turned off the engine and sat, trying to think. Did Champ and Grace Lynn Rose expect more stories and an old man's sad melodrama to force Augusta out her front door to tell all about Bobby Crawford? I thought of the uniform in my closet and wondered if I should hurry home and hide it. I imagined Augusta in the gray isolation of her house, wondering and worrying. I pictured slender fingers edging back curtains and large, fearful brown eyes peering across the street.

"Wiley?" Earl Jones, the dry cleaner, tapped on my window.

I rolled the glass halfway down.

"Something wrong with you, Wiley? Why you sitting so still?"

Intruder. Red, round face. Acne scars. Dark, sharply pressed suit. Fat. Middle-aged. Scent of Old Spice.

"I'm fine, Earl."

"I could help you over to the clinic," he said, his face looming like a full moon in the half-open window.

"I don't need help, Earl. I'm thinking."

"Slide over and I'll drive your car over to the clinic."

"Earl, do you see me shaking or foaming at the mouth?

"No,"

"Then I'm fine—just like I said. Good-bye, Earl."

I rolled up the window.

"Wiley?"

I rolled down the window.

"Earl?"

"If you want one of those papers, you'd better hurry."

Earl unfolded a newspaper and I caught a glimpse of the same headline Champ Crawford had shoved at me. "Dead Hero's Brother Wants Widow Grilled."

"What do you think about this, Wiley?"

"I don't know, Earl.

"Hurry up and get a paper and read it and let me know what you think, Wiley," Earl said, folding the paper under his arm and glancing up at gray sky.

"Do you think it's going to rain, Wiley?"

I rolled up the window and got out of the car. Earl walked on toward his car and I heard the door slam just as I stepped into the market.

"Mr. Frost?"

Behind the counter, young Alma Tate smiled and quit stocking the chewing gum rack. "I just made coffee, Mr. Frost, and I've got fresh donuts from Blinky's Bakery. I believe there's some lemon pastry over there, too. You want coffee, Mr. Frost?"

Pleasant girl. Full of questions.

"You got a *Telegraph*?"

Alma Tate laughed. "You mean the Ransom Enquirer?"

"*Telegraph*," I said, reaching into my pants pocket for my plastic coin case.

"On the rack behind you," Mr. Frost," she said. "Thirty seven cents, Mr. Frost."

I got a paper off the rack, handed her a quarter, a dime and two pennies and started for the door.

"I made a joke a minute ago, Mr. Frost. Finding Bobby Crawford on the common made Ransom famous. Before long we might find ourselves in a detective magazine. Do you think so, Mr. Frost? How about coffee, Mr. Frost?"

Babble, babble.

She kept talking with me going out the door, and I could hear her voice all the way to my car. I got in, shut the door and opened the paper.

By Grace Lynn Rose. *Telegraph* staff writer.

"Champ Crawford, brother of Ransom's late war hero, believes Bobby Crawford's reclusive widow is hiding information about the death of her husband and wants authorities to question Augusta Morefield Crawford."

About what?

Rage began to churn my stomach and I took my eyes off the paper and focused on the front window of the market. Alma Tate fiddled with cash register tape and rattled on at somebody at the counter. Trying to keep my temper, I made my eyes drift left to read every sign tacked to the glass.

Country sausage $1.39 a pound.

Sweet potatoes 49 cents a pound.

Fresh picked flowers $1.50 a bunch.

Pig's feet $2.49 a pound.

"The body of Robert S. Crawford, identified by military forensic experts, was found buried at the Ransom War Memorial Fountain on the Ransom Town Common. Cause of death has not been determined. Police Chief Toby Pugh says his office is investigating possibilities of foul play in the death of Crawford, a Korean War hero."

Why?

Did they find Bobby Crawford with his head in his arms? What about an old, rusty knife still clinging to the bone?

"According to Champ Crawford, Augusta Morefield Crawford must have the answer."

Such as?

"My brother, Sgt. Robert S. Crawford, died in the company of other persons. I believe his widow, Augusta M. Crawford, has information. She must come forward."

Why? Augusta owed no explanations.

"Witnesses have said they saw my brother's wife walking toward the common on the night of the parade—the same night anyone last saw my brother. Some of these citizens have said because of the rain, they stopped their cars and asked my brother's wife if she wanted a ride but she waved them away."

What witnesses? Who?

I lowered the paper to my lap and sat still, feeling the words spill through my mind like a line of fire catching up undergrowth in a dry woods.

Names? Names?

Then I had a fit, tearing the paper, ripping through the picture of Champ Crawford at the War Memorial Fountain, shredding the front page, not caring at all that somebody might see the small cloud of floating paper rising, falling and settling in my car.

"Mr. Frost, what's the matter with you?"

Alma Tate appeared by the door, her expression curious, her face turning from one angle to another like some energized, foam-headed doll.

I rolled down the window.

"Paper got away from me."

"What?"

"The paper. I kept trying to catch it."

Alma Tate sympathetically shook her head but her eyes said she didn't believe me. "Newspapers don't have no wings, Mr. Frost. Don't have no life or no breath and I don't believe they're slippery, either."

I tried to smile.

"Go on home and take a pill, Mr. Frost. You'll be fine."

I pushed bits of newspaper off my lap and started the car. Yes, I'd be fine but only because I'd kill Champ Crawford before I got home.

Deciding to extinguish Champ Crawford didn't disturb me nearly as much as the line of slow-moving traffic on Pickett Street. Cars, pickups, bread trucks, soda trucks, beer trucks and even a John Deere tractor crept along like a funeral line, complete with people, complaining from open windows, unwilling to accept man-made confusion over orderly transit.

Right away, I concluded Champ Crawford's theatrics had created the backup and as I sat there, waiting for an opening between vehicles, I used the time to think of ways to kill him quickly and felt certain every frustrated driver would rejoice at his death.

But my planning time didn't last long.

"Wiley, you ought to get down the street, see what old Champ Crawford's doing." I had left my window down and I heard

Wayland Thomas, Ransom's premier car salesman, call to me from across the street.

I ignored him and concentrated on any kind of break in the traffic.

Playing human megaphone, Wayland cupped his hands around his mouth: "Champ's got Grace Lynn Rose and some TV people down there," he shouted, pointing down Pickett in the direction of Augusta's house. "He says they're going to march up Augusta's steps and confront her at the door."

I looked from the traffic to Wayland Thomas, dressed in a blue seersucker suit and gleaming black cowboy boots. The pointed end of a bright blue and yellow print tie flapped at his belt buckle.

Why tell me?

I blew my horn at two cars blocking my way and edged forward, tapping the brake. The rear of my car bounced up and down with my impatience on the pedal.

"Hey, Wiley? Wiley?" Wayland Thomas had crossed the street and had both hands on my door, leaning to speak to me. "I need a ride to the post office. Can I get in with you?"

"No," I said, furious at being distracted. How could I kill Champ Crawford with these interruptions?

"Just two blocks, Wiley. You got to turn right anyway. You can't get across to the other lane."

"I got things to do, Wayland," I said. "Walk."

At that second, a woman in a gray van motioned to me and I accelerated. Tires screeching, I lurched into the line and through the mirror saw Wayland Thomas start a slow trudge up the street, hands in his pockets, disappointment on his face.

At the next light, I turned left, drove more than a block, turned left again, quickly found Lincoln Road three blocks down, turned left again and stopped at the Pickett light.

How should I kill him? Brain him with the claw hammer under the front seat? Go home first and get my pistol? But could I get the Raleigh paper in jail? Who would look after my farms, see to my Social Security, get my mail and ride by Augusta's house?

Never mind.

The light changed and I turned right, moving in traffic that had begun to thin. Working people. Jobs to do. No time for Champ Crawford. Had the reporters left? I could talk to him, stand behind him, hit him with the hammer and go home.

I leaned over and felt around under the seat for the hammer. But I found only balloons and suckers from the bank tellers, three short pieces of copper pipe from new plumbing at a tenant house, and a nickel.

No hammer. So, I'd just have to run over Champ Crawford.

The car jumped forward when I pressed hard on the accelerator. Thick, gray-brown oak trees and multi-colored houses behind either curb flashed by in a dizzy blur of images and tones. Knowing I'd have to cross to the oncoming lane and go over the curb to get the chair, Champ Crawford, the umbrella and the cooler, I concentrated to the left but glanced to the right at Augusta's house to get my bearings.

Christ. At her gate stood old Champ, addressing a group of reporters with cameras and carrying a sign that said, "Speak!" I recognized Grace Lynn Rose and a *Telegraph* photographer behind her.

Good. I'd get them all.

But just before I swerved right and jolted up the curb, one of the photographers yelled and pointed and they all scattered.

I didn't hit a soul.

I even missed old Champ, but took down about twelve feet of Augusta's fence and demolished the front of my car in a thumping, crashing hail of white painted wood.

That's when I decided I'd better talk to Grace Lynn Rose.

Chapter 8

Opening the front door of the newspaper office, I felt as condemned as any man stepping into an execution chamber. All the circumstances amounted to the same: Catastrophe, no escape.

The front desk secretary ignored me for at least a minute while she finished sealing an envelope. For what seemed like forever, she dabbed a small sponge into a coffee cup of water then patted it across the glue on the envelope flap. The last, quick step involved flipping the envelope, thumping down with the heel of her hand, pressing and sighing, apparently satisfied she'd done her best.

"Help you?" She lifted her eyes to me and spoke, placing the finished envelope on the stack to her right. No smile. A glance at the clock.

"Grace Lynn Rose." I had my hat in my hand and wondered if she thought I had come begging for something.

The woman, mid-thirties, auburn-haired, a bit thin and sharp-faced, said nothing. But she looked me over carefully—like she suspected me of stealing. The look seemed more a true, concentrated study than a simple-minded once-over. In any case, my right leg quivered and I instinctively shifted weight, silently deciding the motion could have made me look guilty of whatever she might be thinking.

"I know you," she said, leaning back in the armless, swivel chair. "You drive around Ransom. River Road, the Boulevard, Pickett."

"I live in Ransom."

"But you drive a lot. Do you have an appointment with Grace Lynn Rose?"

"No."

"Does she know you?"

"Slightly."

"Is there something I can help you with?"

"No. I came to see Grace Lynn Rose."

Pause. She picked up another envelope, pushed back the flap and began dabbing with the sponge. "Grace Lynn Rose is busy," she said, not looking up.

"So am I." My reply, quick and curt, didn't seem to register on her.

The woman picked up the telephone receiver and punched three numbers on the dial. "Elderly man down here says he needs to see you."

Pause.

"What you want to see Grace Lynn Rose about?"

"I'll tell her."

Eyes constricted. Annoyed?

"He won't tell me. Wants to talk to you."

Pause.

"Says she's real busy now. Can you come back?"

"No," I said, my tone sharper. "Tell her Wiley Frost is here."

Pressing down on an envelope, the secretary repeated the message into the phone. "Yeah, sure. I remember now. Yeah. Right now. Sure."

Impatient, I glanced at a row of framed *Telegraph* front pages on the wall to my left. On one, the headline said, "War is Declared" and I recognized a picture of Franklin Roosevelt.

The secretary stood, half-turned and pointed to the steps

behind her. "You can go on up there, Mr. Frost. Grace Lynn Rose is in the far corner—in the little glass office."

I started for the stairs. From behind me came the sound of a finger snap and a sucking kind of deep breath.

"I knew I knew you," the woman said to my moving back. "You got your picture in the paper yesterday when you fainted driving your car and almost killed some reporters and Champ Crawford and tore down that old widow woman's fence. Are you all right now? Can your heart take the stairs?"

I didn't answer.

For spite, I took the last few steps two at a time and arrived in the newsroom with all my breath.

Elderly, indeed.

"Aren't you Mr. Frost?" A balding man in a maroon bow tie and white shirt came around a desk to the right, just inside the door. "Wiley Frost?"

When he spoke my name, the words seemed to reverberate around the room—like the voice of a poor, lost and doomed wanderer calling to himself from the bottom of a sunbaked, lifeless rock canyon. That's because nearly everyone stopped talking. No one pecked at the computers. Every eye in the room focused on me.

"I came to see Grace Lynn Rose."

The man in the maroon tie smiled. "Well, Mr. Frost, you could have been about one day too late. Close call you had yesterday."

"Yes," I said, looking quickly around the room at all the faces aimed in my direction.

"Did you black out, Mr. Frost?"

"Did you have to put a picture of it on the front page?" I asked, showing my best grimace.

The man chuckled.

"News, Mr. Frost. Narrow escape for a lot of people. People in Ransom need to know about that kind of thing."

"I don't think so," I said. "Where is Grace Lynn Rose?"

He motioned to a glass-partitioned cubicle in the corner to my left. Grace Lynn Rose stuck a finger in the air and half-pointed at me—like she would an inattentive waiter. I moved toward her, noticing that a few people had started working the computers and renewing conversations.

Stepping around full trash cans and over short piles of newspapers on the floor, I could hear the hum of voices and machines and didn't feel quite the public spectacle of the day before, when, lights flashing and radios squawking, the rescue people pulled me from my car, strapped me to a board and roared to the hospital.

Still, I sensed inquisitiveness and little mercy.

At the door to the cubicle, I stood for a moment waiting for the young woman at the desk to acknowledge my presence. A framed diploma told me she'd graduated two years before from Campbell University. A brass plaque—a feature writing award— said she'd worked for a weekly in Burlington. For a moment, I watched long, delicate fingers run over the computer keyboard and found myself suddenly absorbed with what I saw on the video screen.

"Champ Crawford says he's undaunted in his quest for a meeting with Augusta Morefield Crawford, widow of Bobby Crawford, Korean war hero whose skeletal remains were found buried in the Ransom Town Common.

"Nearly killed yesterday along with a group of journalists when a runaway car mowed down fencing at Augusta Crawford's home on Pickett Street, Champ Crawford says he'll continue his sit-in and fast across the street until his former sister-in-law appears and talks.

"Police identified the driver of the car as Wiley T. Frost, well-known former Ransom automobile dealer and mortician. Police Chief Toby Pugh says the elderly Frost, who suffers from a heart condition, blacked out and lost control of the vehicle. Frost was treated and released at Ransom Memorial Hospital."

"Did you have to say elderly?" I asked.

Grace Lynn Rose dropped her hands in her lap, turned and looked up at me. "You retired?" she asked, tight-lipped at the interruption.

"Yes."

"You over 62?"

"Yes."

"Draw Social Security?"

"Yes."

"Then, for purposes of description, you're elderly." No smile. Red and blue paisley blouse. Blue pants. Scruffy brown loafers, no socks. Small, well built. Wonderful skin. Slightly elongated face. Perfect nose, lovely teeth. Neat brown hair, pony tail. Thin lips. Gray eyes. Disposition of a dragon.

"You got a chair?" I asked, deciding I'd lost the elderly argument.

With both hands, Grace Lynn Rose pulled a pile of papers and notebooks from a steel chair next to her desk. She swiveled about and dropped the stack on the floor in front of her. Then she turned to me.

"You almost killed me yesterday, Mr. Frost."

We looked at each other, eye to eye. "I don't remember," I said. "Woke up in the hospital, people punching and taking blood and trying to get me to talk."

"How you feeling today?"

"Sore," I said.

"Did you drive down here?"

"Yes."

"Did you feel all right driving?"

"Yes."

It seemed a good time to shift the direction of the conversation. Instinct told me that giving her the wrong answer about my driving could get me nothing but another offer of a trip to the clinic.

Grace Lynn Rose pushed herself straight up into the secretarial chair and crossed her legs. She began swinging the leg that dangled and briefly turned her foot at the ankle—like she might be trying to work sleep from the joint. More likely, however, that reflected pure boredom: She wanted to be done with me and get back to her story.

"You almost killed Champ Crawford, too, Mr. Frost. She

raised one hand and tapped the video screen with a knuckle. "If you'd killed him, no more installments to the Bobby-Augusta story—except for an obit on the lost hero's brother."

A sad sort of look crossed her mouth and her eyes drifted to the computer and hung there for a few seconds like she saw an error or a place needing new or different wording.

"When do these stories end?" I asked, my tone as pleasant as I could make it. "Don't you think Ransom people are tired of this?"

She faced me and laughed, loudly and so long that I felt conspicuous again. "When there's no more story to tell," she said.

"Do you read the stories, Mr. Frost?"

"Yes," I said.

"So do people all over the county and the state. You're as curious as everybody else." She pointed at me, her laughter retreating into a knowing smirk. "You'll read this story in tomorrow's paper. I'll bet you'll be one of the first at the newsstand."

I didn't respond.

"People love this stuff, Mr. Frost. I got big papers in other states wanting me to do stories for them. The whole Eastern United States is talking about Ransom. Tomorrow I'm going to do a story on the star-crossed lovers, how they got together at a formal dance at the Woman's Club and went on to get married. I'm going to write about their great love and how it endured through the war but faded into mystery the day he got his medal."

I couldn't wait.

"Where'd you get your information?"

"Champ Crawford."

"You think he's reliable?"

From the way her eyes held steady on me and the slight twitch of her lips, I could tell she didn't like the question.

"Why shouldn't he be?"

I dropped my eyes and fiddled with my hatband. "Well, he's Bobby Crawford's brother," I said.

"What do you mean?" Grace Lynn Rose uncrossed her legs and leaned toward me, left elbow propped on her left knee, chin resting on her closed left hand. "What do you know?" she asked, her manner warmer, less intense. Coaxing.

"More than you do," I said, turning my hat around in my hands.

"Has Champ Crawford got something to hide about Bobby? What do you know that I need to know?"

I didn't speak.

She leaned back in her chair, crossed her arms and smiled. "I've talked to a dozen people who agreed Bobby Crawford achieved genuine hero status in Korea and honestly got the Silver Star."

"No argument," I said, looking behind her at the wall calendar which had Champ Crawford's name penciled in several blocks.

"Then what are we talking about here, Mr. Frost? Is this fantasy hour? Why did you come to see me?"

Curious now?

"Something wrong with my stories, Mr. Frost?"

Her voice rose a little but I didn't reply right away. Some of the people close by the cubicle stopped typing and looked at us. A few of those standing seemed to be subtly side-stepping in our direction for better hearing.

Grace Lynn Rose, somewhat flushed and grim, uncrossed her legs and put one foot on the swivel base of her chair.

Ominous silence, hanging.

"Are you wasting my time, Mr. Frost?"

"Not if I know something you don't."

"What do you know?"

"You going to write a story about it?"

"I'll tell you after I hear what you say."

Fair, but I wanted a commitment. Hell, she'd been writing every word out of Champ Crawford's mouth. I settled my hat on my lap and edged my chair toward her. She slipped her chair closer to me -- she meant to meet me halfway.

I looked around as though I kept the world's most startling secret and when I spoke, my voice remained just above a whisper. "I knew Bobby Crawford back then and I kept a log about some things," I said.

"What kind of log?"

"I drove the ambulance. Ambulance log. I kept notes on every call. Detailed notes."

Now she whispered: "What's that got to do with Bobby and Augusta? Did they call the ambulance?"

"No," I said. "The hotel clerk called me. I got the doctor and the minister."

Hooked. I could see in her eyes.

"What hotel are you talking about? What doctor and minister? What's the connection to Bobby Crawford?"

At that moment, I stood up and took a couple of steps toward the cubicle door. "I can tell you about all of it. I can tell you about how Bobby Crawford killed a young girl and I got notes in my log and a coroner's report."

"Sit down, Mr. Frost."

"Not now," I said, wanting her to become so curious she'd at least lose a night's sleep. "Meet me at Cobb's Graveyard tomorrow morning. I'll talk about it then."

"I don't know where that is," she said, a look of distress crossing her face.

"Ask somebody. Seven o'clock."

Without a handshake or a look back, I turned and picked my way back through the desks and office debris, found the stairs and jogged down the steps, skipping at least two on the way. To my surprise, I considered justice for Blithe Tanner and peace for Augusta real possibilities.

Chapter 9

In early fall, light comes just before seven and the persistent river mist, thick and chilling, hugs the ground. That gave Cobb's Graveyard all the ghostly isolation of any desolate Scottish moor.

I arrived first. For a while, I sat in the car, avoiding the gray dampness, wondering why somebody hadn't graded out the brain-jarring path through the field or cut grass on graves or seen to broken headstones.

Nobody cared, that's why.

Cobb's Graveyard had always been the end of the Earth: A patch of old Charlie Cobb's farm given to Ransom before the Civil War because it seemed distant and remote enough so nobody had to think about those in the ground. Call it anything: A poor man's last resort, or a dumping site for the unwanted, the evil, the misunderstood or the unidentified.

Churches bought most of the markers and I buried many a body there—from sad, no-name wretches who dropped dead on a street to the banker's son who shot himself over a carnival girl. Looking at the headstones swimming in the mist, I remembered when only a kindly black preacher would agree to say words over Rodney Allen Truelove, seventeen years old.

Alas and Amen. The parents stayed home. A helper and I stood with shovels, the minister laid his hat on the ground and opened his Bible and the carnival left town.

Even with my windows closed, the rattle of the approaching car roused me. An old Ford station wagon, lights on, stopped behind me. The woman in the car shut off the engine and lights, stepped out and slammed the door.

"Mr. Frost?"

I opened my door and eased out.

"You're late," I said. "It's five after seven."

Grace Lynn Rose, in green pants, shiny brown hiking boots and faded army fatigue jacket, whipped at the ground fog with a spiral notebook. "Lucky I'm here at all. This is the pits. How long it this going to take? Christ, I left my tape recorder in the car."

She turned but I touched her arm.

"We'll get to that," I said.

Silence. Just the noise of a few birds.

"I can't see anything," she said, her tone protesting. Her bottom lip pushed forward and quivered a little. Grown woman in a girlish snit.

She looked dazed — it seemed she'd just pulled herself out of bed, dashed on makeup, rubber-banded her hair and jumped in the car.

"Too early for you?"

"No," she said testily. "I like getting up in the dark."

I felt a smile pull at my mouth. Perhaps she deserved a little discomfort. Maybe she needed a dose of reality like Cobb's Graveyard. Then, perhaps, she'd stop writing those stories.

Dream on.

I told her we'd have to wait a few minutes for the mist to burn off. Then I'd make my point.

"What is the point, Mr. Frost? "You said Bobby Crawford

killed a girl and you said you had ambulance logs. I don't see anything here but fog and tombstones. What is this place?"

"I'll show you."

Grace Lynn Rose shook her head, trying to coax her mind into gear. "I'll get some coffee," she said. "I've got a Thermos in the car. Do you want some coffee, Mr. Frost?"

"No," I said, leaning back against the car fender and feeling a little warmth on my back from the rising sun. For a few minutes, she fiddled around in the station wagon. I could hear her talking to herself but couldn't catch the words.

"Find it?" I called over my shoulder and watched a hawk skim the tops of trees along the river bank.

No answer.

Then I heard the door slam and she stood beside me holding the plastic Thermos cup in both hands. She blew on the black coffee and sipped.

"Thermos rolled under the seat," she said. "Terrible road."

"Nobody comes here," I said.

"Why not?" Suddenly, she seemed a little interested and almost pleasant.

"Social Security, welfare. Almost everybody can afford to be buried these days. There's some history here but mostly for the unfortunate."

She drank the smoking coffee.

Watching her face, I continued. "People started burying dead slaves out here in the mid-1850s. Yankee soldiers here, too. Some died of fevers, some mysteriously. Nobody knew their names. My grandfather said four or five got thrown into one grave, no questions asked."

"You going to show me that?"

"Not marked. Lost," I said.

For awhile, we didn't talk. Grace Lynn Rose concentrated on coffee but frequently glanced wide-eyed at the graveyard, perhaps expecting to see some disgusting creature from late-night TV horror arise and approach, remnants of rotten clothing dripping from upraised arms of bare bone. Walking, stalking.

As for myself, I thought about snakes—large, thick cotton-mouths drifting through the weeds to sun on flat grave markers.

Grace Lynn Rose pitched the last of her coffee on the ground and stepped back to her car to deposit the cup. By now, trees along the river had taken shape and mist around tombstones had receded to show the height and color of green-brown grass.

I straightened and walked a couple of steps, trying to get circulation up in my legs. "This way," I said. "Watch where you step. Look down."

"Why?" she asked, her face contorted in almost childish apprehension.

"Snakes," I said.

"Shit," she mumbled.

I knew all about Cobb's Graveyard. Pointing to a clear stretch of earth, I speculated slaves and Yankees had been buried there. Grace Lynn Rose said nothing but walked along, pausing to look at faces of tombstones. I found a long, sturdy stick to push grass and dirt from flat markers so we could read inscriptions.

She stopped before three stones, all nearly black with age, two broken at odd angles—just below the tops. Another, whole but badly chipped, leaned backwards and seemed ready to topple. She knelt near the center stone and read the names aloud:

"Geraldine Mercer, 1842-1859

Robert A. Mercer, 1822-1893

Florence B. Mercer, 1852-1873."

I didn't comment but walked on, sweeping the stick through the grass, thinking that would frighten the snakes. Grace Lynn Rose came up behind me.

"Mercer had two wives. People married young, Mr. Frost. Women died in childbirth, I suppose." The sun, a reddish half-ball, began to heat my face. I stopped and looked at her. She stepped along, looking down, just like I'd told her to.

"Old man Mercer killed his wives," I said, my tone purposely dry and matter-of-fact. "My grandfather told me he called them unfaithful to a jury both times and they let him go."

Shaking her head, Grace Lynn Rose glanced back at the three headstones. "Both?"

"Yes," I said. "Strangled."

I stopped. With the end of the stick, I pushed back grass knitted across a flat marker at my feet. Then I got down on one knee, snatched at weeds and brushed dirt away with my hand.

This time, I read the inscription:

Alonza C. Crawford, 1850-1876
Hanged.

She crouched beside me. "Who?" Her question sounded almost absent-minded, a girl struggling to sort out an abundance of new discoveries.

"Another Crawford," I said, trying to inject dripping prejudice into the words. "Convicted, carried outside, yanked up a on a tree limb with a rope."

Grace Lynn Rose shivered and stood up. She wrote Alonza Crawford's name, date and tombstone commentary in her notebook. "This one kin to Bobby Crawford and Champ Crawford?"

"Great-uncle," I said, standing.

She continued to write. At first, I could hear her pen scratching across the paper but the sound soon got lost in the growing, rushing noise of leaves moving in a new and cooling breeze.

"What did he do?"

Taking a breath, I poked along, jabbing at the grass with the stick. "Old story says he stabbed a man named Henderson twenty-six times in his own yard while the whole Henderson family screamed from the front steps," I said, trying to remember details from my grandfather and father. "Max Lee Henderson. He nearly bit Alonza Crawford's hand off trying to get the knife." I looked at her. "Whole thing started over a stray mule."

Grace Lynn Rose looked down at her pad, made a few more notes and looked over at the tree line, up at the brightening sun and back at me. Her mouth stayed tight but her eyes seemed a little softer, her manner less aggressive.

"We got to get on with this, Mr. Frost. Show me what you

brought me to see."

I pointed with the stick. "In this corner. Step carefully."

Dew-heavy grass swished about my feet, sending a cold wetness creeping up my pants. "Over here," I said. But I couldn't find Blithe Tanner's grave until I recognized an old, red plastic flower pot I brought last Easter. Full of black-eyed Susans. Empty now, cracked and weathered, the pot sat halfway down in the hole I carved that day with my pocket knife.

I got down and chopped around the marker with a sharp stone and it occurred to me I should pay someone to clean the stone and grave. Then I decided I'd do it myself one day.

Grace Lynn Rose bent over to read:

Blithe Tanner
Died May, 1951

Then she stood, clutching the open notebook in both hands and pressing the pen between a couple of fingers. She glanced at her watch.

"Who's this?"

Impatient again?

In the few seconds it took for me to get to my feet, she backed away like she meant to go to her car. Grime blackened my hands, both shoes squished from the dew and wet pants stuck to my legs. Losing her at that point would have been worse than anticlimactic.

"This is the girl Bobby Crawford killed."

Grace Lynn Rose shook her head just like channel eight's six o'clock news anchor. "Where are the logs you told me about? How did Bobby Crawford kill this girl?"

For a second, I ignored the questions and thought of magazines at the supermarket checkout. Did Grace Lynn Rose read about two-headed babies in Peru and Princess Diana?

"Captive," I said, my heart suddenly up in my throat.

"Who?"

"This girl here," I said, pointing to the marker. "Bobby Crawford kept her captive."

Grace Lynn Rose laughed—like she'd just learned the final answer to some maddening crossword—and closed her notebook.

She stuck the pen over her ear. "What have you got against Bobby Crawford?" she asked, teeth flashing and grinding.

I slapped both hands together, trying to dislodge clay and grit. Thinking of Blithe Tanner tied to the bed that way, I gathered myself. And feelings—old, hard and deep—dictated my next move:

"I'm going for breakfast at the Sheraton," I said, "and then I'm going to the post office and the bank. Then I'm gong home for a nap."

We walked toward the cars. Zero conversation. She almost skipped ahead, her eyes on the ground, watching for snakes, I guess. About the time I reached the front of my car, she slammed her door and started the engine. Both hands on the wheel, she looked at me.

"Blithe Tanner," I said, not caring whether she heard or not. "Don't forget her name."

Chapter 10

When she caught up with me the next day in the showroom at Reasonable Chevrolet, Grace Lynn Rose seemed subdued and even a little pensive as she sat on one of the bright, flower-print couches.

Perhaps she wondered about my reaction to her latest "undaunted" Champ Crawford story—the one I saw on her computer. Of course, she didn't know I exorcised my outrage by walking around a car lot with Wayland Thomas, listening to him spout and speculate how long it would take Champ Crawford to starve. He even suggested Augusta make peace by bringing the crotchety old bastard some molasses cookies. Good God.

Grace Lynn Rose stared out the big front window, turned through magazines and waited for me to stop haggling with Wayland Thomas over a new car. At one point, I thought if I couldn't get Wayland down three hundred dollars more she might have to see me another day.

"Can't do it," smiling Wayland said, twirling his pencil. "I swear to God, Wiley, I've cut this until it's screaming. It's embarrassing to take a deal like this to the boss. He'll laugh. How do you like people laughing at you?"

I didn't. So I thumped on his desk with a knuckle.

"That's my offer," I said. "New cars got computers, Wayland, and it costs money to fix a mind. One of these new ones could be more expense than my old one."

Grace Lynn Rose stirred on the couch, turned slightly and caught my eye over her left shoulder. I looked down at Wayland Thomas's paper.

"Wiley, you're trading a car with a ripped-up front end. Hell, it's got picket fence rammed all through the hood, lights are cracked, grill's gone and the fan's hitting the radiator."

"Only seven years old, eighteen thousand miles," I said, insistent.

In the press of discussion, I took my eyes off the woman on the couch. When I looked again, she'd started talking to Terry Tuten, another salesman, about a slick, yellow showroom convertible. They pointed and chatted, voices drifting to me in friendly, pleasant tones. Head down, Wayland figured and fumed and didn't see Terry and Grace Lynn Rose approach. He didn't even look up when Terry leaned on the top of the booth.

"Wayland, you got a key to a demonstrator convertible?" he asked. He flipped a grin at me. "Miss Grace Lynn Rose wants a test drive."

Without stopping his pencil scratch, Wayland Thomas pulled a key with a stringed tag from his pocket, handed it to Terry Tuten, grunted and squirmed in his plastic chair and glared at me. He hadn't forgotten I made him walk the other day. "No, Wiley."

I shook my head and just then, Grace Lynn Rose called to me: "Mr. Frost, want a ride in a convertible with the top down?"

Tired of Wayland Thomas, I stood.

"Yes," I said.

I picked up my hat and followed her toward the door.

"Wiley?" Cowboy boots thumped behind me. Wayland put a hand on my shoulder and I stopped. "Aren't we dealing, Wiley?" he said, a plaintive, almost pathetic lilt in his voice.

I put on my hat and squinted at him. "Wayland, I'm going

riding in a convertible with the top down." With that, I hurried through the door and down the steps to the little green convertible with Grace Lynn Rose at the wheel.

"I rescued you," she said, smiling and pulling into the traffic. "You could have petrified there—just like some old piece of wood."

"Not old," I said quickly. "Elderly."

She laughed, mumbled, "sorry" and turned right at the corner, heading toward the west end of town—out past the shirt factory and the small mill village houses.

I discovered right away that Grace Lynn Rose liked speed and slipped down in my seat, trying to keep my hat.   The speedometer zoomed past fifty in a thirty-five zone. When we flew by a new speed limit sign, she hit the accelerator and I watched the needle touch seventy, then drop back to fifty five. Still, we seemed to rocket past the mill, reminding me of riding with Augusta in her white Buick convertible.

"Strong. Fast." she said, grinning and glancing at me.

"Too much for you?"

"Yes," I said, finally taking off my hat and allowing the thirty-odd strands of white hair on my head to fly out of control.

So she slowed.

"I want to see your logs and talk to you for the record," she said, looking straight ahead. "How did Bobby Crawford kill Blithe Tanner. Strangulation?"

Too fast, again.

"I'm not going to talk racing around the country like this. We have to have a sit-down discussion, not a passing conversation."

Grace Lynn Rose didn't like that.

"You can tell me how she died, can't you?"

"Pneumonia," I said.

She turned the car onto the gravel approach to the softball park and stopped. Dropping her hands in her lap, she looked square into my face. "He didn't strangle her or shoot her or stab her or at least smother her with a pillow?"

"She just died."

"That's nothing," she said. "That's no kind of a story—not like Champ Crawford finding out how his hero brother died. We need spark and flame."

"Bobby Crawford's not a hero in this story."

"You still haven't told me what you've got against him." Grace Lynn Rose pulled the windshield mirror around and checked her makeup, fingering spots around her nose, smoothing beneath her eyes and patting her chin like she thought it might be ready to crumble. Then she settled straight behind the wheel. The engine hummed. I ran my hand over my hair and said nothing.

"This afternoon," she said.

I nodded. "At the store building on my Clay Root farm," I said. "One-thirty."

"Where's that?"

"Route eleven twenty-one, three and a quarter miles from the Cherryburg highway. You'll see the turn. Big wagon wheel mailbox. Store building's white and got a rusty Pure Oil sign."

I put on my hat.

"I'll never find it," she said, shaking her head and getting a grip on the wheel.

"Ask somebody," I grumbled.

Grace Lynn Rose didn't like that. She spun tires in the gravel, threw up a cloud of dust and rocks and lurched onto the pavement with such force my heart fluttered.

At one-fifteen, mildly elated after out-dealing Wayland Thomas, I arrived at the store and parked a new, unblemished car under the old wagon shed. A minute later, I heard distant rattling and saw the Ford station wagon on the dirt road, barely outrunning a cloud of thick, gray dust.

When she turned up the lane, Grace Lynn Rose glanced at her watch, then smiled at me. She stopped next to the rust-eaten Pure Oil sign, got out, pulled at the shoulder strap on her purse and closed the door.

"See?" She tapped the face of her watch.

At the store door, I entered the last number on the combination lock, snatched down and pulled the lock from the hasp. Then I pushed open the door. Right away, the deep, damp, musty smell struck my senses, making me think more ventilation or simple household deodorizer couldn't hurt.

Walking between counters, I pulled on overhead lights and looked up and down aisles for mice or squirrels that might have gotten in through the flooring. Around the ceiling, spider webs abounded but no bats.

Not far behind, Grace Lynn Rose took a breath.

"Oh," she said, open-mouthed astonishment crossing her face. "Another world."

Frost Dry Goods and Seed always looked the same to me but a visitor needed explanation. "My father's lament," I said. "My grandfather left it like this the day he died in 1930. He took his lunch to grandmother's grave. My father found him dead against an oak stump. The store closed that day and never reopened."

"Time warp," she said, walking slowly up and down the aisles, fingering and sometimes picking up dusty coffee and tobacco tins, high-top shoes and women's hats of dyed straw and fake, now faded, colorless flowers. She lingered in front of a crank Victrola, inspected seed bin labels and swiveled the rooster on a dusty weather vane display. She smiled at a bottle of Lydia Pinkham's Nerve Tonic.

"This is a story by itself," she said.

"I have a better one," I replied, heading for the office behind the cash register counter. She followed me, walking half-turned, still examining my grandfather's merchandise. At the office door, I glanced back and her expression had taken on a soft, dreamy look. Perhaps she imagined—as I often did—haunting sounds and voices of a long-ago day when children whispered and nervously counted coins for candy, women tugged and stroked bright-colored fabrics and men smoked and condemned Herbert Hoover by a hot wood stove.

I turned the key and opened the door, found the light and

walked inside the small room lined floor to ceiling with bookcases, all filled.

"Records," I said.

Grace Lynn Rose stepped up beside me. "Of what?" she asked, eyes scanning shelves of papers, collected in thick, loose-leaf, metal-clasp folders, standing upright.

"Every transaction at Frost Ford and Funeral Home until I sold it."

"You sold cars and embalmed people in the same place?" She looked horrified.

"Next door to the service area, actually. But there was just a partition between the paint shop and the embalming room."

Since I used the office for farm accounting, I tried to keep my grandfather's desk, straight-backed chair and a classic red leather Morris chair clean and dust free. I walked to the desk, gathered up some bank statements, encircled them with a rubber band and dropped the stack into the top, right-hand drawer. Just to be sure, I brushed at the Morris chair's seat and arms with my handkerchief and asked Grace Lynn Rose to sit.

For a few seconds, she seemed reluctant to leave her reading of labels. What if I had opened the 1956 volume and showed her pictures of dead Wilton Pennington, the poor soul who fell under a hay rake that year? The sight might have shocked her into sitting.

Finally, she took the chair, dropped her purse on the floor and looked moved, but most likely confused. "I could write a book on just this—on this store and on stuff in your records."

"No," I said.

"Why?"

"Because it all belongs to me. I'll show you what you need to see and tell you what you need to know. Fair?"

"News management," she muttered, pony tail switching while she tried to adjust the tilted back of the Morris chair.

"Private ownership." I said, turning my chair toward her and feeling satisfaction at having parried her comment.

Grace Lynn Rose got the back of the chair where she wanted it and settled herself, legs crossed, notebook resting on one knee.

"Well, Mr. Frost?"

I sat in the desk chair, took off my hat and put it on top of a filing cabinet to my left.   Turning back to face her, I saw a small tape recorder standing on the desk.   Through a tiny, clear plastic window, I saw a tape turning.

"No," I said, punching it off. "We have to talk first."

She slapped her pen down on the notebook and shook her head, exasperated.   "The dawn of man took less time than this, Mr. Frost."

"I'm looking for a little justice," I said, realizing I couldn't be laboriously cryptic if I wanted to keep her interested. "I got things to tell. You can quote my words and describe me and talk about my background but everything has to be from me—directly, word-for-word. And I want to see what you write before it's published."

That did it.

Grace Lynn Rose stood, grabbed her tape recorder, jostled it up in her arms with notebook and purse and started for the open door.

I spoke quickly: "I can tell you Bobby Crawford brought a young girl to Ransom in the Spring of 1951, kept her locked and bound in a hotel room, fed her jelly sandwiches three times a day and let her loose only for the bathroom — at his convenience.   Pure abuse, I'd say."

She stopped and turned around. "You'd let me quote you?"

"Yes, I said that—but under my terms."

I had her complete attention.

"Our hero did this?"

"Military hero," I said, temper rising. "Rest of the great legend isn't so great."

Grace Lynn Rose took a step toward the Morris chair.

"Ransom's darkest secret," I continued. "Whole town has worshiped—literally—a man who survived Korea only to come back home and commit an act for which, alive or dead, he's never been held accountable. He killed a young girl just as dead as if he shot her."

I stood and got my hat off the filing cabinet.

"I've got an appointment," I said, walking quickly toward

the light switch.   "Norfolk newspaperman's got a room at the Holiday Inn."

Silence.

Clutching the purse, notebook, pen and recorder in her arms like a good mother holding a special child, she raised her right hand, palm out. I couldn't decide if she wanted to take an oath or parley.

"What if I agree?" she asked, chin up, mouth intense, eyes anxious, visually caressing the bookcase volumes as a hungry dog might behold a meaty hambone.

Chapter 11

May, 1951.

After brushing dust from the binder with my hand, I gave the bulging file to Grace Lynn Rose. Finally, I could hear Champ Crawford's silence.

"On the desk," I directed, handing it over with my right hand and motioning to the desktop with my left.

"I'll get started," she said, placing the file on the desk, ignoring me and turning to the first entry. Small, ringless fingers smoothed yellowed, mold-edged papers and photographs.

"In a minute," I said, my voice dry and short, not wanting her to get ahead of me. "This is my system. I'm trying to remember dates, deciding if I need June."

She slapped the file closed like a little girl caught peeking, then warmed her best recitation voice: "Bobby Crawford arrived by train Wednesday, May 13, 1951," she said, voice unemotional, eyes impatiently roaming dark, half-pulled curtains and bright, odd spears of light shooting into the room. "He rode with his wife on the convertible and got his medal at the courthouse. After that, Bobby

Crawford took Augusta to her house, walked her to the front steps, passionately kissed her to the applause of a crowd at the gate, got back in a car and rode to the Ransom Hotel to celebrate with his friends."

Right out of the social pages. I put the June file back in its place, wishing she'd omitted the passionate kiss.

"How did you know?"

"Old newspaper clippings and Champ Crawford," she said, "He told me he drove Bobby to the hotel and they had a party that lasted long and late." The reporter smiled when she spoke and her expression seemed to acquire distance—like she'd been there and remembered the party as she might a country club cotillion, complete with icy, lightly-spiked fruit punch, the swish of long dresses and conversation that sounded like Canada geese whispering to each other long before dawn.

Really.

I took my chair. She hung over my right shoulder as I turned papers and old black and white photographs.

"Ouch."

"Willie Carlisle," I said, holding up the photograph. "Nice man. Store owner. Robbery. Got a blast of birdshot in the face. Got another one in the stomach at close range. Lived 18 minutes after I got there. See the pellets—some just under the skin on his cheeks."

She didn't look away. "Let's get on with it," she said, waving a pointed finger just below my eyes.

I pretended not to hear and kept turning, slowly filtering through the pictures and my handwritten comments about death and injury. Some took me back to sleep-shattering phone calls, shivering in the cold on black, winter nights, smelling blood of murder, suicide and highway madness, enduring cries of pain from the back of the ambulance while I raced to Ransom Memorial.

Then I found a picture of Tim Slusher, one day old.

"I delivered this baby," I said, remembering the fear and tediousness of the moment. "He's over 40 now. Good citizen."

"I know him," she said. Then: "May 13th, Mr. Frost. Are we ever going to get there?"

I ignored that, too, and took a few seconds to pry apart some stuck-together photos and fiddle with a piece of slippery onionskin paper that seemed destined for the floor.

"Here."

"Damn," she said, her tone reminding me of my farm manager, who kept field hands jumping with sharp, one-word comments, mostly expletives.

"At 11:06 on Wednesday, May 13, 1951, call received. Woman with a high fever at Hotel Ransom. Arrived at the hotel at 11:31."

She leaned down further, fingers running along lines of an odd sweeping scrawl. "Who wrote this?"

"I did."

"What does it say?"

"I'll read."

She sat in the Morris chair, plunked the tape recorder up on the desk and pressed the record switch. Again, I turned it off. "I'll read. You take notes. Record later. You agreed."

More grumbling and muttering. But she quickly got her notebook arranged on her knees and focused on me with a half-stare, waiting.

My voice seemed an odd, hesitant croak as I slowly deciphered my own hasty handwriting and started the story of that night at the Hotel Ransom. "Night clerk Joel Honeycutt at front door. Told my helper and me room 310 wanted ambulance. Honeycutt took us up in elevator to third floor and left us. At 310, Bobby Crawford opened door."

I paused, running a forefinger over the lines of my log, attempting to speak and make sense at the same time. Head down, Grace Lynn Rose scribbled on her notebook.

"So what did he say when he opened the door?" She kept her eyes on her note taking.

"Come in," I said, not looking up.

"That's all? Shit."

I continued: "Two rooms. 310 adjoined 312. Three men in room, including Bobby Crawford. He indicated subject in 312 and sat down at a table with the two other men. Helper and I entered 312 and found a young, black-haired woman in double bed, covered by sheet."

Pause.

"Well, did she say anything?"

"She groaned," I said, irritated at the interruptions.

"What did Bobby Crawford say?" This time, I had complete control. She looked up at me, expression all business, eyes narrowed, concentrating on my every word.

I read from the log: "Bobby Crawford identified woman as Blithe Tanner of San Francisco, California. He said she came to Ransom to visit friends and got sick. Examination indicated subject semi-conscious, delirium from fever. Weak pulse, deep and heavy chest congestion, wheezing, labored breathing, wrists restrained to the bedposts by leather belts. Naked. I unstrapped her wrists and told Bobby Crawford to get a doctor."

"All that? What did Bobby Crawford say?"

"He said no."

The newspaper reporter stopped writing and looked at me. "Why?"

"Drunk," I said, shrugging my shoulders and going on: "Explained urgency. Repeated request for doctor. Bobby Crawford said no again. Then he told one of the men in 310 to call Dr. Jamie Felton."

I paused over a word.

"Is that all?"

"No," I said.

I pointed to the tape recorder. Grace Lynn Rose let her notebook pad rest on her knees and thumped the record button.

Pushing my chair back from the desk, I sat very still for a moment, trying to think of words that would describe the scene, not distort or embellish it. In my mind, I saw the hotel room's sorry yellow wallpaper, burn-spotted lampshade, sheer, lace-looking curtains and a coil of leather belts on the floor.

Watching the tiny tape turning in the recorder, I spoke carefully. "Here is what I saw: Bobby Crawford and the two other men played cards at a table and all were so drunk they could hardly hold their chairs. The card game didn't stop. Right on shuffling and dealing.   Bobby Crawford had on his Army uniform, tie loose, shirttail out. He drank whisky from a pint bottle he held between his legs. The others had bottles on the table."

"Then what?"

"I couldn't understand why those men didn't want to help— except that whisky brought out meanness. I felt the woman's forehead again, poked a thermometer in her mouth, put my ear to her chest, pulled the thermometer and read 106 degrees. Then I walked to the open door. Bobby Crawford had his back to me, smoking a cigarette and taking frequent drinks from his bottle."

Grace Lynn Rose leaned forward in her chair and slipped the tape recorder closer to me. "Drinking whisky and playing poker with a sick, out-of-state naked girl tied to a bed? That's torture!"

I didn't answer, but glanced at pictures on the walls—stern portraits of my father and grandfather as old men and young men. Then I studied framed snapshots taken at hog killings, deer hunts and in corn and tobacco fields during peak harvests. What would my people think of me telling tales?

But at that moment, I couldn't consider the question and turned back to the file and Grace Lynn Rose.

"I spoke to Bobby Crawford and asked him about Dr. Felton. 'When he gets here, you'll be the first one to know, Wiley Frost,' he said. Then I told him the woman might die if we didn't get her fever down. He laughed and said she was too hot for her own good anyway. The other men laughed, too.

"'I need some ice,' I said. 'Need to ice this woman down, get her fever down.'"

Raising a hand, she stopped me.

"They kept on playing cards?"

"Yes."

"Did the doctor come?"

"Yes. I'll tell you." Impatience, impatience.

"I had to ask for ice a half-dozen times before Bobby Crawford ever acted like he heard me. Finally, I blurted I'd call the police if he didn't get some ice. At that, he growled and grunted, wobbled to his feet, pulled his wallet from a hip pocket and pitched it to the man across from him. He told him to go to the desk for ice. Man said the desk didn't have ice. Bobby Crawford said find ice, buy it if he had to."

"Did you know the man?"

"Yes."

"Who?"

Instinctively, I hesitated. But it didn't matter.

"Waverly Barnhill," I said. "But Waverly Barnhill never came back. I had to send my helper, Marty Chesnut, for ice and pillowcases to pack around her."

She put down her pen, fingered the pony tail and adjusted the rubber band.   She wrote Waverly Barnhill's name in her notebook and circled it.

For a moment, neither of us spoke. She looked over her notes, mumbling to herself, underlining words and groups of words. Then she looked up at me.

"Did you get her fever down?"

I described putting ice in the pillowcases and placing them around Blithe Tanner's body, knowing full well we'd soon have a wet bed to change.

"Her fever dropped a little and I kept expecting the doctor to come and tell us to take her on to the hospital but time passed and I got anxious and walked to the door and yelled at Bobby Crawford about the doctor.   Dealing cards, he didn't say anything at first. Then he snickered and I heard 'whore', among other things."

Grace Lynn Rose shook her head. "The doctor...?"

"At that point, I suspected nobody had called Jamie Felton or any other doctor. I told Marty Chesnut to stay with the girl. I'd go to the front desk to call a doctor and police."

"And?"

"There were two men in the room: Bobby and one more. Before I could get to the door, the man with Bobby got up and put himself between me and the knob and stood there, giving me a drunken, stupid smile. About the same time, I heard some squalling and realized Bobby Crawford had my helper with his arm twisted behind him.   He pushed Marty into 310 and hard against the wall. That knocked the breath out of Marty and he sort of slid down the wall, gasping.”

"Then?” she asked, eyes wide, mouth expectant.

“Bobby Crawford turned to me.   He took a pistol from his pocket,” I said, “and pushed the barrel against my forehead.”

Chapter 12

Her pen stopped.

"Say again?"

"No," I answered. "Listen."

"I did but did I hear you—that he put a pistol to your head?"

"Yes."

"Did he hit you?"

"No," I said. "I believe he wanted to entertain everybody in the room. I didn't think he'd shoot me but worried that he'd just come back from combat and might have felt nothing about killing. I remember he got very close to me and had terrible whisky breath."

Hunched over her notebook, the reporter wrote furiously. Pen flew over the paper, creating a nearly unreadable scribble—even worse than mine.

I waited for her notes to catch up with my story.

"What did he want?"

I took a deep breath.

"Trademark Bobby Crawford. In those days, people like Bobby and his friends carried pistols or at least had them in their cars.

The pistol amounted to pure reflex. He thought I'd do a little fixing on Blithe Tanner, leave and keep my mouth shut. Of course, he didn't want a doctor! When I got uncooperative, he thought his pistol might change my thinking."

"About what?"

"Why do you think they had her strapped to the bed?"

Her expression turned blank.

"To keep her from running," I suddenly shouted, sounding like a frothing tent preacher and not a bit sorry my voice made Grace Lynn Rose jump. "They wanted no interruptions. Bobby Crawford helped himself to her, along with the others. Not strong enough to fight. They didn't care about her being fevered, conscious or unconscious."

Leaning back in the Morris chair, she shivered. "Unbelievable," she whispered.

Calming myself, I got a rubber band from the desk and put it around two fingers, then three, then four. Then I started back to my thumb.

"What did you do?"

"Well, I didn't get shot," I said, trying for a speck of low humor. But she didn't catch it so I answered the question: "First, I yelled about getting a warrant for him. Then I yelled for him to put the gun down and get away from me and Marty Chesnut. Then I swore he wouldn't be anybody's hero when I got through with him."

"And then?"

"He pulled back the hammer."

The reporter took a breath and wrote quickly in her notebook.

"He kept the gun on me for another minute, staring at me, eye to eye, that awful breath in my face. Then he eased the hammer down. Right then, I heard noises from the other room—coughing, groaning, bed springs twanging like little Blithe Tanner might be trying to stand. Bobby Crawford pointed to the door of 312. I pulled Marty Chesnut off the floor and helped him into the next room. Bobby slammed the door behind us."

Newspaper reporters amaze me. One minute they're full of shallow questions and the next they offer insight in proportions that confound the mind.

"A real beast," she said.

"What, our hero?" I said.

She didn't respond, but gave me a hard look as she stood, placed notebook and pen on the seat of her chair and walked—to the window, to the wall pictures, to the refinished antique butter churn in one corner. For a second, she paused at a spider web running down from the top of one of the bookcases, then wiped it away with a sudden slash of her hand.

Then she turned to me: "You felt sorry for that girl. Did she die right away?"

Without speaking, I pointed to the Morris chair and pondered her question while she slowly took her seat. If everything I had told her got published, my motives had to be unquestionable. Using Blithe Tanner to dissolve Bobby Crawford hero-worship would free Ransom, reverse the collective mindset, and chase Champ Crawford from in front of Augusta's house. Small justice at last, I reasoned. But would that make Augusta come out of her house? Could anything dilute the pain of lost and lonely years?

Not for Blithe Tanner, Augusta or me.

Nevertheless, I took the simplest route: "Yes, I felt sorry for Blithe Tanner. And no, she didn't die right away. She died the next afternoon."

"No doctor ever came," the reporter's tone sounded suffocated by resignation, perhaps caught in her own feelings about Blithe Tanner.

The rubber band snapped off my fingers and landed somewhere on the floor. I didn't pay much attention.

"I got Jamie Felton," I said. "But by then, only God could help her. Pneumonia's too strong a killer."

She raised her hand, motioning she had to put in a new tape. I waited until she'd snapped the cover shut and pressed the record button: "Right after Bobby Crawford pushed us into 312, Marty

Chesnut and I did what we could.   At that point, we'd become prisoners like the poor girl struggling to get out of bed.   Marty and I both spoke to her and our words seemed to calm her. We found sheets in the closet and changed the bed with her on it, shifting her from side to side like nurses do.   All night, we took turns sponging and by morning she rested easier and I even thought her breathing might be better."

"How about Bobby Crawford?"

"I could hear a little from the next room. They got loud, talking and laughing, and I heard the outside door slam a couple of times.   They played cards and cursed Waverly Barnhill for not coming back. Bobby said he didn't like playing poker with just two people."

"How did you get the doctor?"

I picked up a pencil, leaned forward and tapped the eraser end on the desk.   "When I took over from Marty at 8:15 the next morning, no noise came from 310. I decided they'd passed out and thought I might try to slip by to the desk phone downstairs. After all, Bobby Crawford only shut the door to 312; he didn't lock it. I cracked the door and looked inside the other room. Nobody. Not a soul. Cards, colored chips and full ashtrays littered the tabletop and empty whiskey bottles stood on the bureau and the window sill."

"Then you called."

"Yes. I didn't take the elevator. I ran the stairs to phone Jamie Felton about a sick girl at the hotel. He got there a half-hour later, looked her over and pulled me to one side. 'She can't live," he said. "Breathing's near nothing and pulse's fading. Call me. I'll do a death certificate.'"

At that juncture, the desk chair started punishing my spine, so I stood to stretch and walk a bit. Grace Lynn Rose—perhaps from the intensity of my story-telling—seemed relieved at the break. She turned off the recorder and for a few minutes we didn't speak. I ambled up and down, heels scraping and thumping on plank floor-ing.   Through the curtain, light had faded so I tried to get my thoughts together to finish.

I stepped to the desk, sat again, and turned on the recorder.

"We kept sponging and turning, hoping Dr. Felton might be wrong—that so young a life might be spared. She rallied a few times, opened her eyes and looked at Marty and me and cried softly—like she knew—and I told her we'd stay with her."

"Did she talk?"

"A few times, just briefly. She told me about the train trip and the men who had bound her and taken turns with her. She spoke of Bobby Crawford, Waverly Barnhill and two other men. One of them blindfolded her and called her cherry lips. Then she said she felt hot and tired and wanted to go home to California. I asked her if she had family and never got an answer. Fell unconscious again."

The reporter sighed and leaned back, looking up at the ceiling, attempting to understand, I suppose, the people and events I'd described and given life. At one point, I wondered if she might be touched enough to cry but remembered good reporters stay tough, don't get too deeply involved.

"In about an hour, Blithe became conscious again and asked about Bobby Crawford. I told her he'd gone out. She said she needed to talk to him about throwing her in the river. Gave her back her clothes, she said, pulled her down to the river and pitched her off the bank. To get rid of the fever, he said. Then he took her back to the hotel, took her clothes again and pushed her back into the room."

"When did she die—what time?"

"About 5:20. It's here on the death certificate," I said, picking up the paper and waving it toward her. "At four, her breathing got so rough I thought she'd go then. So I tried to find a minister to come pray for her. Most visit congregation members on weekdays but I got Phillip Rayner. He said he'd come and got there about 4:45."

"Do you go to church?"

"Do you want the rest of this?" I asked, testiness showing.

"Go on," she said, unmoved.

"Phillip Rayner motioned me out of the chair I had next to the bed and sat down, Bible open. As he took the chair, I whispered her name to him and said she came from California and hadn't spoken about her family and would die in a few minutes. I also told him what Bobby Crawford and the others had done. He felt her pulse, touched her wet, matted hair, closed his eyes and prayed aloud for Blithe Tanner's soul, asking the Almighty for eternal peace and nearly shouting when he appealed for punishment for the men responsible for that child's death. Her eyes fluttered a little and then opened wide—like she saw something coming and couldn't get out of the way. Then she slipped away. I closed her eyes. Phillip Rayner sat with head bowed, repeating the 23rd Psalm until I touched his shoulder and told him she'd died."

Silence.

Maybe I told the story so well it seemed somebody had died right in my office. A late afternoon breeze moved trees near the window in a soft, rushing rhythm. Besides our breathing, that's all Grace Lynn Rose and I heard while we pondered a young girl, Bobby Crawford and events of a distant time.

Suddenly, she collected herself: "That's all?"

Like everything had been nothing.

I don't know why I overlooked the remark, kept my temper and continued: "Phillip Rayner closed his Bible and left. Marty Chesnut left to call Dr. Felton and the police. Alone there, I pulled back the sheet and looked at her tired and rigid face—a mask, not even a countenance. She could have been smiling and laughing—if her life hadn't been stolen."

My voice rose and cracked a little but I didn't care.

And while my listener may have felt twinges of pity for Blithe Tanner, any sign of that faded quickly once she saw me affected. She couldn't show her own feelings, I suppose. Maybe that's the reason she got real serious.

"What about Bobby and the others?

"Police couldn't find Waverly Barnhill or Bobby Crawford," I said.

"What happened to the other two?"

Suddenly, the weight of the past shifted, crushing all my designs into what I mentally pictured as fine, floating powder, caught in the whirlwind of words on tape, sucked into a semantics mill or oblivion. Weariness dogged my thinking: The truth was, after so many years, who cared about who did what to whom? Besides me, who said Ransom wanted to be freed of Bobby Crawford? Besides me, who dreamed Augusta might return to the living world?

Nobody.

I thought of poor Champ Crawford, old man speaking his mind, carrying on a crack-brained crusade from a lawn chair, drinking soda, amusing passersby. Maybe somehow he'd already paid his price. As for the fourth man, I never expected to know his name. So, out of some lightning stroke of part pity, part truth, I held up four fingers, counted Bobby Crawford dead and Waverly Barnhill forever missing. Then, picturing Champ Crawford, waving signs at passing cars, I lied and told her the third man had died.

"And the last one?"

"I don't know. Remember, the girl got blindfolded. Never saw him, never heard his name called."

She shook her head and turned off the recorder. "Now you say we got two dead men, one who vanished and another who remains a mystery, in a town where everybody knows everybody and everybody's business?" she asked, a cloud of frustration crossing her face.

"Where's Marty Chesnut?"

"Working at the washerette."

"I'll talk to Reverend Rayner. I'm going to read him this quote of yours and see if he really prayed for 'innocent' Blithe Tanner." She chuckled.

"Why?" I didn't understand.

The reporter closed her notebook and dropped the recorder into her purse. "A girl like Blithe Tanner can't come across the country with two men, submit to a hotel room with two more and be innocent—in a strict moral sense."

Then she laughed loudly—like virtue wouldn't melt in her mouth.

Furious and straight up in my chair, I shook a finger at her. "Fourteen years old! How do you moralize that?"

Chapter 13

Grace Lynn Rose drew back in her chair. Her face went from pink to pale to glowing red.

"Don't consider that a judgment," she said. "But I think Blithe Tanner could have avoided such a dreadful end."

"Possibly," I said, rapping the desk with the flat of a hand. "But then you've missed the point here. This story shouldn't be taken cynically. There's validity. It's about inexperience, blind trust and betrayal. It's about consequence—dying hard and lonely!"

Raving. I stopped.

She cocked her head.

"Mr. Frost, what happened to Bobby Crawford?"

Suspicions now? Pushing back in my chair, I put both hands together as though seeking prayerful communication. "I didn't tell you about the funeral," I said.

She looked at me, glanced at her watch, took a breath and fished the tape recorder from her purse. "Did you have a service?" she asked, tone low, controlled.

"Cobb's Graveyard," I said. "the day after she died. Friday, May 15."

"So soon? Anybody do an autopsy?"

"She died of pneumonia. Doctor certified.""

"Oh," she said, turning on the recorder.

To avoid any confusion, I let her read my copy of the death certificate Dr. Felton signed at the hotel. She said nothing after she scanned the paper and returned it to me.

"We wrapped her in a sheet and blanket and belted her to the stretcher. Marty Chesnut and I carried her down the stairs because of the small elevator car. In the lobby, I passed a police detective asking questions of the day clerk."

"Did you talk to the police?"

"Yes," I said. "Told them what I saw. Told them I wanted a warrant for Bobby Crawford. Police looked for him but didn't get too excited about it. I guess it seemed a pretty sorry task to question a man about a dead girl when he'd gotten the Silver Star in front of the whole town the day before."

"You took her to your funeral home?"

"Yes. Got her in the embalming room, did the job, got on the phone and got a funeral together."

"What sort of funeral?" she asked, her expression grim and immobile. Her eyes reminded that young people often consider talk of older folks boring and painfully time-consuming. Or, she had real suspicions about me. Or both.

"I called some ministers and told them the circumstances of Blithe Tanner's death. All had pressing matters—for the near and distant future. Nobody wanted to get involved with a female transient who died in a worn-out hotel."

"Then you did the funeral yourself?"

"No," I said. "Phillip Rayner did."

"Why?"

"I didn't ask," I said, wishing I knew more about Augusta and Phillip Rayner. "His wife gave us a plaid suit. It made Blithe Tanner look like a little Scottish girl.   He brought people from the Bible classes. We stood around the open coffin and sang, 'What a Friend

We Have in Jesus' and 'Amazing Grace.' I prayed Blithe Tanner heard every word. Marty Chesnut slipped a red rose into her hands, Mr. Rayner said Amen.   Then we sealed the lid and lowered the coffin."

"Sad," Grace Lynn Rose said.

"Bright, even warm sunny day," I continued. "Gray weather or rain would have made the whole thing worse. Since none of the people knew her, only a few stayed around while we closed the grave. Working, Marty and I didn't pay much attention. Then we found ourselves alone."

"If I ask the police to look up their records on Blithe Tanner, what do you think I'll find?"

"Young girl from San Francisco died in the hotel."

"You're the only source for this story. These logs and death certificate...what kind of corroboration am I going to get?"

"No need. Use these papers. I'll make copies for you."

She paused and stared at me.   No uncomfortable feelings raced through me, no panic ensued. I just stared back.

"Can I believe this?" She broke her gaze and dropped her eyes to her notebook, glanced up and around, seeking nothing, aimless.

"Ask Marty Chesnut," I said. "Ask Phillip Rayner."

Watching the old station wagon sway away in a cloud of dust, questions about talking with Grace Lynn Rose jumbled my thinking.

Had I said too much?

Not enough?

When he read her story would Champ Crawford understand that if he didn't remove himself, chair, umbrella, cooler and signs I'd tell The *Telegraph* about his role in the Blithe Tanner story?

But by the time she got out of sight, I decided that she didn't believe me and wouldn't publish any story. That meant survival of Bobby Crawford's legend and Champ Crawford spending eternity harassing Augusta. Probably Phillip Rayner wouldn't remember anything and Marty Chesnut would answer her inquiry with a coupon for a free load of wash. Jamie Felton died two years ago.

Since I promised Grace Lynn Rose copies of the log entries and death certificate, I climbed the old store's stairs, locked the door behind me and got back to my desk, fumbled and sifted through papers, trying to collect what she needed.

Reading along, I discovered an entry about Augusta on the same log page with my handwritten comments about taking Blithe Tanner's body from the hotel room: "7:10 p. m., Thursday, May 14—Admitted Augusta Crawford through funeral home back door. Stayed approximately five minutes. Looking for her husband."

Sitting at the old desk, confronted by the past, the words made me smile. Even then, I practiced caution, neither describing Augusta's state nor accurately recording the time from my opening the back door to closing it behind her.

But I have remembered her every movement, every word.

Except for dressing, I'd finished Blithe Tanner's body, washed my hands and walked out to the hall, closing the embalming room door. Augusta's loud voice and persistent knocking broke the mood of my sad solitude.

I stepped to the back door and shoved back the bolt. Dressed in white cotton blouse and dark brown skirt, Augusta stood in the evening glow with frustration on her face and both hands by her sides.

"Have you got a body here?" she asked, voice sharp, controlled, muted anger coming from the back of her throat.

"Yes," I said, trying to understand her mood. "I got four bodies."

"Who?"

"Old man Johnny Glass, Judson Irvin's new baby, a ship-out to Baltimore and a poor girl."

"Hotel girl?"

"Yes," I said.

"I want to see that body."

With that, she rushed by me and walked down the hall,

opening doors to offices and sitting rooms—everything but the embalming room, just behind me and up a short corridor on the left.

"Why?" I asked the question but already knew the answer.

She turned and hurried toward me—like news of the world's impending end had just reached her. "Police said they're looking for Bobby about this girl who died. They said he brought her to Ransom and they had a big party in a room he rented for her."

Trying to project a look of concern for her, her husband and the unwashed of the Amazon jungle, I folded my arms and tried to radiate sincerity and manly strength.

"She's here," I said. "Girl named Blithe Tanner—from San Francisco, California. How did you know?"

"Police came to the house."

"Have you talked to Bobby?"

"No. But I don't believe the police."

"What else did they say?"

"That a girl had died and you had her."

"Oh."

"Where's Bobby?"

"I don't know."

Suddenly, she took my hand and began to gently twist and turn like she wanted direction from a blind horse and couldn't decide the best stimulus.

"Where is Blithe Tanner?"

"Augusta, we got to leave her alone."

"Help me, Wiley."

I remember thinking if she saw Blithe Tanner, she'd know the truth, divorce Bobby and marry me. Protest, I told myself. But not too much.

"I'll help you, Augusta," I said, not giving one thought to her pain—there, tugging at my hand, or when she saw poor Blithe's body. How could I have been so single-minded and ruthless? Did I care more about purging Bobby from her mind—by any means—than Augusta herself?

Did I drive her behind locked doors?

"Help me, Wiley."

I took her hand, as I might to lead a child, and pulled her the few steps to the embalming room and opened the door. Scents of alcohol and embalming fluid hung in the air, making me think of dry cleaners.

Inside, I found the light and when I snapped it on, Augusta gasped, not ready I suppose, for the sight of the form on the table covered by a white sheet.

"Go home, Augusta," I said, adding to my weak protests.

She squeezed my hand. "Take me up to her," she said.

We walked slowly to the table and for a moment, she stood, her eyes running over sheeted, protruding forehead, nose, breasts, knees, tilted feet.

"Take off the sheet," she said.

"Augusta?"

"Take off the sheet, Wiley."

She saw the large tattoo and didn't make a sound. But with one finger, she traced the shape of the big, blue heart between Blithe Tanner's breasts and each letter of Bobby Crawford's name in the center.

When I finally got her to the pine deacon's bench in the hall she'd stopped shaking. But the tears continued and I left her clutching my damp handkerchief to find a box of tissues.

Then I sat beside her and watched as she pulled tissues from the box, my silence respecting her sniffling and coughing. Wait. Don't push.

"Wiley, have you seen Bobby?"

"Yesterday," I said, wanting to be less tattletale and more wellspring of strength.

"At the hotel?"

"Yes."

She took another tissue.

"Bruises—wrists and arms and around her mouth and eyes. Who did that? Did she die hard, Wiley?"

"She died quietly," I said, trying not to tell her everything I knew. She'd cried enough.

Augusta blew her nose again and wiped her eyes. "I have to find him, Wiley. I don't know where to look or what to say."

"I understand," I said, holding back the torrent of words imprisoned just behind my teeth. I put my arm along the back of the deacon's bench and touched her shoulder. Like getting a signal, she collapsed toward me, shaking again and snatching tissues from the box I held between us.

"Son of a bitch," she said.

I kissed her cheek.

"Scum," she said.

I kissed her ear.

She pushed toward me, dropping her face between my left shoulder and neck. I could feel the tears—droplets running down my shirt collar.

"Should I let him alone, Wiley? Should I just go home?"

"Yes, Augusta. Go home."

I kissed her neck. She lifted her head and kissed my mouth. Her hands ran over my shoulders, into my hair and behind my head. She kept kissing me and I acted instinctively, allowing one trembling hand to fall to the buttons on her blouse and I almost died when she started pulling at my belt.

Suddenly, she dropped her arms and stood.

"Not now," she said, moving toward the door.

"Augusta?."

I followed her to the door, hoping she'd change her mind and come back to me. But she opened the door and paused only to kiss my mouth again.

"Someday," she said, turning and walking quickly toward the back gate, sand-blonde hair stirring like a wind-touched streamer.

"Someday," I said from the open door, hiking my pants back to proper level and buckling my belt.

"Someday," said Bobby Crawford, who stood about thirty feet to my right, pissing on my ambulance.

PART III

Chapter 14

Just as I'd slammed the door on Bobby Crawford that night at the funeral home, I ended a kindly but tedious relationship with Grace Lynn Rose. Abruptly. Finally. Without remorse.

After all, her story made me a suspect in the death of Bobby Crawford and drove me to kill Champ Crawford.

Oh, yes.

Pure ambition triggered it. Grace Lynn Rose had set out to make a name for herself and considered the Bobby Crawford story the vehicle she'd ride to bigger things. The lines quoting me reflected she'd listened to me, but she had reproduced the information for self-promotion, not truth.

"Prominent Resident Wanted Revenge."

"Wiley Frost Claims Sgt. Crawford Imprisoned Girl, 14."

By the time I read those headlines on the *Telegraph*'s front page four days after the interview at the old store, my heart twittered and twitched so I thought surely my last moments had arrived. But, of course, the merciful Almighty spared me to climb new mountains, all of which seemed higher and darker.

Blind Reggie Tingle started it all when he stumbled up my steps to bring the paper when he should have had his son put it in the box at the gate.

"Wiley?"

Reggie must have caused the doorbell to stick because it kept ringing and once I got the screened door open, I had to pry at it with my fingernails to stop it.

"Is that you, Wiley?"

Reggie's nasal whine ate into my patience and I pulled my robe tighter. The cold, early morning air chilled my bare feet. "It's 6:25. What do you want, Reggie?"

"Here's your morning paper, Wiley." He handed me the rolled-up, rubber-banded newspaper.

"Why didn't you put it in the box, Reggie?"

The blind man backed away from the door, long white cane tapping the front porch floor in steady rhythm, feeling planks, anticipating rocker chairs, marking the doormat's edge.

"Did you do it, Wiley?"

"What?"

"Kill Bobby Crawford. Did you throw him in that hole on the common, Wiley? Did he struggle or holler when you threw dirt on him? You must have really been mad, Wiley. Didn't he try to fight you? What did you hit him with?"

Just out of bed, it took me a minute to get consciousness attuned to Reggie Tingle's questions. "What are you babbling about, Reggie?"

"Read the paper, Wiley. Chief Toby Pugh says he's going to talk to you about Bobby Crawford's death. Champ Crawford says he's going to talk to you, too."

I slipped the rubber band down and opened the newspaper to find stories by Grace Lynn Rose, pictures of Bobby Crawford's tombstone and Champ Crawford, drinking a grape soda in his lawn chair across from Augusta's house.

My whole body took a sudden chill and I shivered, happy that Reggie Tingle couldn't see. Pictures of me being escorted into the famous old Raleigh gas chamber flashed through my mind. I could feel the straps on my arms and legs and heard the heavy door slam and the wheel turning to seal the chamber.   Then the pellets dropped.

Plunk.

I folded the paper and stuffed it under my arm.   "Reggie, I have to read this before I can decide what to say. Maybe a suspect like me shouldn't say anything."

Reggie Tingle turned and tapped his way toward the steps. "You can talk to me, Wiley," he said over his shoulder. "I won't say nothing."

Already I knew even this brief conversation with Blind Reggie would take a half-hour to circulate Tammie's Coffee Shop, dominate the talk on Richmond Street and zip through the court-house like a gun-shy bird dog.

"I'll think about that, Reggie," I said, keeping my voice even and pleasant.   "You come back tomorrow. But put the paper in the box."

Reggie tapped slowly down the steps, over the walkway and to the door handle of his son's chugging, gray Toyota pickup. "You can trust me, Wiley," he said.

Without commenting, I closed the screened door, flipped on the hook and locked the oak door.   Then I routinely checked windows and the back door.   Champ Crawford didn't have to leave his sidewalk camp for his admirers to get serious about my new status.

In the kitchen, I put the paper atop the refrigerator, out of sight, out of mind.   But all through making coffee, it grew.   Shaky hands took forever to get the filter in the basket.   Then I couldn't find the coffee scoop and when I did, I missed the basket and spent considerable time cleaning the counter and sweeping the floor.

By the time I finally got to the table with coffee, the newspaper might well have been a ravenous panther, waiting from a high perch for the moment to tear away my life. So I calmed myself, sipping coffee and studying gathering patterns of warm mist on the sides of the cup.

Then the phone rang.   7:14.

I stood and walked the few steps to get the wall extension. Police Chief Toby Pugh sounded pleasant but somewhat official.

"Good morning, Mr. Frost. Have you seen the *Telegraph*?"

"No," I said.

"You need to read the stories, Mr. Frost, and I need to come out and talk to you."

"What for?" I tried to make my voice sound intolerant so he wouldn't think of me huddled and quaking, waiting for the Ransom Police to dish out doom.

"Your interview with The *Telegraph*. I want to talk about you and Bobby Crawford."

Female scoundrel.

"I don't know how I can help you, Chief. I told Grace Lynn Rose what I knew about some goings-on here years ago. I thought it might give people a better idea about those days, put things in perspective, you know."

"Didn't turn out that way, Mr. Frost."

"How did it turn out?"

"Talk all over town, Mr. Frost. People think you know how Bobby got in that hole. Story said you wanted revenge on Bobby."

"Not revenge, Chief, justice."

Silence.

"Oh, well, Mr. Frost, we'll talk about this. What time?"

"Anytime after I've gone for breakfast, nine or so."

I hung up the phone.

For a moment, I stood by the phone, wondering if I should call *The Telegraph* and speak to them about their reporter's powers of interpretation. But Grace Lynn didn't understand justice, only revenge. Therefore, I decided not to speak to her again. Ever.

I got the paper from the refrigerator and flattened it out on the table. The stories and pictures spread all over the front page with continuation lines to back pages, additional pictures of the closed front curtains at Augusta's house and me lugging a garbage can to the curb for last Tuesday's pickup. I didn't look muscular or menacing but old and very determined about garbage.

"Retired Ransom businessman Wiley T. Frost says the late

Sgt. Robert S. Crawford and friends forcibly detained a 14-year-old girl in a local hotel when Crawford received the Silver Star for heroism."

True.

"They held her captive, according to Frost."

True.

"Frost, a retired automobile dealer and mortician, says the girl died of pneumonia but that criminal neglect and abuse by Crawford and others at a marathon poker game led to her death. Frost says he's been seeking revenge on Bobby Crawford ever since."

Didn't say revenge. But not completely untrue.

"During his interview with the *Telegraph*, Frost contended he felt the girl, Blithe Tanner, believed to be from California, might have lived if Crawford and his friends hadn't prevented her from receiving medical attention. According to Frost, who ran an ambulance service in Ransom for many years, Crawford used a pistol to keep Frost and a first aid worker imprisoned in the room with the dying girl and refused to call a doctor."

True.

"Throughout his interview with the *Telegraph*, Frost readily and carefully traced events which led to the funeral and burial of Blithe Tanner in old Cobb's Graveyard, four miles west of Ransom off state road 621. But Frost, the owner of several large farms in Ransom County, evaded questions about the final hours of Sgt. Crawford."

Wild-eyed speculation. But true.

"In fact, no record or witness account of Sgt. Crawford's last movements exists. The Korean war hero, a legend in the community, simply vanished years ago from the Ransom Hotel room where Blithe Tanner died, not to be found until the recent day when workmen uncovered his buried remains in the common."

Then, for God's sake, she quoted old Anson Rule: "Wiley Frost came to the common and watched our excavations of the specimen later identified as Sgt. Crawford. I remember him standing over the site, peering anxiously, watching my every movement with trowel and bush. I never thought such a fine man could be involved in such a deadly act."

What deadly act? Recopying the old log entry, eliminating the record of Augusta at the funeral home? Taking Bobby Crawford's clothes? Of those things, I'm guilty. But would anyone want to hear about Bobby staggering around my parking lot screaming he'd caught me with his wife and would kill me? Would anyone want to know I slammed the door when he hollered he'd kill Augusta, too.

Then the phone rang again. 7:36.

Avery Tucker, the lawyer: "Wiley, you need a lawyer and I want you to know I'm at your disposal."

"I'll call if I need you, Avery."

"When?"

"When I need you, Avery."

I hung up the phone without waiting for a reply.

7:38. Another ring, another lawyer: "Wally Upchurch, Wiley. I can defend you on any charge. Do you have my number?"

"No," I said.

This time I didn't hang up the phone but cut Wally off with a flip of the button. Then I pulled the receiver around the corner in the hall and buried it in a basket of clean underwear.

When I got back to the table, the coffee had turned cold so I dumped it in the sink, poured a fresh cup and sat again before the newspaper.

"Champ Crawford, brother of the dead hero, says he believes Frost knows something about his brother's death. Crawford, an elderly former sawmill operator, says he thinks answers lie in Frost's relationship with Augusta Morefield Crawford, the Sergeant's reclusive widow."

Now, I thought. Hitting home.

"Champ Crawford charged Frost with being involved romantically with Augusta Morefield before her marriage to Robert S. Crawford and has concluded that led to Frost's vengeful feelings against his brother."

Old Champ ran with the ball all right, cleanly steering Grace Lynn Rose away from Blithe Tanner's death until the end of the interview. Finally, she pointedly asked him if he was involved. No, he said. He knew nothing.   He worked at the sawmill that night.

But he knows I saw him, dealing cards, smoking cigarettes, pouring straight whisky into a water glass, throwing it back — a true saloon cowboy. Champ Crawford helped his brother kill Blithe Tanner.

All the way back from the Sheraton, I drove slower than usual, wondering about Toby Pugh's questions and how I might answer without lying.

Not even the lovely, brilliant colors of fall leaves could keep the voice of Dixie Corbin, the fat waitress, out of my mind. "Trouble knows your name, Mr. Frost," she said, serving cold eggs and biscuits so hard they could have been shot for missiles.

"When you going to talk to Chief Pugh?" she asked.

"Gravy," I said.

With a stained, gray-brown cloth, she wiped puddled water from around my glass.

"Bring the gravy," I said.

"Oh," she mumbled, waddling back to the kitchen.

I fumbled through the rest of the *Telegraph* and started the crossword in the Raleigh paper.

"Gravy." Dixie Corbin thumped the bowl on the table. With the spoon, I stirred a couple of turns, watching bits of sausage reluctantly surface, then sink out of sight.

"Concrete," I said.

Dixie smiled, her mouth opening to show yellow teeth and a tongue that seemed as long as a hound's. Round, thick cheeks quivered and right away I suspected bad nerves or simple meanness.

"I like Bobby Crawford stories," she said, folding her arms across her chest, acting like a spoiled, fat princess. "I think I'm related to him."

Fried eggs and blood retaliation?

"Check," I said, promising myself breakfast at the Hilton tomorrow.

"Don't talk too much," she said, a little laugh in her voice and a rippling jiggle in her huge bosom.

I turned off Richmond Street and onto Pickett—to pass Augusta's house. Fear, intimidation and threat clawed through my brain like combatant alley cats, all instinct, all survival.

A few cars passed around me, roaring by, drivers looking back with blank messages on moving lips. Not far from Augusta's house, tears caught in my eyes so I edged to the curb and cut the engine, to wait until my vision cleared. I got out and stood by the car.

"Murder! Murder!"

What a mistake. First, I recognized the shrill voice of Champ Crawford and then saw a thin, blurry form stalking toward me. Fervently wishing I'd parked somewhere else, I touched my eyes with a handkerchief and looked toward wide, wild eyes, chicken neck and wagging pink gums—all bearing down upon me like a toothless swamp brute.

He stopped a few steps away and pointed at me with a soda can. "Tomorrow, me and Police Chief Toby Pugh going in Augusta Morefield's house with a warrant to search. Going through the door — just like elegant company."

I blinked and leaned back against the car.

"Kiss my ass, Champ Crawford," I said.

"Murder!" he yelled, moving away, heading back to his chair-cooler camp across the street.

"You want your name in the paper?"

"Don't matter," he shouted over his shoulder. "Nobody'll believe you anyway. People think your old brain's mush."

Just before he got to the curb, Champ Crawford turned and pointed at me again. This time, he spoke in an almost pleasant tone. A distant, curiously peaceful expression flowed over his face. "Bobby's coming to Ransom. We're going to make a judgment on you and Augusta Morefield. Me and him. Right here. Tonight."

I started to chuckle, crossed the street, and faced him, standing not two feet away. "Is he bringing old Lucifer, Champ?"

"Tonight, Wiley Frost."

I spat in the street. Champ Crawford stepped down off the

curb and shoved my chin around. Without thinking much, I pushed back, thumping the top of his breastbone with the heel of my hand. He stumbled backwards over the curb and sat down hard on the sidewalk.

Rocky Marciano couldn't have done better. I turned and started to my car.

"Bobby and me'll see you tonight." Faint and choked, Champ's voice reached me about the time I stepped over the white line in the street.

I didn't stop walking and didn't look back.

"Come on," I said, voice hoarse and menacing, heart thumping, flushed with victory and more than ready to take on a silly old man and a ghost.

Chapter 15

The sight of Toby Pugh's black patrol car at my house dissolved the euphoric rush from knocking down Champ Crawford.

So when I turned into the driveway heading to the garage, I didn't return his friendly wave. And walking around to the front of the house, I practiced aloofness by looking up, concentrating on a gentle shower of brightly colored leaves.

When I reached the foot of the front steps, Toby Pugh got up from his seat in one of my rockers. "Mr. Frost, I just want to have a private talk. Why don't you sit here with me," he said, pointing to a rocker like he owned it.

A voice in my head said frown. I frowned.

"Nothing's private in Ransom, Chief Pugh. Your car signifies wrongdoing. You on this porch talking to me makes it worse. We'll go inside."

He didn't complain and waited for me to unlock the door. Going into the living room, I didn't hold the door for him, showed him no manners. I didn't even speak, just pointed for him to sit on the couch.

I took my TV chair across the room.

Toby Pugh fumbled with a small pad and a pen. "I just need a couple of answers, Mr. Frost. Won't take long and you can get on with your business."

Suddenly, the room grew cold as some forgotten underground chamber. I envisioned myself, afraid and desperate, clawing for daylight on a door that would never open. Then I remembered the uniform in the closet and felt pure, sour fear surge into my mouth.

"You going to search me?" I asked, keeping voice and tone steady but maybe a little childish. Then I quickly imagined Champ Crawford, Toby Pugh and his men storming through Augusta's house, rooting like Gestapo, looking for anything to reveal something about that wet and miserable night on the common.

Toby Pugh laughed.

"Mr. Frost, I'm interested in your recollections. What can you tell me about Bobby Crawford?"

"He's dead," I said.

The police chief, wearing dark brown pants with a red cardigan sweater over shirt and tie, smiled a painfully patient smile, silently telling me he had all day, if necessary, to deal with a stubborn old man.

"I'll be straight with you, Mr. Frost: Did you put Bobby Crawford in that hole?"

"No," I said.

"Did you throw any dirt on him, did you cover him up?"

"Do you want me to swear?"

For a few seconds, Toby Pugh wrote on the pad. He looked up at me a time or two and it seemed like he might be drawing my picture instead of taking notes about me.

"No, Mr. Frost, you don't have to swear."

"Then are we finished here?" My words came out gruff and impatient. I wanted the police chief out of my house before he decided to take a friendly look in the plastic bag in my closet.

Toby Pugh leaned back on the couch. "Mr. Frost, did you see Bobby Crawford after he left the hotel?"

"Yes," I answered.   "About seven in the evening, the day after Blithe Tanner died."

"Where?"

"In my parking lot."

"Doing what?"

"Drinking whiskey, pissing and hollering."

"Did you call his wife?"

"No," I said.   "I let him take care of himself."

"What does that mean, Mr. Frost?"

"It means I locked my door and left him drinking whiskey, pissing and hollering."

Toby Pugh hummed. He kept his eyes on the pad and hummed up about three octaves and then down the same three -- an aspiring tenor warming up.

"Did you have a relationship with Mrs. Crawford, Mr. Frost?"

The hair prickled on my neck and my face warmed several degrees.   But I didn't falter: "What's the value of your question?"

"Curiosity," he said.

"Personal or professional?"

"Both."

Knowing others could answer the question, I took a deep breath, glanced at a small water spot on the ceiling and back to Toby Pugh. Now, he sat on the edge of the couch, pad hanging loose in his left hand.

"We talked about marriage."

"Then Bobby Crawford came along?"

"Yes," I said, my mind gently recoiling at the pictures from those days, spilling again from my memory.

"Did you have ill will against him?"

"No, not particularly.   Augusta had her own mind. I couldn't say much."

Toby Pugh reacted with silence until he started tapping his pen on the pad. For a full minute, we sat there, across from each other, not moving but listening to his tapping which soon sounded like pounding, tribal drumbeats.

"I don't want to cause you trouble, Mr. Frost."

"Then why don't you get on with your work? Haven't you got an armed invasion planned for Augusta's house?"

At that, Toby Pugh turned red.

"Champ Crawford got Judge Boyd to force that. Hate to bring grief to that poor woman."

"Then don't do it."

"Judge ordered it."

I stood and asked him again if he'd concluded his interview. He slipped the pad and pen into an inside pocket, nodded and started for the door.

"Am I suspected?"

Toby Pugh squared around to face me, one hand holding open the screened door. For so early in the day, his face showed weariness and a troubled mind.

"Found a skeleton on the common, Mr. Frost. Then we identified it as Bobby Crawford, local hero. I got a judge and a community clamoring to know how he died."

Toby Pugh backed out on the porch and let the screened door slap shut against the door frame. "Mr. Frost, I deal with simple things—Saturday night icepick stabbings, marital problems, drunks. This isn't simple. If we have enough reason, a Grand Jury will probably look into it."

Oh," I said.

He didn't speak again but turned and walked down the steps to his car. I waited until the car pulled away, then closed and locked the doors. A few seconds later, I yanked the plastic bag from the bedroom closet rack, put it on the bed and spent the next five minutes making sure I had all the pieces of Bobby Crawford's uniform.

Early that afternoon, after a lunch of hamburger and a tablespoon of cole slaw, I decided to find a remote dumpster for the uniform and folded it all into a green plastic bag. Then I walked out the back door and down the steps, pretending to strain with a load of trash. I headed to my car.

I put the bag down into the trunk, dropped the lid and turned to see a *Telegraph* car pass the front of the house.

Stalking me? How about Toby Pugh's men? Had I become Ransom's priority criminal?

I backed down the driveway, acorns crunched under tires, leaves fluttered, touched and slid from the windshield. My hands turned cold on the steering wheel but muddled thinking overcame complete confusion and I decided only a real spy could handle the Bobby Crawford intrigue. A stumbling amateur like me could pretend to be unruffled and get by with a lot. Maybe.

I edged backwards into the street, took time shifting gears, took pleasure in the number of cars stopped, waiting for me to move, and finally drove toward Green Apple Drive, turned right and headed for the post office.

At nearly 10 a. m., Ransom traffic seemed reasonable. A few log trucks, fresh out of the woods, swayed along, huge tires leaving clumps of red clay on the pavement. Young mothers turned into playschools to deposit small children or tugged them along the sidewalk, lecturing and pointing fingers, smiling only when greeting passersby. Elderly couples walked dogs, pulling or being pulled.

Nice.

But the *Telegraph* car loomed in my rear view mirror.

I pulled to the curb by the post office. The *Telegraph* car turned the corner and parked on Simon Street. With ease and at my customary slow pace, I carefully took each of the steps up to the brass-glass doors, pushed inside and walked toward my box around the corner from the counter.

But the old postmaster, Dinky Hodges, saw me. He leaned over the counter to look at me. "Somebody following you, Wiley?" He grinned a mocking grin; seemed he enjoyed other peoples' troubles.

"Yes," I said, walking out of his sight to my box.

"You're famous," he said. I could hear his giggle and his face, thin, skeletal—almost like that of dead Bobby Crawford—rippled through my mind.

I opened the mail box door, then quickly looked over gas

and telephone bill envelopes, a circular from a pizza house and two envelopes addressed to "Wiley T. Frost, Murderer."

Closing the box, I walked around to face Dinky Hodges. "Did you put this in my box?" I slapped the envelopes down before him, pointing the blank return address corner and underlining "Murderer" with my forefinger. "I don't want this trash."

"Addressed to you, Wiley."

"Do what I say."

"You going to knock me in a hole?" he said, laughing.

Without answering, I left the envelopes on the counter and headed for the door. Rage ripped through my chest and drove into my stomach, giving my brain a clear vision of Dinky Hodges' expression if I'd grabbed his neck and pushed both thumbs into his Adam's Apple.

"*Telegraph* car's been following you."

I stopped and looked back but didn't speak.

"They've got a photographer on you," Dinky said, chuckling. "Recording you like a documentary, Wiley."

"Piss on you, Dinky."

He giggled. I opened the door and ambled down the steps like I didn't care about anything, stood still on the sidewalk for a minute, reading and turning the pizza circular, acting like nobody nearby had a camera on me.

But I could see the *Telegraph* car and the camera lens—round, long and black—poking from the passenger window. In my head, I could hear the whir of shutter repetitions and wondered if a shot of me and my mail would be more appealing to *Telegraph* readers than me carrying a garbage can.

I opened the gas bill and scanned figures. The camera lens edged further out the window. That boiled me into impulsiveness. I pushed the envelopes into my jacket pocket and crossed Simon Street. The lens quickly withdrew out of sight. About the time I got to the driver's side window, the engine started and the *Telegraph* car began to edge out of the parking spot. I walked along the curb until I looked at Grace Lynn Rose, eye to eye.

"You made up your own story," I said, my voice even, far too pleasant.

She let off the accelerator and the car drifted back against the curb. The photographer, a thin, sharp-faced young man I'd seen a few times, slid down in his seat holding the camera between his knees.

"Interpretation," she said. "It's a good, interpretive story," she said, smiling like she had all the rocks in the quarry. "Everybody's talking about it."

"Quit following me," I said, anger in my tone. "Quit taking pictures."

"Public street, Mr. Frost," she said, racing the car's engine and looking at me like she'd ensnared me and a Pulitzer Prize.

Then she pulled into light traffic and headed up Simon toward the common, leaving me with exhaust fumes in my eyes and nose. I got a handkerchief from a hip pocket, wiped my eyes, blew my nose and looked up to find people standing on the post office steps, peering through shop windows, stopped in their cars on Simon Street, whispering on Maxie's Drug Store corner.

Nobody waved. They just looked at me.

Hell with them, I thought.

"Wiley Frost?" Turning to my right, I saw the short, stubby little man who had called my name. Witt Arnold, a psychologist at Ransom College, had one hand resting on a parking meter and the other in his pocket. "Come see me, Wiley," he said. "You and I can find the truth."

Profanity and obscenity came to mind but I suppressed the urges, said nothing, recrossed Simon Street and picked my way through scattered clusters of people. Catching sight of my car, I walked down the sidewalk in front of the post office, glanced at Dinky Hodges staring through the door glass like a pale-faced ghoul and finally got around to grasp my driver's side door handle.

Refuge? For an instant, I looked at the people—so still, so intent, so mesmerized by me, a man they believed a killer. Then I opened the door and sat behind the wheel.

"Wiley Frost?" asked the old man sitting on the passenger side. He held a Budweiser can.

"Get out," I said.

The old man, thick-chested and friendly, wore a gray poly-ester leisure suit with open white shirt.   He laughed and despite baldness, a red, puffy face with sagging jowls, he looked familiar. "I'm your old friend, Aubrey Winslow.   Remember?"

Chapter 16

The years fell away and I remembered Aubrey Winslow at the wheel of his patrol car, determined to find Augusta after that melee at the pavilion by the river.

Trying to appear unruffled, I eased the car slowly into the street. As we drove aimlessly down Hannaford Pike, it occurred to me that Aubrey should be dead from alcohol. Then he pulled out a cigarette.

"I haven't been in Ransom for over forty years, Wiley," he said, puffing and blowing smoke.

"How've you lived this long?" I really wanted to know.

He laughed, showing a few yellow teeth.

"If I'd had sense, I would have never left Ransom and gone to Reno. But Wiley, have you ever seen a casino, bright lights and so many women begging for a touch?"

"No," I said, paying more attention to the rear-view mirror than Aubrey's ramblings. "I couldn't leave Ransom."

He looked at me like I might have been a midway oddity, a weary freak squinting in the sun on a dusty stage.

"You've missed a lot of world, Wiley," he said, pointing to a stand of woods. "Out there, beyond Ransom, it's evil and raw." His eyes seemed glazed—from the beer or nostalgia, I wasn't sure.

"It gets raw and evil in Ransom," I said, taking off my hat and putting it on the seat between us. "I haven't missed anything."

For a few seconds, Aubrey didn't speak. He just drew on the cigarette, blew smoke toward the crack of the window glass and watched the wind whip it away.

"I'm going to help you, Wiley," he said, pushing the cigarette out the top of the window. He settled back in the seat and took a swallow from the Budweiser can. "All the way in Reno, Nevada, I read about you and Augusta, Bobby and Champ and the young girl, Blithe Tanner. She died at the hotel, didn't she?"

"Yes," I said, wondering if I should curse him for presuming I wanted his help or just let him out at the next gas station. Or, change the subject.

"Aubrey, after you left Ransom, what happened to your wife and children?"

"My last wife? She died."

"In Reno?"

"No, here. I left her here."

"Here?"

"She didn't want to go. I called her every week. She lived in a house on Tommy Woodberry's farm—behind the chicken plant."

"All those children?"

Aubrey shook his head. "Scattered," he said, "like a pack of homeless kittens."

His tone made me sad. Imagine, losing a wife and children like that. "I guess you don't see them, do you?"

He laughed. "Hell no. They'd skewer me if they knew I'd come to Ransom. Hate me for not being dead, I suppose."

"Oh," I said.

Aubrey finished the beer, folded the can in his big hands and dropped it on the floorboard. I imagined waves of beer flowing into new carpet but said nothing, hoping he'd get out soon so I could get rid of the can.

"Wiley, what are you going to do about Champ Crawford?" Aubrey asked, picking at dead skin on his hands.

"Nothing," I said. "Can't do anything."

Aubrey Winslow chuckled. "Not so."

Following up on his comment didn't seem a way to answer the Champ Crawford question. Sadly, I had become resigned to Champ's grubby, makeshift camp and considered myself powerless to prevent the intrusion on Augusta's house planned for the next day.

"Champ's easy," Aubrey said, reaching for another cigarette. He fired up with a flaming Zippo lighter and sent more smoke drifting under my nose.

I gave him a skeptical half-laugh. "It would take a plague to run him away. Now, he's got battery-powered TV. He likes to watch himself on TV. Somebody interviews him every day, you know."

Aubrey flicked an ash out the window.

"I'm going to kill him, Wiley."

I didn't answer.

"I'm going to shoot him."

Who was this man? Instant, pure fright smashed into my already troubled brain. My stuttering heart caused my foot to flap on the accelerator. The car surged forward, dropped back. Forward and back.

"Shit, Wiley. You always drive like this?"

At a wide spot on the shoulder, I pulled off, knowing I had to stop or run my new car in a ditch. Pushing the gearshift into park and gripping the wheel, I faced Aubrey Winslow.

"You're not serious," I said, trying to offer a sensible comment to counter the insanity as thick in the car as cigarette smoke.

Aubrey pushed the cigarette out the window, sighed and looked at me. "I got a reason."

I sat back.

Aubrey squirmed a little, trying to cross his legs but gave up and planted big feet side by side on the floorboard. "Out there, over the treetops, Wiley -- a different world. I'm as sane as you except

I admire John Wilkes Boothe."

I must have looked shocked. Aubrey had been a plodding, good-hearted policeman, not an assassin. For a minute, we didn't speak. He sat quietly, gazing across a plowed-up field, smiling at gray-brown corn stubble, maybe reminiscing about one of his many wives or children.

Then he turned to me. "I've been gambling all these years, Wiley. Sometimes I shot somebody to pay table debts. I shot people in the back, in the head or through the heart. That's a kindness."

My face and hands felt frigid and my heart still twitched.

Somehow, I spoke. "Aubrey, I don't want you to shoot Champ. All I want him to do is stop talking about Augusta and me in the paper."

Aubrey rolled down the window about an inch. "I'm going to slip up behind him and shoot him in the back of the head." He aimed a pointed forefinger as he spoke.

"No," I said.

"I'm going to free your soul and mine, Wiley."

"No, Aubrey." My voice rose and broke slightly but he didn't pay attention.

"Yes, Wiley. We'll both feel better." He looked stern and sounded unyielding. "Wiley, I had a niece named Blithe Tanner who lived in San Francisco."

Then he asked me if I'd seen Champ Crawford in the hotel room that night.

I nodded.

On down Hannaford Pike, wide-open fields gradually disappeared and thick, briar-infested woods closed in on the road. A hawk sailed against gray sky and sparrows moved in small, dark clouds from tree to tree. A few doves, breasts puffed, balanced on power lines.

"Right turn," Aubrey said, jerking a thumb at the narrow logging path leading into the woods. "Speed up, Wiley. Hell, you can't expect to run away from somebody if you poke along like this."

I turned right, hoping the *Telegraph* car in my mirror would stay on the pike and leave me in peace. Aubrey got excited. You'd have thought he was a teenager with a hot car, eluding the Sheriff for a world's worth of story-telling.

"Gun it," he shouted, laughter in his voice.

Mud holes. Big.

"I can't," I said, silently admitting to life beyond control. "This is a new car."

"Have some fun, Wiley." Aubrey snapped his head around to check the *Telegraph* car, now on the path and negotiating holes even slower than me.

The car shuddered and slowed in a muddy rut and I pressed hard on the accelerator. Mud flew everywhere, including the windshield. "I'm going to stop and clean this off," I yelled, pointing to great, dark splotches on the glass.

"Don't," Aubrey said, his tone suddenly lowered and his manner more determined. Then he snatched a pistol from a shoulder holster. "If they don't break an axle in a minute, I'll stop them."

My brain froze. Trying to control the bucking wheel, I couldn't fathom one more thing. "Aubrey, I'm going to stop and let you out."

He looked at me with a scolded child's eyes. "In this woods?" he asked, his voice rising and straining. "It's a two-mile walk to where I'm going."

"Put up the pistol."

"I'm your friend, Wiley."

I slowed the car. "I don't need a friend, Aubrey. I need peace."

"Oh," he said, pushing the pistol back into the holster and securing it with a leather strap. "Speed up, Wiley, or we'll get stuck."

He paused and looked back. "Like them," he said.

Glancing into the mirror, I saw the *Telegraph* car had stopped and two people stood near the rear wheels, hands on hips, wondering, I suppose, how they'd get back to Ransom.

"Where're you sleeping, Aubrey?"

I wanted to get him out and go home.

"Turn left on the next path you see and get back on the highway," he said, lighting a cigarette and rolling down the window.

"I love chasing around," he said, sounding satisfied, just as if he'd done the driving. He pushed back against the seat and blew smoke toward the window.

"We didn't have to run like that, Aubrey," I said, busy trying to miss more water-filled holes. "God knows what the paper'll have tomorrow." He didn't reply so I concentrated on listening to the beer can clink against his shoes.

"Turn." Aubrey pointed to a track to the left that seemed less muddy but more suitable for 19th century horse carts than automobiles. "This'll take us out on the Dairy Road. I'll get out about a mile from there."

"Where?" The question didn't come from intense curiosity but more from just wanting to know where we'd be going next and how soon I could get rid of him.

"Brick house in some oaks," he answered, smiling. "Not far."

A minute or so later, the car struck the asphalt and dirt thundered and popped from under the car. Aubrey threw out the cigarette and rolled up the window.

"You know somebody out here?" I asked, curious but trying not to appear nosy.

"Friend," Aubrey said. Then he got quiet and I wondered if he might be thinking of the person in the house or Champ Crawford.

"Aubrey," I said, using my firm and businesslike voice. "Don't shoot Champ."

He stared ahead, face immobile, hands folded in his lap.

"It's settled. I'll shoot him."

"No." I found myself pleading and didn't know why.

"Champ Crawford won't bother you anymore."

"Listen, Aubrey."

"Champ Crawford won't bother me anymore."

Fear crowded my stomach. I felt my face turning red, my heart seemed ready to leap through my eye sockets. Should I tell

Champ Crawford a crazed killer was on his trail?

"Here." Aubrey Winslow's voice returned my focus to the road. "Turn," he said, pointing to a blacktop driveway on the right.

I eased into the turn and stopped.

"Everything's done, Wiley. You'll get your peace."

Words began to flow to my mouth as I started to make one more stuttering attempt to stop murder. But Aubrey ignored me, opened the door and stepped out on the ground. He paused for a second, then slammed the door.

"Aubrey?"

He came around to the driver's side, leaned down—close enough for me to smell foul breath. "My dead sister put her girl on a train to visit in Ransom. I'd got the gambling sickness and already gone to Reno."

Aubrey paused and looked straight at me.

"Somewhere, she got off the train," he said. "Now I know where. People responsible for that child's dying need to get shot, Wiley."

"Forty years," I mumbled, thoughts in a whirl.

With that, he walked toward the house. I inched the car forward until a small woman with long, gray hair opened the front door, stepped barefoot onto the porch and sat down on the top step. She wore a lavender cotton dress and held her arms against the afternoon chill.

"Aubrey?" I called.

He stopped and looked back at me, lips half-parted, hands by his sides. "Do you remember my sister, Lorraine, Wiley?"

"No," I said. "This doesn't matter anymore, Aubrey."

"It'll help my heart, Wiley."

When he got to the steps, the woman stood and I recognized her. She took his hand and led him into the house. Even after the door closed, I couldn't forget the jangle of the bracelets on her arms and ankles.

Chapter 17

When I finally stepped into my living room shortly after 6 p. m., eliminating Champ Crawford no longer appealed to me. But instinct told me the deep anger I had seen in Aubrey's eyes would drag me into more confusion.

Should I keep silent and allow him deadly revenge? Should I warn Champ? My head throbbed, my eyes watered and I ultimately made the poorest decision of my life.

After closing the front door, I quickly circulated through the house, closing blinds and pausing to listen for odd sounds. Moving through the kitchen, I remembered Bobby Crawford's uniform in my car. So I flipped on the backyard floodlight, illuminating everything from the mud-spattered car to the edges of the garage building to the approach to the back screened door.

For once, I felt like a soldier, expecting attack and thinking defensively. Who might come? Blind Reggie Tingle? Toby Pugh? Nobody?

There in the kitchen, my mind swept along in a stream of uncertainty. I imagined a fearsome, faceless enemy, rattling the back screened door, snatching it away, sailing it into the yard.   Then my ears manufactured sounds of breaking glass and my eyes conjured a thick, hairy hand, snaking through a smashed kitchen door window and snapping back the inside bolt.

"Did you do it, Wiley?"

Old blind Reggie's voice floated through my head.

"You going to knock me in a hole?"

Dewey Hodges cadaverous face leered at me.

"I'm going to shoot him, Wiley." Aubrey's death sentence tumbled through my thinking.   Repetitions of his words continued like a mad echo and I imagined Champ Crawford falling from his lounge chair, a bullet hole behind an ear.

All that made me squeeze a kitchen chair under the back door knob and wonder about paranoia. But then I convinced myself Toby Pugh would take me to Raleigh in chains, just ahead of a howling mob, and supervise my execution with Rev. Phillip Rayner as a mumbling, prayerful witness.

But what if Aubrey got Champ? Did that mean I might have a chance at reconciliation with Ransom?

No. Not by murder.

I walked up the hall to the living room, muttering a poor prayer for an end to distress, turned on the TV, and sat down in my chair.   On Channel 4, I got the conclusion of a talk show about stroke and paralysis. On Channel 6, I found Champ Crawford being interviewed live from his encampment on the local "Ransom Journal" program.

"Tomorrow," he said, lips curled back like a grinning giraffe's, gums shining, chin rotating like a cow chewing something. He pointed toward Augusta's house.

But he didn't say what "tomorrow" meant and smirked like he held a burning secret. The reporter, a pretty brunette girl in a flower-print blouse, gently pressed him.

"No comment," said Champ, coy, and as puffed up as a bogus potentate.

"Oh," said the reporter, pausing and looking toward the camera for guidance.   "Then tell us about your favorite country singers, Mr. Crawford."

At that point, old Champ stated his admiration for Eddy Arnold, Tennessee Ernie Ford and Tammy Wynette. He even hummed a few bars of "Sixteen Tons," and the brunette girl applauded.

I turned off the television and listened to slow, passing traffic, wondering who might be among the curious, interested in a glimpse of a suspected murderer's house. Would they soon want autographs or strands of my sorry, thinning hair? Perhaps I should set up a table out front, a macabre version of a child's lemonade stand. I could sell T-shirts emblazoned with my face or lapel buttons spelling out my name.

I couldn't stand the thoughts.

Then the doorbell rang.

I decided not to move and held onto the chair, hoping the caller would tire of waiting in the evening chill and go away.

But that didn't happen.

By the time I got to the door, I'd decided not to open it. But I did peep through the front curtains. In the light of the porch bulb, I saw two dark forms and right away suspected Toby Pugh's detectives or a couple of Crawford cousins.

"What do you want?" I called through the door, hoping they might be Mormon missionaries.

"Wiley Frost?" The voice sounded faint but determined. I heard thumping, a restless movement of feet on the porch.

"Not here," I said.

"Open the door," the voice said.

"No."

"Why?"

"None of your business."

Muffled laughter answered me.

"I'll call the police," I said.

"No, you won't."

I cracked the door the length of the chain. In the sliver of dim light, a small, female face loomed at me.

"Grace Lynn Rose, Mr. Frost."

"What do you want?"

"Pictures. Candid shots. Wiley Frost reading the newspaper about the Bobby Crawford investigation, watching the television reports, going through picture albums with Augusta Morefield's picture."

Two large hands pushed a camera above her head. Strobe light exploded and I heard the lens whirring.

"No," I said, half blind, pushing the door shut. "Go away." Had I come face to face with the ferocious enemy I expected?

Aubrey's round, red face darted through my mind.

"Go find Aubrey Winslow," I said, impulsively calling through the door. "He's new to town.   He can tell you about gambling in Reno, Nevada."

Panic sent thoughts and intentions colliding.   Could Grace Lynn Rose provide enough inane distraction to take Aubrey's mind off Champ Crawford?   What if Aubrey decided to eliminate a nuisance and shoot Grace Lynn Rose? Surely I'd get blamed for that, too.

"Dairy Road," I said, hoping Aubrey might be pleased to have his name in the paper. "West on the Boulevard.   Turn left at the first crossroads. Brick house in some oaks."

Low voices, unintelligible chatter.

Shoes thumped on the porch and steps.

I quickly turned off the porch light and retreated trembling to my chair, realizing that in the interest of sanity, I must speak to Champ Crawford.

Five hours later, I stood in the deep, black shadow of a mimosa tree on Pickett Street, convincing myself I could run Champ Crawford away, save his life and spare Augusta the pain of public scrutiny.

My body shook like a victim of St. Vitus Dance, and the message that I could get close to Champ Crawford if my teeth stopped clicking broke through to my consciousness.

A bone-chill hung in the air. During the seven-block walk

from my house, I fiddled with the collar of a long, gray raincoat and pulled down on my dark hat brim, trying to stay warm and keep my face obscured.

Old man walking. That's the notion I wanted for anybody's recollection of a lone figure on Pickett Street after 10 o'clock. Shadow within shadows, unknown.

Under the raincoat, I wore Bobby Crawford's khaki uniform, tie and all, long pants turned up. The belt had nearly stopped my breathing. With every step, I heard myself gasp. The too-big, rubber-heeled GI shoes thunked on the sidewalk and I tried to walk on the grass to eliminate noise. From time to time, I pushed one hand into the right side pocket of the raincoat, feeling for the small, tan cap I'd put on once I got close to Champ.

The long walk made my knees ache and I wondered if I'd ever get back to my house and bed. Considering my dress, I couldn't wave down a late-running cab. I decided to concentrate on Champ Crawford's threat to Augusta and push distractions from my mind.

My mission seemed simple: I'd appear and tell Champ murder stalked him in Ransom and he must leave or die. Seeing the uniform, he'd think brother Bobby had truly returned in some mystical miracle. With distance and darkness, he might be frightened into believing an apparition and escape Aubrey's bullet.

I left the mimosa, slipped silently along on damp grass, hoping to come up behind him, then step down to the sidewalk and speak. But how close could I get? With fire dancing in a steel barrel and a kerosene heater glowing, could he recognize my face?

No. Not an old man awakening from sound sleep. And from the wheezing and grunting, Champ appeared to sleep well in the down bag in the lawn chair. Snores echoed from tree to tree. Roosting birds, obviously disturbed, twittered and stirred in the branches above me.

I moved closer. Did he have a dog with him?

No.

Did he have a pistol?

Maybe.

Which way to run? Could I run? How far?

I eased ahead—to just outside the camp's circle of light.   In the darkness, I pulled out the army cap and dropped the raincoat and hat to the ground, reminding myself to grab both if escape became necessary.

I put the cap on my head and moved into the light.

Champ Crawford lay on his back in the lawn chair, mouth open, snorting like an old gas motor.   The red sleeping bag, zipped to his neck, made him look like an skinned caterpillar.   Watching him closely, I moved further into the light, knowing I'd have time to run before he could unzip and level a pistol.

"Champ.   Brother Champ."

My voice sounded low, urgent and hollow.

Champ didn't move.

"Brother?"

Nothing.   I became impatient.

"Brother, wake up," I said, speaking louder, trying to sound like a late-night TV ghoul.

More snorting.

I backed out of the light and fumbled around the trunks of several trees, gathering acorns and short sticks.   If I couldn't rouse him with my voice, perhaps I could ping him into consciousness.

Back in the light, I lobbed a couple of acorns at the chair. One hit the arm and glanced to the ground.   The other sailed into the darkness.

"Brother Champ...."

I flipped a stick end over end.   That popped on the sleeping bag and tumbled away.

"Champ?"

In the next instant, I unloaded a handful of acorns, lobbing them high so they dropped like a mortar barrage.

Champ Crawford sat up.   He looked around, pulled his toboggan hat down about his ears, rested his head and closed his eyes.

"Brother Champ..."

He sat up again.

"What?"

"Brother Champ..."

Then he focused on me.

"Who?"

"Poor dead Bobby," I moaned.

He didn't speak but his eyes covered me from feet to cap and fixed on the gleaming Silver Star pinned to the shirt.

"Bobby?" His eyes grew wide. He unzipped the sleeping bag and drew both hands outside. He rested them in his lap.

"What do you want?"

"Go away from Ransom," I said, adding a little high-pitched tremor to my voice—to intensify the strangeness of the moment. "Someone has come for your life."

"Who are you?"

"Poor dead Bobby."

"No."

"Yes," I said.

"Who's come?"

"The girl's kin."

"No," he said.

"Yes," I said.

With both hands, he pulled the toboggan from his head and sat straight.   In a second, I knew I'd be seeing the pistol barrel. Instead, he shifted his legs about and stood on the ground. Hobbled at the knees by the sleeping bag, he suddenly raised both hands like a revival preacher and fell on his face.

He never moved or spoke again.   I didn't turn him over or check his pulse.

I knew.

Dead as a stone.

I stepped back into the darkness and tried to calm myself by mumbling over and over that old age killed Champ Crawford. But what if I'd stayed home? Did his fingers twitch?

Surges of guilt shot right through me, mixing with nearly consuming panic. "Sorry," I whispered, like a lonely child who'd just lost another playmate. Turning toward Augusta's house, I slipped on the raincoat and hat and folded the tan cap into a pocket. The old Morefield house reminded me of a grotesque castle, cloaked in darkness except for an upstairs light and an unmoving, silhouetted figure in the window. Then the light disappeared and I walked on the grass until it seemed safe to take the sidewalk.

Chapter 18

No sleep.
No breakfast.
No lunch.
Boiled eggs and oatmeal for dinner.

By the time the news of Champ Crawford's death hit newspaper and television the next morning, my stomach had shrunk and twisted into a large and painful knot. Nausea swept over me and only sips of ginger ale calmed the turmoil.

I took the telephone off the hook to silence its unceasing ring. I could hardly believe people called to thank me for freeing Ransom from old Champ's disagreeable presence and to ask how I murdered him. Toby Pugh called to see if I'd left town. To all, I offered resentful responses and little time.

In the early morning dark, I slipped to the front porch for the *Telegraph*. Even then, slow traffic passed my house. At the time I mentally noted the flow of cars but felt no apprehension.

By lunchtime, after reading the paper and watching TV news about a vagrant finding old Champ, I heard more cars and imagined an angry, milling crowd at the doorstep, waiting for an appearance.

Or a public lynching.

At any moment, I expected Toby Pugh with a warrant, charging a smelly, rag-tag hobo had identified me walking away from the sad old dead man in the grass.

But in the evening—after a day of fear and television, I heard a soft tap on the back door.

"Wiley?"

I moved closer to the door, wondering if the mob had chosen to take me through that entrance.

"Who are you?" I asked, my voice surprisingly strong, without quaver.

Could I die like a man?

"Aubrey."

For a second, I didn't answer, trying to let the voice tone filter through my brain for simple purposes of recognition.   It sounded like Aubrey.

"Last name?"

"Winslow. Open the door."

"What color is your hair?"

Pause. Deep breath on the other side of the door. "I don't have any hair."

I pulled back the bolt and cracked the door. "Aubrey?"

"Jesus, Wiley." With a disgusted expression, Aubrey Winslow pushed into the kitchen and quickly walked up the hall.   I followed as fast as short legs could move. He strode into the living room, peered through the edges of the front curtains, checked the locked door and turned to me.

"People watching your house, Wiley," he said, edging along the windows, checking locks. "Four or five cars out there—no lights. People just sitting."

I sighed.

Aubrey Winslow sat down in my TV chair and motioned me toward the couch. He pointed a finger at me. "You must be the best hit man in the east, Wiley. They can't find a mark on him. How'd you do it?"

The last question, an odd compliment, rattled around in my head for a few seconds. I hadn't purposely killed Champ Crawford.

"Not me," I said, my voice soft—like an anxious, errant child's. I looked hard at Aubrey, silently expressing disappointment at such an inquiry.

Suddenly, Aubrey stood. He pulled off his coat, dropped it on the chair and sat again, midriff rolling up and down his body like he had a wad of jelly stuffed into his shirt. I noticed he didn't have the shoulder holster and pistol.

"When I heard about Champ, I felt anger, Wiley," he said. "You know I wanted to kill him myself. Did he die ugly, did he scream and holler? How much do I owe you?"

"Not me," I repeated, feeling a wave of weakness which made me want to slide my soul to the floor and leave the rest of me on the couch, blank and silent.

Aubrey shook his head. "You got to tell me what happened, Wiley. Everybody in town thinks you killed Champ Crawford."

"They don't know anything," I mumbled.

Outside, a car stopped. Then an engine started. Aubrey got up, stepped to the side of the front window and looked through the curtains. "Detectives. Shift change."

Headlight beams swept the window, capturing Aubrey Winslow as a huge, momentary silhouette. A second later, he dropped back into the chair.

"Toby Pugh's insisting on an autopsy. The Crawfords disagree. It'll probably end up in court."

"Aubrey, where does that leave me?"

"For now, guilty," he said buttoning his shirt.

"They got witnesses?"

"No."

Aubrey Winslow rubbed the top of his shiny head, scratched at one ear and then the other. "Wiley, you got to tell me if you saw Champ Crawford last night. Then you got to tell me what you did. I can't help you if you don't tell me."

After my experience with Grace Lynn Rose, telling anybody anything held no appeal. On the other hand, I needed to tell somebody and Aubrey seemed loyal, close-mouthed and wary to the point of dishonesty.

"I stayed home all night."

"That's a lie, Wiley. Old Champ and Toby Pugh planned to search Augusta's house today. You meant to stop that, didn't you?"

For a moment, I didn't answer.

"I don't deny I wanted them to leave Augusta alone," I said, picking at a fingernail.

"Then what did you do?"

Again, I took a minute to gather my wits.

"Aubrey, I dressed up in Bobby Crawford's old uniform and walked up there, made sure Champ could see me and called to him. I made my voice sound as though it came right from the grave. I told him to go home."

"Where'd you get the uniform?"

"I won't tell."

"Okay," he said, grimacing at the ceiling. "Then what?" Sweat appeared on Aubrey Winslow's broad forehead. He dabbed at his face with a pocket handkerchief.

"He stood up and dropped dead."

His eyes glued on me, Aubrey stood and took a few steps away from the chair. "Where'd you get the uniform?"

I shook my head and sighed.

"I see," he said.

For a few minutes, Aubrey didn't speak. He bent over and picked up the paper from the ottoman. His eyes rolled over the pages, particularly the front, and he made grunting, burping sounds as he read.

"Barbecue," he said.

"What should I do, Aubrey?" My words emerged, plaintive, almost panicky.

With his hand, Aubrey slapped the paper. "Look at this Wiley. See these pictures? That's old Champ dead on the ground, sheet over him, sleeping bag around his feet like ankle irons. Here, Miss Grace Lynn Rose speculates Toby Pugh has suspects, including Wiley Frost."

"Nothing but trash," I muttered.

Aubrey didn't pay much attention, shook his head and continued: "A retired mortician, Frost had clashed with Crawford since Frost charged Crawford's brother Bobby, a Korean War hero, with the abuse of a young woman at the Hotel Ransom in 1951. The alleged victim later died."

Aubrey glanced at his watch, allowed the paper to float to the floor and turned on the news. Voices blared into the room. I rose to turn down the volume but Aubrey motioned me back to the couch.

Reluctantly, I sat, ears and brain under attack by the newsman's booming voice, pictures of a body on a stretcher, a rescue truck, rotating red and blue lights and endless repetitions of Champ Crawford's name.

Then the stream of pictures and words wound down to a single, well-dressed young man, microphone in hand, standing before Champ Crawford's deserted camp. Behind him, the camera caught overturned chair, scattered soda cans and ice chest. The black oil drum stood flameless -- a monument to nothing.

Lean, blonde-haired, handsome, young newscaster Webb Allen edged toward the camera. He didn't speak but turned his eyes toward Champ Crawford's rubbish. Then, having executed a perfect dramatic pause, he looked back into the camera, faking a grave and troubled expression.

"New mystery here, folks. First Bobby Crawford's skeleton is found on the town common and now his older brother is dead. Rescue workers failed in attempts to revive Champ Crawford. Police are still searching for evidence."

Webb Allen, round-faced with a clipped Yankee accent, tossed his head like a restless racehorse. "Police report they found a folding army cap. Tan. Khaki. One investigator says it looks like World War II-Korean era. They found it on the ground a half-block from here."

Aubrey Winslow pounded the chair arms, jumped to his feet and struck the TV's off button with the heel of his big right hand. He glared at me.

"For God's sake, Wiley. Didn't you check?"

Embarrassed and a little frightened, I shook my head.

Red-faced and panting, Aubrey put both hands together and looked to the ceiling. I suspected he might be asking for his deliverance, not mine.

"Where's the rest of the uniform, Wiley?"

"Under my bed," I said.

"For God's sake," he bellowed.

"Time, Aubrey. I couldn't burn it and I couldn't bury it—not with those people watching the house."

"You should have done something last night."

"Too cold," I said, standing to face Aubrey. "I had to get home, get out of the chill."

Aubrey put a hand on my shoulder and squeezed, a gesture I thought resulted from impatience more than sympathy.

"Come on," he said, sounding much like a snarling guard dog. I followed him down the hall and stayed right behind him. He turned into my room, eased to his knees and started fishing around under the bed with one arm.

"Where, Wiley?"

"In the middle," I said.   "Plastic bag."

Seconds later, he stood and dumped the pieces of the uniform onto the bed. "Unbelievable, Wiley. How could you do something so stupid?"

"Do you mean putting it under the bed or getting it in the first place?"

Without speaking, he looked at me, eyes wide and nervous. Then he pulled the ball of khaki apart and spread out the pants, socks, tie and shirt. He put the black shoes, now scuffed from the night's rough treatment, off to one side.

"Everything but the cap," he said, fingers moving over the Silver Star still pinned to the breast pocket of the shirt. "Soul of Ransom here on your bed." His last words struck hard and I wanted to say Ransom had a college, an imposing courthouse and people with sniffles, enlarged prostates, decent marriages, new babies and good hearts. I wanted to argue, to say Bobby Crawford had been a scoundrel, not a universal light.

But I didn't.

Just after 10 p. m., Aubrey and I slipped over the wire fence in my backyard and came out Miss Regina Toll's driveway on Scott Avenue, one block over. Walking along, we avoided the glow of street lights, sticking to shadows of houses and trees.

I carried the plastic bag. "To the cemetery?"

"That's where things get buried, Wiley," he said, glancing back at me and lifting a forefinger to his lips.

No moon.

A dog barked.

A door slammed.

Voices. Dark figures moved behind drawn curtains. A pickup truck, only one light shining, pulled over and parked at the curb in front of us.

"Here, Wiley." Aubrey crouched behind a tree, his face and form lost in the shadow.

Clutching the bag to my chest, I got down behind him. "Get on home, Aubrey. This is my problem." He didn't answer but nodded toward the man who shut off the truck light and got out.

"Tippy Horton," I whispered.

"See how he puts one foot in front of the other?" Aubrey whispered. "He's tucking in his shirt and smoothing his hair. Look." He laughed.

"Trying to sight the steps," I said.

"No. He's looking for a place. He wants to have one last drink."

We watched Tippy Horton and relaxed a little. I sank to one knee behind Aubrey. Tippy sat on the bottom front step, in the faint glow from the front window. He pulled a pint bottle from his belt, lifted it high, and drank the last swallow. "Watch. If he's got a wife, she'll put an end to his evening right about now."

"How do you know?"

Aubrey, a large, formless lump before me, turned slightly and I could make out a smile. "Too many wives and too many nights of my own."

That's when we heard footsteps on the sidewalk, leather heels on concrete, popping in regular cadence, advancing. Huddled against the tree, we listened, hardly breathing, hoping the walker would pass without seeing us.

"Shit, Wiley." Aubrey stirred, cursing quietly and laboring to stand on cramped legs. Finally, he pushed himself upright against the tree. I stayed on one knee, clutching the plastic bag against my chest.

The footsteps stopped. I stood and tried to ask Aubrey about the silence but he snatched the bag from my arms and ran.

Chapter 19

I don't know what happened to Tippy Horton.

But I remember staring up, into the face of Rev. Phillip Rayner, Augusta's Rev. Rayner. What in hell was he doing here? I felt foolish there on my knees so I quickly tried to focus on how to survive the conversation. Certainly I owed Aubrey apologies for trouble on my behalf and would offer amends — if I ever saw him again. We'd discuss our long friendship and not the cruel dampness of ground moss on old knees or his leaving me in an awkward situation.

"Wiley Frost?"

Phillip Rayner sounded like the voice of doom. He looked down at me from the sidewalk with what seemed a mixture of surprise and pleasure — like he'd caught me dead drunk, primed for a temperance lecture.

I stood.

"Are you ill, Wiley?"

Damn Aubrey, I thought, trying to gather myself for questions and answers. Low class, illiterate fat ass. Miserable barbarian.

Thug. Communist. "No," I said, hoping my tone carried enough irritation that Phillip I. Rayner could consider himself intruding and go away.

But he didn't and I faced him.

He stepped closer, trying to get a whiff of my breath.

"May I help you home?"

That made me furious. "I can walk by myself."

"Have you been robbed or hurt? May I get a policeman for you?"

Oh, hell no.

"Meditating," I said. On my knees. In the dark.

"Yes, yes. You have trouble, don't you?"

Phillip Rayner must have been seventy or more. He wore a black felt hat and he'd raised the collar and lapels of his dark wool topcoat. But white shirt and tie showed.

"I'm going home," I said.

"Then I'll walk with you."

"I'll walk by myself," I said, feeling old envy rising to my mouth. After all, he'd seen Augusta and I hadn't. Rayner didn't seem disturbed by my rejection. But he didn't comprehend I wanted him gone. "Are you at peace, Wiley Frost?"

For God's sake. What is peace? I ignored the question and moved down the sidewalk. The minister followed, heels thumping.

"Confess," he said.

I stopped and looked back at him, laughed and continued walking.

He ran a couple of steps to catch up with me and once at my side, clutched my elbow. "Confess to killing Bobby Crawford and his brother," he said in a voice that sounded like a whine to me.

Fingers dug into my elbow and I found myself turned toward Rayner. Even in the dim light, I saw an uncharacteristic imbalance in his eyes. His voice seemed ready to burst from his body.

I pulled my arm away. "What do you want?" I asked, roughly pushing his hand.

"Think of Augusta. Our weary, lost child," he said, head bowed, hands clasped.

"I do," I said, hoping resentment, suspicion and perhaps a little hatred surfaced in my words.

Suddenly I felt overwhelmed, and to this day, I'm ashamed to say I spat at his feet.

The preacher, shocked and offended, just mumbled: "I have nothing further to say." He stepped into the street and crossed to the sidewalk on the other side. In spots of stray light, the shoulders of his topcoat glistened and I finally felt the fine mist falling about me.

"Wiley? For God's sake, get up. Follow me."

I sat on the curb, wet as a water rat. I didn't look at Aubrey when he spoke. But then I raised my head and saw he had the sack of army clothes. He motioned to me with his left hand and kept his attention on the street, repeatedly glancing left and right.

"What happened?" He sounded impatient, like a sneak thief who couldn't find his way up a gutter pipe. I cleared my throat and tried to speak.

"Phillip Rayner," I said, "Augusta's preacher."

"I remember him. What's he doing out in this rain? What'd I tell you about preachers? Got no sense." He started walking up the sidewalk.

"Come on, Wiley."

I heard urgency in his tone and guessed that he wanted to get to the cemetery, bury the clothes and get out of the rain. Somehow, I just felt like sitting and drowning.

But a second later, Aubrey had me by the arm. He pulled me to my feet and to the sidewalk across the street. As we started up the sidewalk he looked at me once, glowering with a clear degree of disgust. So, I walked with him and kept his pace.

"What did Rayner say, Wiley?"

"He thought he'd found another drunk to feed to the temperance women," I answered, wishing I'd remembered to wear my hat and raincoat.

"What did you say to him?"

Really, I didn't want to talk about it.

"Sorry I ran off, Wiley," Aubrey said, trying to break my sudden silence. "But what if he'd told Toby Pugh about two wet old men carrying a bag of army uniform clothes?

It didn't matter.

"He wanted my confession," I said. "He wanted me to say I killed Bobby and Champ."

Aubrey took a breath, shook his Chesapeake retriever head, and tried to clear his eyes. "Did you ask about him and Augusta?"

The question cut and I couldn't reply. Only when we turned on Third Street, a half-block away, could I get my thoughts and tongue coordinated and away from visions of Phillip Rayner in Augusta's bed. Stepping along, I strained to keep feelings inside and brain calm. No screams—on the outside, anyway.

"All these unhappy years," I said, keeping my eyes on Aubrey's face, hoping for agreement, "I've made myself believe Augusta sat in that house—in royal isolation, listening to music, reading old books and thinking of me."

"Wiley, that's likely not the case," Aubrey said, not slowing his stride.

I didn't answer.

We turned onto an unpaved street with so many back fences it looked like a string of fortifications. Even in the dark, I recognized Pollard's Alley.

Aubrey stopped for a second and motioned me closer. He put a finger to his lips. "Whisper," he said, pointing to one of the white, wooden gates. "If we wake up one dog, we'll have them all raising hell."

God. I imagined a chorus of barking loud enough to bring a fleet of Ransom police cars hurtling into the alley, sealing both ends. I could see Aubrey and me in the middle, hands up, blinded by scores of headlights, cringing before gun muzzles and blaring megaphones.

"Find another way," I whispered. Besides, I didn't want to

pass Augusta's house.   Not tonight.   Not wet.   Not tired.   Not frightened.

Aubrey said nothing.   He just cast a disapproving paternal glance my way and motioned me ahead.   I followed, not knowing what else to do.   We were prowlers.   Hardly a sound, even on fine gravel.

We passed Mayor Oscar Ernest's gate and I felt reluctant to go further.   Seeing the Morefield house and not Augusta made the old loneliness creep back—like a painful, chilling, weakening sickness.

As we walked on I struggled to control my feelings.   Then I remembered sliding back the gate latch on a long ago night and pictured her on the wide back porch, waving, mischief in her smile, knowing she'd have to slip through the house and up to her room to avoid explaining our lateness to her father.

"Wiley?" Just ahead of me, Aubrey Winslow signaled me forward and suddenly I stood in the dark at Augusta's back gate.

Aubrey raised himself on tiptoes to look over the gate. "Light," he said.   "Movement."

Since I could see nothing without standing on a box, Aubrey relayed all he saw.   Hating myself for being short, I stood with my back to the gate, begging the Almighty for six more inches of height.

"It's a shadow," Aubrey whispered. "Shades down.   I can't see much."

"Let's go on," I said, anxious.

"You ought to knock on the door, Wiley." Aubrey sounded like a child, trying to help, speaking without thinking.

"No," I said, walking away, heading toward the end of the alley. "She'd only turn off the light."

A second later, Aubrey's big shoes crunched in the gravel behind me and I presumed we'd turn left on Pine and head for the cemetery, a good three blocks away. So I kept walking, my thoughts dwelling on how soon we'd get finished, how soon I'd get to bed and how soon Aubrey'd go away.

Then I realized I no longer heard Aubrey, his rough breathing or the occasional snap of his lighter.

I stopped and looked behind me.   I saw sidewalk, trees,

parked cars and late flowers, wet-heavy and bent from continuing drizzle. Aubrey had abandoned me again.

No matter. He knew we had to bury the uniform. He'd show up.

I walked a half-block further to the stone fence and iron gate of Ransom Hill Cemetery and stood in the rain, water in my shoes and running down the collar of my soggy windbreaker.

When the hand lightly touched my arm, I nearly fainted. "Son of a bitch," I mumbled, bracing for a billy club against my skull. A chill passed up my back about the same time I heard Aubrey snicker.

"It's me, Wiley," he said.

I fumed: "Son of a bitch, Aubrey!"

"What if I'd said 'boo?'"

Brainless ox.

"This is a cemetery, Wiley." He laughed again.   "Dead, Wiley. All gone. You know about dead people. They don't talk and they don't bother anybody because they don't give a damn."

"Where've you been?" My voice sounded most unfriendly and I didn't care, considering how Aubrey had frightened me.

"Pissing," he said.

I didn't question him further.

The drizzle had not slackened but Aubrey lit a cigarette, drew smoke and held it by his side, cupped in his right hand. With the other hand, he held the bag with Bobby Crawford's khakis. He pulled twice more on the cigarette, thumped it away and stepped toward the low, stone fence. He pushed himself up and, for a few seconds, hung at the top. Then he slipped over the other side.

"Come on," Aubrey whispered.

So I followed—over the fence and in among the headstones, expecting the kiss of the living dead at any moment.

"Wait," I blurted.

"Here," Aubrey answered. "I've found Miss Millie Harper."

For an instant, I thought he'd found a breathing human in

the black masses of stones. By the sound of his voice and flickering cigarette lighter, I discovered Aubrey stood not five feet away. Hadn't Millie Harper just died?

"Dig." Aubrey's voice shot at me. I could see a little and watched him go to his knees and start at the clumps of sod packed onto Millie Harper's grave. I got down beside him and sunk my hands into water-soaked earth.

All through the process, Aubrey continued whispering instructions: "Lay each piece of sod carefully off to one side, pick up another and place it beside the first one. Try to think in some kind of order, Wiley, so we can put the top layer of dirt back just where it was."

By this time I surmised Aubrey planned to bury the bag on top of Millie and while I thought the act a sacrilege, I didn't argue, considering the consequences of the uniform being found with me.

"Dig." Aubrey sounded urgent and impatient. My hands worked faster, like a shovel, scooping and arranging wet clumps of grass and dirt into small piles at my side.

Finally, he stopped digging and held up one hand.

The hole seemed more like an opening for a stomach sectioning—about two feet deep and narrow. Aubrey stuffed the bag into the hole, pushed down with both hands for a deep planting and threw in fill dirt, patting and packing as he worked.

"Wiley, I'm not playing in this mud, I'm putting the dirt on solid so nothing—no storm, nothing, not even an earthquake—can push it back out the top."

Then Aubrey stopped and looked up at me. "I want you to remember this, Wiley," he said, "in case you have to do it again sometime."

I ignored the remark and threw mud into the hole.

When we packed the last of the wet sod over Bobby Crawford's uniform, I got off my knees and brushed at my pants, trying to knock away some of the clay caked to my hands.

The rain had stopped and clouds had moved to uncover a

sliver of yellow moon. Aubrey stood on the other side of the grave, mumbling that hands amounted to a better tool than a ten-dollar shovel.

"Nothing like hiding something in a fresh grave," he said, making it sound like a delicious experience, like bread just out of the oven.

But I wondered if Millie Harper, 89 years old and recently dead, could endure eternity with a bag of men's clothes buried on top of her.

"This is fine," Aubrey said, looking up at the thick, moving clouds. "We'll get some more rain here tonight. Wash away sign."

I brushed at my face, knowing I had mud smeared across my cheeks.   "This isn't right, Aubrey," I said, my voice low but not frightened.   "I hate using Millie Harper."

Aubrey chuckled.   "Don't worry about Miss Millie, Wiley. The clothes don't fit her and from what I knew of her, it's the closest she ever got to a man."

I didn't find that amusing.

"You know what I mean," I said, purposely letting a touch of anger slip through my teeth.

For a few minutes, we didn't speak.   Using the glow of his cigarette lighter, Aubrey smoothed excess dirt into cracks of the sod pattern. I pulled away some rocks, stood and threw them into the empty field next to the cemetery.

Soon enough, Aubrey and I faced each other across the grave.

"We should pray, Aubrey."

"Why?"

"Using poor Millie."

"Nothing but chance, Wiley. Could've been anybody."

No more arguments. I gathered my thoughts to offer some kind of solace and explanation to Millie Harper.

Aubrey grunted.

"Millie, we ask you to understand what happened here tonight. Nobody meant to disturb you. Aubrey said we had to do this. Forgive us and find your peace."

"I don't want no forgiveness," Aubrey whispered.

Well, I did. I ignored him and went on.

"Millie, I hope you'll understand the intrusion and not think too unkindly of Aubrey and me. I can't call Aubrey a fine Christian gentleman but I'm almost sure he doesn't have even one tattoo."

"Amen," I said.

Aubrey moved toward the stone fence. "Come on, Wiley," he said, waving one hand for me to follow. "This is getting on my nerves."

I didn't care. "I'm going home now. I know I got pneumonia."

Aubrey stopped, then turned and walked back to me. He leaned down in my face. "You've got to see Augusta," he said. "Tonight."

He backed away and stood still for a moment, muddy hands groping in his pockets for cigarettes and lighter.

I started walking toward the stone fence.

"You got to find some answers," Aubrey said, smiling in the trace of moonlight. "If you don't, you're going crazy or to jail or both."

I was too tired for more amateur analysis. I kept walking.

Chapter 20

There may be much that's unsavory about Aubrey Winslow but not much of it has to do with his words. When he says something, most of the time it's the truth.

Sometimes though, Aubrey doesn't tell the whole truth so when he said he'd picked Augusta's back door lock with a coathanger wire, I didn't believe him.

"I did. I did." Aubrey said, coughing and defending himself as we turned again into Pollard's Alley. "I stopped to piss and thought of it. All you've got to do now is walk in the door and into the kitchen. Then go wherever there's a noise or a light. You'll find her."

He laughed when he spoke but his tone seemed positively serious, confronting me with prospects of once more confirming suspicions about Augusta's life. So before we'd gone a quarter way up the alley, I felt an odd, burning worry about facing a woman who'd become strange and fragmentary in my mind. Had I imagined seeing her again would establish a glorious, enduring bond? Why now did doubt and fear rush to my soul, leaving me with a sour, dry mouth?

"I'm not a burglar," I said, protest in my voice.

Aubrey stopped at Augusta's gate and whispered: "Wiley, don't complicate this. Go tell Augusta Champ Crawford's dead and gone and won't bother her. Tell her you'll take care of her."

Even in the low light, I saw Aubrey's lips draw tighter, relaying to me that no matter the circumstances or consequences, seeing Augusta amounted to a right and honorable thing. Nevertheless, a picture of the Ransom County Jail skipped through my thoughts.

Quietly, Aubrey lifted the gate latch and we eased to the foot of the steps. "No," I grumbled, trying to ignore the sickening swirl in my stomach.

Aubrey stopped dead still. "Wiley, I'm tired of you mooning over this old woman so long and not knowing a thing about her. Find out about Phillip Rayner. Tell her you love her. Anything. You're wearing me out. This is worse than the night we caught her in Sarah Wingo's woods."

I paused; the old fear returned. Once I stepped inside that house, I'd be set up for one more taste of rejection. "What if she's got an alarm?" I asked.

"Run," he said.

"What if she's got a gun?"

"Hit the floor and crawl."

I stood there, looking down. I was trying to focus on the blur of a doorknob swimming in darkness. Voices rose from distant corners of my mind. I heard those who had called me murderer now call me a sneak thief and intruder as well.

And Augusta? Would she speak to a man who slipped into her house, threatening her solitude and whatever peace she had found?

I looked at my watch. Past midnight.

Quickly, I began to practice: "Augusta, it's Wiley Frost. I'm sorry to call so late but I've loved you for fifty years and thought I'd say hello again."

No.

I should be more specific, more authoritative, in control.

"Yes, Augusta, it's me, Wiley Frost. I've come to take you into the light, to open your eyes, to give you new vision and commitment to life."

Poor.

"Go on," Aubrey urged.

"No," I said.

"I'll bet you ten dollars you can't find her."

I thought about that for a minute, grasped the knob and turned it slowly.

I wished for a flashlight until I stepped into Augusta's kitchen and saw a soft florescent light glowing over the sink. A table lamp in the hall barely illuminated a rug, some chairs and the slant of the long, elegant staircase that white-gowned Augusta might have descended had we married.

Did I smell Mr. Morefield's pipe? Did I hear the purring of Augusta's fat yellow cat? Did I feel Mrs. Morefield's touch on my arm and find myself again attracted to her smile and rice pudding?

Ghosts.

Damp and shivering, I stopped and listened. A step on the stairs? A thump on the second floor? A sigh from the library? Imagined or real, all the sounds came at once and I felt bombarded by indecision. Which way? Would spirits lead me?

Forward, I decided. Five steps forward—without regard to discovery or danger. I made no sound and stopped just at the bottom of the stairs. For a moment, I listened, poised to escape to a deep shadow.

Hearing nothing, I advanced, nearly to the front door. On my left I saw the parlor room where Ransom ladies had gathered on Sundays, to drink tea and chat ferociously. I recalled the attentive butler, Marvin Lee, refilling cups from a silver pot. Unforgettable female voices jammed together in a stream of pleasant inflection and inference while poor, plain Elizabeth Lightfoot, Augusta's cousin, gently urged less chatter and more substantial topics.

Laughter. Whispered secrets. Light hearts. All of it poured

through my head, prompted by dark outlines, ancient furnishings, silence, and shadow.

I glanced right, thinking of the library. Thin, broken streaks of light, rectangles standing on end, cut the darkness on the far side of the huge living room.

A closed door. But had I found Augusta, only a wall away? The thoughts sent my tired heart into erratic twitters giving me an alarming, rush of weakness. Instinctively, I stepped further into the living room, looking for something to grasp to steady myself.

"Not now," I muttered, trying to order away shortness of breath and dizziness. I groped along the back of a sofa, thinking I'd find a seat—until the spell passed. But when I ran my hands down the sofa's left arm, I touched warm flesh.

The shock should have killed me.

Then a word: "Bobby?"

The voice from the sofa sounded soft, kind and firm. Nevertheless, I detected a faraway quality, the kind of plaintive twist of tongue from one who'd suffered pain and silence.

I couldn't speak. Emotions ran wild inside me. I wanted to cry. I wanted to sink to the floor and just lie there, listening and hoping I'd really heard Augusta's voice.

"Bobby, I'm so glad you're here. Come close."

Finally, I found my trembling voice: "Augusta?"

"Yes. Come, sit here." Her hand gently grasped my arm and I felt her guiding me. Shuffling, I moved around the corner of the sofa.

"Here," she said.

Heart askew, mind awhirl, I sat.

"I like the quiet," she said. Sometimes my father comes and we talk politics. He still doesn't care for Republicans."

Although the voice and form reminded me of Augusta Morefield Crawford, I strained for signs to clearly identify her. Should I strike a match? Find a lamp? Touch her face? Hold her hand?

No. Somehow I knew light could destroy this dim world I'd entered; and I dismissed the notion. In my heart, I knew Augusta sat next to me. And I understood remaining close to her meant pretending to be Bobby Crawford.

Augusta stirred. She patted my arm.

"Shall I order coffee? I'll call Marvin Lee. He might not like being awakened so late, but he'll bring coffee—in robe and slippers. He's such good company. So kind."

She'd half-turned toward me and a trickle of light from the hall lamp filtered into her hair, backlighting strands, creating countless thin silhouettes, curled and positioned. Even with darkness distorting her face, I recognized features—thin, small nose, tiny ribbon of mouth. The particular elegance of her speech and the tilt of her head moved me, returning me to those days when I felt her face meant abundant life.

"Marvin Lee?"

After Hell and eternity. Augusta.

"Marvin Lee? Can you step here, Marvin Lee?"

She took my left hand in both of hers, slipped to the edge of the couch and lifted her face—as she would if someone approached. "Marvin Lee, Mr. Crawford is here. Would you make coffee, please. Serve us here."

I said nothing.

Augusta held my hand, sometimes gently squeezing. She slipped back on the couch and crossed her legs. I could see enough to tell she wore a sweater and a dress of some sort. Finger rings touched my skin and right away I imagined Bobby Crawford's wedding band on her left hand and wondered what happened to the dinner ring I gave her after her first year at Woman's College.

She kissed my cheek.

"You must come earlier. Would you like to help with the plants or sit in the library and listen to music?"

Bobby Crawford liked Hank Snow so I didn't answer.

"Marvin Lee gets LIFE magazines from the market. I look

at the pictures."

Her hands felt warm and smooth. Should I speak?

"Marvin Lee? In a minute, I'll go to the kitchen to investigate." She laughed, easily. "There may be pineapple cake. Do you like cake?"

I cleared my throat. "Yes."

Augusta laughed. "Marvin Lee? Bring cake with the coffee. Remember, no nibbling."

A nervous chill passed up my spine and I shivered. Suppose she came to her senses, discovered Wiley Frost next to her? Would she send me away and burrow deeper into hiding?

"You're cold."

"Yes," I said, not wanting to explain the dampness of my clothes, the chill or the overwhelming sadness closing over me.

Without speaking, she rose and walked a few steps away and returned to her seat. I felt a wrap going around my shoulders and her fingers at my neck, tucking and straightening the blanket she'd given me.

"Cold like Korea," she said, sitting back and taking my hand again. "How you must have suffered!" Her voice drifted, traveling the air like whispered afterthought. I caught hints of resignation, anger and maternal protectiveness.

For him. Not for me.

"Blankets remind me of the picture you sent. You sat on the ground with other soldiers and you wore a blanket around your shoulders. You'd pulled down the earmuffs of your cap and tied them at your chin. But you still smiled."

Always smiling.

I didn't interrupt. Augusta paused, her mind replenishing itself with recollections to share, to overflow into the darkness she trusted.

Then she spoke: "I dreamed of you dead. When some of the others came home dead, I expected you with them."

Pause.

Her strong, steady tone continued: "I never believed you'd come home alive. After the parade, when you left again, I waited.

Now you've come home.   There's so much to say."

Silence.

Then her voice rose: "So much happened! Remember the parade and the band and the flag bearers? You had Ransom at your feet. Do you remember waving to old friends?"

Augusta stood.   "Marvin Lee's taking his own time, isn't he? Sometimes he can be so slow and deliberately does everything his way.   Father complains and swears he'll find a new man."

I turned my head and watched her walk quickly through the living room entrance and disappear into the hall toward the kitchen. "Forget the coffee," I called, hoping she'd accept some other line of thought.   "Come back. Sit with me. I must leave soon."

Seconds later, she came back into the room, stood next to the couch with hands on her hips. I couldn't clearly see the expression on her face though her stance hinted girlish pouting.

"Sit," I said, trying to inject comfort and reassurance into my words.   "There's not much time."

Augusta sat.   "Leaving already!" She encircled my arm with hers. "Come back tomorrow," she whispered, the heat of her mouth and breath in my ear.   "Come back in the light."

Attempting to recover my senses from the tingling in my ear, I paid little attention to her withdrawing her arm and standing. "Yes," she said.   "Come back tomorrow."

Hell.   Sure.

Augusta suddenly turned, walked to the library door, opened it, stepped inside and closed it.   I heard a muted snap and the slivers of light around the door vanished like the end to an instant of lightning.

Alone again.

Good.   She'd never understand a thing about Champ Crawford and I surely didn't want to tell her Marvin Lee'd been dead for thirty years.

Chapter 21

At 8:20 a. m. I peeled back the bed covers and sat up. Early morning chill quickly enveloped me, recalling the drizzle of the night before. I shivered and tried to think despite a thunderous headache.

Aspirin. The word flashed through my poor brain like movie house popcorn dancing aimlessly behind hot glass, going nowhere. In pajamas and sock feet, I stood, took a few tentative steps, then slowly reached the hall, turned left and shuffled to the bathroom cabinet. I dumped four pills into my hand, popped them into my mouth and drank a half paper cup of water.

Coffee? Breakfast? No. I had to sit down.

In the hall, I found the thermostat and pushed the heat up five degrees and walked down the hall to the kitchen. There, on the table, like a mocking demon, sat an empty bottle of Kentucky Colonel whiskey. I'd warmed damp old bones beyond necessity.

Daylight, Augusta said.

I sat down at the table and her voice came to me from the night before, almost as if she were standing at the kitchen counter.

Tomorrow, Augusta said.

The pain in my head magnified—to the beat of at least 10,000 Cossack horses, racing across a sparse, dreary plain, never slowing, eyes aflame, galloping into cannon range with bearded madmen on their backs.

I propped my head on my hands, praying for the aspirin to work and closed my eyes, drifting back to the night, to Aubrey and the deepening fear that I had seen Augusta at her best. Curiously, I no longer worried about Bobby or Champ Crawford or feared Toby Pugh. The worst of judges and juries couldn't punish me more severely than the horror of Augusta's derangement and a whiskey hangover.

In slow motion, my head dropped to the table top. I heard myself whispering, begging for a clear head, Hell's fire for Bobby and Champ Crawford and for Phillip Rayner to dissolve, vanish forever. I even conjured a slimy, snorting dragon possessing Augusta and speculated how to save her without sorcery, horse and lance.

Finally, I stood, wobbled around to the coffee maker, filled it and waited, cursing murderous consequences of indulgent self-pity. Clutching the edge of the counter with both hands, I let go just long enough to reach the whiskey bottle and trash it.

I felt cold cereal and milk sloshing in my stomach as I struggled over Regina Toll's fence about 10:45. The food might have eased the nausea but nothing could have helped my burning eyes and bad head.

Walking might help, I thought. Besides, at least one police cruiser had been parked across the street when I got the paper. Heads bobbed in the car and arms languished out open windows, prompting me to leave my car in the garage.

But the peaceful, solitary potential of walking to Augusta's house didn't last because anonymity doesn't exist in Ransom. People know each other, so they speak to everyone—out of curiosity or courtesy. And they believe inquiring into the business of others defines virtue.

That's why I crossed Scott Avenue to avoid Cotton Agley.
"Wiley," he yelled, coming at me with uplifted hand and a smile.
"Which way you headed?" The question meant nothing because
Cotton Agley knew Scott Avenue led to Pickett and downtown.

I didn't stop.

"I read about you in the paper," Cotton said, stepping up the
curb.

I said nothing.

He pulled up beside me, puffing and complaining about
being out of shape. Since I knew he'd passed 75, it seemed a blessing
he could walk at all.

Then he put his hand on my arm, slowed my pace and started
clapping his hands. Because of my headache, I didn't understand or
appreciate the gesture.

"Shut up, Cotton," I snapped, remembering that before he
became a dried-up, white-haired old man he'd been a lawyer and
liked attention.   But that didn't mean he could clap me to death.

"Headache, Cotton." I kept walking.

"Allergies," he said.   "Time of year."

"Go away," I said.

"I'm applauding you, Wiley." Step for step, he stayed with
me.

"Myself, I never cared for any of the Crawfords," he said,
shifting his gaze from the ground to me. "Bobby Crawford shot my
sheep."

I walked faster, trying to tire or outdistance him.

"Sweet ewe," he said, glancing across the street to a tree
trimmer snipping small oak limbs with a clipper on a long pole. "For
fun, he shot her in the rump. Poor thing died of blood poisoning."

I didn't react.

"That's not the worst he ever did," I said.

"1948," Cotton said. He got tears in his eyes and he didn't
notice my indifference.

Cars passed; some tooting horns. Cotton Agley waved, a
royal holding court on foot. He called names and sometimes just
nodded. I kept my eyes straight ahead, walking as fast as recurring

dizziness would allow.

We crossed Albemarle. I stumbled up the curb. Cotton kept talking while I staggered a little, trying to regain balance.

"I never had respect for nobody as mean as Bobby Crawford. But take a man like Phillip Rayner. He's helping out at the Widow Crawford's this morning."

"Compassion," Cotton continued, with more charity. "That's a damn sight better than shooting a man's sheep."

Pure jealousy burned through me and I couldn't think of who to blame for those feelings, Phillip Rayner or Augusta. But I decided quickly that since Augusta possessed no reasonable will or direction, in all fairness, the blame must rest upon Phillip Rayner.

Cotton Agley didn't care. He left me at Cedar, saying he needed a nap. He wished me a nice day. I didn't wish him anything.

With three blocks to go, I got a distant glimpse of Phillip Rayner's old Plymouth. He'd parked by the curb in front of Augusta's house, in full view of all Ransom. I suppose the sight of his faded blue car stood as a monument promoting him from mere shepherd to champion of the sad and lonely.

However, I'd seen enough heroes. And the closer I got to Phillip Rayner's Plymouth, the more it resembled a red, rocket Oldsmobile, reminding me of the man to whom I'd lost Augusta. Now I found myself competing for an old woman's sanity.

Glancing around for police cars, I turned up Third Street and headed again for Pollard's Alley, this time determined to see Augusta in the daylight and with Phillip Rayner.

My stomach had settled but my head still throbbed and I wished I'd brought along the aspirin bottle. I needed to think straight, I told myself, or bringing Augusta out of the darkness would remain dream only.

About halfway down the alley, I slipped behind a tree while Geraldine Williford's maid placed a bulging plastic garbage can beyond a fence and silently withdrew, closing the gate behind her. In a few seconds, I stood at Augusta's gate, next to her garbage can, and wondered who put it out.

I'd brought along coat hanger wire if I needed to open the door. Of course I realized my inexperience at lock-picking and if the door hadn't been unlocked I would have spent the morning, prying, punching and cursing.

In daylight, the kitchen seemed more familiar and more the way I remembered it in the days when Marvin Lee ambled around with silver trays and dishes of pastry. An ancient glass orange squeezer sat on the counter top next to the refrigerator. I recalled the oval, pleasant face of Marybelle Reed, the cook, and how she told of twisting a million oranges so Augusta could have fresh juice whenever she wanted.

The muffled sound of music drifted to me but I couldn't identify it. It came from the library, I thought, and after I'd seen Phillip Rayner out the door, I could listen with Augusta. Maybe I could make tea.

Slipping along in the hallway, apprehension surged to my throat, fouling my mouth with the same taste I experienced the night Aubrey's spotlight caught Bobby Crawford and Augusta squirming on the blanket in the dark pine woods.

At the entrance to the living room, I edged my face around the door frame. The act of peeking didn't raise any moral questions in my mind. Simply, I wanted to see Augusta and Phillip Rayner together. After that, I'd decide my next move.

Late morning sun streamed through cracks in the drawn living room curtains, steaks of light making white powder of dust on picture frames, tabletops and figurines. The piano and orchestra music from the library began to swell, capturing the soul of rhythm and snatching it away to dream, where ordinary humans might imagine themselves in concert, conducting, lost in a powerful musical current.

Recognizing Chopin, I stood still for a moment, absorbed in the piano and silently wished I'd used some of those forty years to learn the keyboard.

Then someone turned down the music. I moved to the right of the cracked library door and looked inside. I could only see filled bookshelves and a table.

"And this?" Augusta asked.

"Yes," Phillip Rayner said. The music dropped lower and the voices became clear.

"Bobby, can you smile for me?"

"Yes," the man said. I heard him clear his throat at least twice.

"Will you come back?"

"Yes."

My fingertips lightly touched the middle of the old mahogany door and gently pushed, not enough to attract attention. Phillip Rayner sat straight in a wingback chair, both hands on both knees, like Sundays when he waited for the end of the choir's anthem.

"Beautiful," he said. "Your name is cherry lips."

"Tonight?"

"No," he said.

"Oh," she replied, her tone dull.

For a moment, neither spoke.

"You should come at night. My father comes at night."

"What does your father say about me?" Phillip Rayner asked, a slight smile on his mouth.

"He says I should run you away."

"Will you?"

"No."

"Then Bobby says move this way and that," Phillip Rayner said, turning his head from side to side in time with the music.

I pushed the door open further and saw a gray-haired, 61-year-old woman, blindfolded, nude, swaying to music, humming along with Chopin.

When he reached the door, I stepped from behind the staircase and spoke his name. Phillip Rayner's expression hardened and he didn't offer a word.

"You called Blithe Tanner cherry lips."

Rayner said nothing. He seemed to look past me, perhaps into some gray, remote corner of his thinking that didn't consider blame or articulate explanation.

Then words burst into my mouth, spilling through my teeth and into his face. "How could you violate a shattered soul like Augusta?" My voice was jammed into high pitch. Rayner opened the door and backed onto the porch. In an instant, I stepped the distance between us and slapped his face, never considering the man to be a head taller than me, and demented at that.

PART IV

Chapter 22

Ten days after I discovered Augusta and Phillip Rayner, I still boiled with a rage that at times cut my breath short or sickened an already delicate stomach.

Augusta, bless her, cooperated nicely, called me Bobby and occasionally asked why Bobby now visited nearly all day, every day. The presence of the practical nurse I hired didn't generate any inquiries. Augusta called Esther Coleman mother, stayed close to her and seemed to appreciate companionship. Large and efficient-looking in her white uniform, Esther Coleman said she'd reached her fifty-ninth year, reared eight children, sent four to college and buried her husband three years before.

Most of all, Esther Coleman alleviated worry.

"Nobody," she said, "will get in this house without your good word, Mr. Frost." I thanked her, told her no more than necessary and gave her another twenty dollar bill.

Finally, I slept soundly most nights. But sometimes I dreamed of young Augusta, her beauty and enthusiasm for life. An instant later, the dream shifted to the older Augusta, living over forty years of days in a dusty house, wearing dresses from her teenage years, haunted by people long dead and misused by Phillip Rayner.

While I held terrible anger for the man, the relief of knowing everything somewhat eased my mind. Care of Augusta took precedence over malice. Each day, sitting with her on the library sofa or driving home alone, my mind flooded with questions and I realized each answer must be pursued painstakingly.

Legal custody? I'd call a lawyer.

Bobby Crawford's death? I'd speak to Toby Pugh.

Champ Crawford's death? Heart attack. Forget it.

Call Phillip Rayner's church? His wife?

No. I decided. First, Augusta must be protected from scandal and that meant using Grace Lynn Rose to alter Ransom's focus on the strange woman who lived in the big house on Pickett Street.

When she answered the phone at 9:35 on a Wednesday morning, Grace Lynn Rose sounded busy, if not harassed. That translated into her tone which I mentally characterized as arrogantly self-absorbed, if not rude.

"I got no time," she said, her words clipped and punchy. "State your business. Quickly."

"Miss Rose?"

"Yes. I've got a deadline here."

"Wiley Frost calling."

Silence. She didn't speak right away but I could hear newsroom chatter, people telling other people to hurry and the clicking of computer keyboards. Somebody screamed for a headline on a state budget story. Somebody else swore and demanded another minute.

"Aren't we enemies?"

Trying to gather my wits, I hesitated, then took the offensive: "You don't tell the truth."

The comment must have stirred her because she cleared her throat before speaking again. "I write what I see, Mr. Frost," she said, anger in her voice. "If you don't like that, talk to the editor.

Complain, Mr. Frost."

"No," I said. "Bargain with me."

The request brought no instant response and I suspected she'd put her hand over the mouthpiece. "Not now," I heard her say in a voice hardly audible.

Then she returned: "What kind of bargaining, Mr. Frost? You got more to say about Bobby Crawford, Blithe Tanner, sadness and strife? Who killed Bobby Crawford, Mr. Frost? Who dropped the old army hat near Champ Crawford?"

Overwhelming. But I kept my head.

"Tell me something else, Mr. Frost: Why do you park your car every day at Augusta Crawford's back door? That's a fine place to start. Story's getting stale and I'm tired of writing old news."

The comment didn't disturb me. I'd seen the *Telegraph* car following me. One can't expect some new and unusual ccurrence— like my car at Augusta's back gate—to proceed unnoticed in Ransom. Besides, I realized long ago that Grace Lynn Rose's resourcefulness complemented her dishonesty.

"Do you want to bargain?" I asked.

"If I bargain, what do I get?"

"Interview with Augusta Crawford."

For a moment, she kept silent but I could hear her breathing and guessed the wheels in her brain had picked up speed.

"What's she got to say?" she asked, her tone cautious, even tedious.

"Why don't you ask her the questions you asked me? I guarantee an answer for any question."

"This got conditions, Mr. Frost?"

"Yes."

"What?"

"That you write a true story and stop following me."

More silence.

"You want a bargain?" I asked, pushing, insisting.

"What happens if I don't agree?"

"I'll give everything to TV news."

Pause.

"Yes. When can I see her?"

"I'll call," I said, hanging up the telephone.

On Friday morning, Grace Lynn Rose strolled up Augusta's walk like a queen bee loose on the world. She carried recorder in one hand and yellow pad in the other.   Her tall, dark-complected photographer, Willis Everett, followed her, looking much like a Latin American revolutionary with straps of cameras and light meters crossing his chest, bandoleer-style.

"I guess this is the great story of my life," she said, sarcasm thick.   "I can't wait to see the siren who launched a thousand traumas."

"Kindness," I said, my voice touched with irritation and a sudden loss of patience. "Or go away."

"Allright," she said, not looking at me.

I opened the front door for Grace Lynn Rose and Willis Everett.   As they stepped inside, disbelief washed over their faces; they'd stepped into an alien world, complete with cobwebs, dim light, threadbare rugs and furniture that outdated their ages.

"Dungeon," whispered Willis Everett.

"God, turn on the lights." Grace Lynn Rose pointed to the drawn curtains in both the sitting room and the living room. "Who could live like this?"

"Augusta," I said.

I motioned for them to follow me into the living room. Grace Lynn Rose stared, mouth open, at paintings, tapestries, cane-bottomed rockers. She stepped to a table beside a large, stuffed chair, and ran fingers over a rack of pipes, each carefully in its place.

"Mr. Morefield smoked a pipe," I said. Getting carried away, I added: "Prince Albert, Half and Half, Rum and Maple."

Grace Lynn Rose faced me. "How'd you get in this house, Mr. Frost? How'd you get in charge?"

I ignored the questions and walked into the library.

❖

Of course I found Grace Lynn Rose intelligent.   But I honestly admired her intuitive nature and investigative instincts. She already tried to corner me and hadn't yet met Augusta.

I stood aside and nodded for Grace Lynn Rose and Willis Everett to enter the library.   Augusta sat on a sofa at the far end of the room.   Slowly, she turned the pages of an old world atlas book, frequently stopping to study a map or to trace a river or mountain range with her finger.   She didn't look up when Grace Lynn Rose and Willis Everett crossed the room and took straight-backed chairs in front of her.

I moved over to the sofa and sat next to Augusta.

Immediately, Willis Everett pulled up a camera and I whispered for him to wait.   He looked at me like a baseball pitcher working with a disagreeable plate umpire.   However, he did lower the camera, glancing at Grace Lynn Rose, who said nothing and kept her eyes on Augusta.

I leaned over and patted Augusta's hand.   "Where are you now?" I asked.

She smiled.

"South America," she said.   "Through the Darien, on to Columbia, headed for the Amazon." Like a child, I thought.   Surely, even Grace Lynn Rose could understand the toll of turmoil and isolation on a fragile heart.

"Visitors," I said.   With a hand, I motioned toward the reporter and photographer.   "Feel like talking?"

Augusta Crawford didn't speak and I couldn't decide if she'd welcome her first real visitors in over forty years, withdraw to a sullen heap on the sofa or become angry at the intrusion.

I persisted.

"Friends," I said. "From the *Telegraph*.   They're here to ask you about your travels.   Can they take your picture?"

Augusta clasped her hands in her lap.   "I've been away," she said, smiling.

About thirty seconds into the interview, I expected Grace

Lynn Rose's questions to cynically dissect and batter Augusta's sad state of mind.   But that didn't happen and I came to admire compassion I didn't know she had.

"Where've you been, Mrs. Crawford?" With recorder humming in her lap and pen poised on the yellow pad on her knee, the reporter spoke softly and slipped to the edge of her seat, watching Augusta's face and hands.

"I've been to England and Germany and the low countries," Augusta said, her cheeks showing a little pink.

"Who is this man here?" Grace Lynn Rose shook a hand in my direction.   "What's his name?"

Augusta looked at me. "This is my husband, Mr. Crawford. Don't you know?"

For a second, reporter and photographer looked at each other. Augusta unclasped her hands, took my right hand in her left and smiled at me. Her brown eyes seemed alive and purposeful.   I returned the smile but couldn't help but wonder about the path of her thoughts.

"Isn't your husband dead, Mrs. Crawford?"

"No," she said. "You see he's here."

"His body's been found, Mrs. Crawford."

"No," Augusta said, turning another page in the atlas book. "He's here." She squeezed my hand.   "He's here to stay, now. Sometimes we talk to my father.   Sometimes Marvin Lee makes coffee for us."

"Who takes care of you?"

"My husband and my mother."

Grace Lynn Rose turned to me.   "Is this real?" she asked.

I nodded. "The woman she calls mother is a practical nurse."

"Mrs. Crawford, do you know Champ Crawford?"

"Yes."

"Do you know Wiley Frost?"

"Yes."

"How do you know Champ Crawford?"

"Mr. Champ Crawford is my husband's older brother."

"How do you know Wiley Frost?"

Augusta didn't answer right away.   Then: "Dear Wiley. Wiley Frost is an old and dear friend. Before my marriage, we went to dances and barbecues and the pavilion by the river."

Grace Lynn Rose pushed back in her seat and made a few notes on her pad. "When did you last see your husband's army uniform, Mrs. Crawford? Specifically, the tan, folding cap."

Augusta thought for a second. "When Bobby got his medal after the war."

"Could it be here—stored?"

"No," Augusta answered. "Marvin Lee cleaned the attic and discarded old things. I remember the hat and I expect it ended up in the trash."

One eyebrow arched, Grace Lynn Rose looked at me again.

I returned the gesture with a shrug, crossed my legs trying to control my surprise at Augusta's answers.

"How long ago did Marvin Lee clean the attic?"

"Before I left on my trip," Augusta said, beginning to ramble. "We had piles and piles of useless things here. I told Marvin Lee to throw it all away. My husband couldn't wear the uniform anyway. He gained weight." She squeezed my hand again.

Grace Lynn Rose leaned over to whisper to Willis Everett. "Everything's new here," she said, her voice showing excitement. "She accounted for the cap, didn't she?"

"Yeah." Willis Everett, obviously more interested in pictures than stories, agreed. "Can I shoot?" He glanced at me.

"In a minute," I said.

At that point, it occurred to me The *Telegraph*'s star reporter showed no concern for credibility. Even if Augusta's statement about the cap satisfied Toby Pugh, how could a newspaper claim a mental cripple as a source for answering the key question about Champ Crawford's death?

Stop worrying, I told myself. Sit still. Admire how Augusta drifts and fascinates them.

"Mrs. Crawford, where do they pick up your trash?"

Augusta's eyes took on a pleasant shine. "By the back gate."

I dared not speak.

Grace Lynn Rose whispered to Willis Everett: "Some wino could have picked the cap from the garbage. It could have been passed around for years."

At that point, nervousness made me cough.

"Reasonable to me," said Grace Lynn Rose, slipping back in her chair and sort of swaggering with her shoulders. "No other explanation."

"Marvin Lee's dead," I interjected.

Grace Lynn Rose looked at me. "We've got enough."

I didn't argue. "Ready to take pictures?" Willis Everett smiled. Augusta smiled. I smiled.

"How old are you, Mrs. Crawford?" asked Grace Lynn Rose, her expression soft, her eyes aglow and at least a little triumphant. No doubt, she thought of all the TV reporters she'd leave in the dust.

"Twenty-two next month," Augusta said.

Chapter 23

On the front porch, it became my turn and I tried not to lie. By then, however, I'd resigned myself to just about anything.

"You've taken over her care, Mr. Frost?" the reporter asked.

"Yes," I said, silently vowing to continue straight talk as long as I could. "Mr. Rayner supervised Mrs. Crawford's affairs for many years. His wife's not well. He's needed at home."

"So you'll pay the bills, have the food sent in and keep a nurse with her. What's her medical state?"

Sitting on the top step and sounding more and more like a PR genius, I confirmed Augusta Crawford hadn't had a physical examination in many years and that I'd see to treatment, physical or mental.

"How'd you get in the house?"

At that point, I lied, figuring Phillip Rayner had enough survival instincts not to dispute me. "Mr. Rayner and I met here. We decided I'd be responsible for Mrs. Crawford.

Noting my comments on her pad, she stepped back as Willis Everett's camera clicked off several frames, making me wish I'd looked in a mirror first. The photographer backed off to the fence to take wide shots of the house and Grace Lynn Rose came forward again.

"Mr. Frost, have I just witnessed fine acting?"

"She has no sense of reality," I said, hoping she'd go to her car, leave and ask no more questions. "I think doctors would agree."

"What can I believe?"

"Whatever you wish. Some. All. Nothing. She remembers some things," I ventured. "Like the hat."

Grace Lynn Rose smiled at that, like I'd just spoken truth she needed to believe. "Do you think she knows her husband's dead?"

"She said he's alive."

"Will her mental condition satisfy Chief Pugh's questions about Bobby Crawford's death?"

"I don't know. He can question her," I said, suddenly weary of constant self-protection and supplying vague answers to vague questions.

For a second, Grace Lynn Rose drew circles on her pad. "How long have you been taking care of her?"

"About two weeks," I said.

"Has she made sense about anything? Any rational comments about Bobby Crawford, Champ Crawford or the Blithe Tanner incident? Did she know anything about that?"

Scratching for anything. But her question sent my brains bouncing like bingo balls. My mouth got dry and I prayed not to sweat. Quickly, I reviewed my feelings about Phillip Rayner and silently declared myself competent to distinguish between justice and vengeance. He deserved to make payment. Not to me. To Blithe Tanner and Augusta Crawford.

"She told me the name of the fourth man, the one who blindfolded Blithe Tanner at the hotel," I said, almost sensing the heat of the Devil's fire for liars. "I've confronted the man and he didn't deny it."

Grace Lynn Rose's eyes widened.

"Who?"

"I know the name," I said emphatically, tightening my lips

like a fourth grader who'd been admonished for talking and directed to zip his mouth.

Grace Lynn Rose kept her eyes on me, breathing in nervous pants, likely trying to think of a question or a deal she could make with me to get the man's name. After enticing this dangerous animal into a cage, I'd closed the door and locked it.   Greed, without consciousness or shame, constricted her eyes.

"You want to tell me?" Her voice suddenly sounded kind and pleasant, almost childlike.

"No," I said, not mistaking sugar-coated coaxing.   "Not now."

"When?"

"Maybe never."

Of course, that didn't satisfy her so she pushed from another direction.   "Mrs. Crawford told you the man's name?"

"Yes."

"How did she know?"

"She called me Bobby and asked me to promise never to go back to the hotel again with those men.   And she called off three names. Two of those men are dead. The third lives here in Ransom.

The reporter's face reddened and I speculated to myself that she might be losing a struggle for patience. But she didn't interrupt.

"She wanted me, Bobby, to apologize to the young girl and she wanted the other three men to apologize, too."

"How did you react?" Grace Lynn Rose asked.

"I apologized," I said.   "That made her happy and we didn't discuss it further."

At that point, Grace Lynn Rose ran out of questions.

"Mr. Frost," she said, a touch of begging in her voice, "I need a name."

"No," I said.

"Then I'll go ask Mrs. Crawford myself."

"No."

She slapped the side of her head with the legal pad and nearly dropped the recorder from her other hand. Quickly calming herself, she batted her eyes a time or two and smiled. "Mr. Frost, can we bargain?"

A bit charmed, I laughed.

"Sure," I said. "Forty-eight hours after you publish your story, if the man doesn't make a public confession, I'll tell you his name.

"Forty-eight hours," she said.

"Forty-eight hours," I repeated, certain that I didn't yet trust Grace Lynn Rose.

Three days passed before the paper published Grace Lynn Rose's story and Willis Everett's pictures. At 9:15, after I'd read every word, I telephoned the *Telegraph* office to thank her for straightforward reporting.

However, a newsroom person answering her phone said she'd gone out to cover a story and would return shortly. Any message? I gave my name with the simple message: "Thanks."

At 9:45, I stepped out of my house, headed for the car and a quick stop for sinus tablets and then drove on to Augusta's. I felt warmed and satisfied, easy. Only Phillip Rayner became a recurring thought. Could Grace Lynn Rose's story push him to public confession? What if he chose to keep silent? It would be my word against his. But who would believe a murder suspect like me—a man who quoted a reclusive old woman of questionable sanity?

The questions grew as I walked the short distance to the garage. In my right hand, I carried a list of chores to be handled before reaching Augusta's.

J.T.'s Amoco: Gas

Bank: Money for Esther Coleman.

Erika's Boutique: New dresses for Augusta.

Jiffy Appliance: Repair work on the phonograph.

Carolina Telephone: Phone installation.

Luck's Food Store: Settle Augusta's account and place new order for delivery.

Near the garage, I picked up my plastic garbage can and bits of trash some worthless dog had scattered on the ground, snapped the lid handles tight on both sides and wiped my hands with a pocket handkerchief. I had turned toward the car, worrying if I had enough gasoline to get to the station when someone quietly called my name. "Mr. Frost? Wait a minute, wait a minute."

Police? Grace Lynn Rose?

No. Billy Ray Stevens, thirteen years old, head poking around the back corner of the garage.

"What you want, son?" I didn't have much time for conversations with a long-haired blond boy wearing a Disney World T-Shirt, overworn sneakers and blue jeans full of holes.

"Over this way," he said, motioning for me to come with him. "Man wants to see you."

"I got no time, Billy Ray."

"Man says to come. Says for you to give me a dollar." Having to pay for inconvenience exasperated me but I moved along behind Billy Ray Stevens, curious as who might be waiting.

Phillip Rayner. Already?

We crossed Regina Toll's fence and headed down her driveway. Billy Ray Stevens stopped at the curb.

"Man's on that bench—in the park. Gimmie a dollar now." He pointed across Scott Avenue to the solitary figure sitting, smoking on a bench in the small park adjoining Stephen Foster Elementary School.

Handing him the bill, I made a mental note to never do business again with Billy Ray Stevens or the man on the bench, for that matter. But curiosity had me in its grasp: I wanted to know the man in the park who'd made me pay a dollar to see him.

Billy Ray Stevens vanished and I eased down the curb and took my time crossing the street, fearing if I made too much noise, the man might leave and I'd not see his face.

A big man, he had his back to me and wore a weathered brown suit and a chesnut-colored slouch hat. Balls of smoke rose above him and I could see his left hand frequently going to his mouth. The movement did nothing but produce more smoke.

He must have heard me coming and turned. I saw Aubrey Winslow, sweating, crimson-faced, cigarette in hand and trouble on his face.

Truthfully, I'd hardly thought of Aubrey. Facing him across the bench pushed a shot of guilt into my head. How could I have neglected him when he brought Augusta and me together?

"I should have come to see you, Aubrey," I said, my voice sounding hollow, even wimpish. "I should have thanked you for what you did for Augusta and me."

He looked down at the ground, then at me. "I don't know I did you a favor, Wiley. If you're planning to spend the rest of your natural life with a woman with a feeble brain, I didn't do a thing. Augusta just got herself a new caretaker and you got a headache."

The sharpness of his comment surprised me. But I moved around the bench toward him.

"Sit," he said.

Maybe I wanted to complain a little so I didn't wait for him to speak again. "She doesn't know my name, Aubrey. She calls me Bobby."

But I won no sympathy.

"She's old, too," Aubrey said, lighting another cigarette off the glowing stub he held in his left hand. "All the silk and shine's gone off her, Wiley."

Aubrey Winslow's voice trailed off. He looked out across the playground, eyes wandering over vacant slide, swings and see-saw. I found myself looking at the same things, trying to make sense from his words. Could he be angry with me? Augusta?

"I don't understand," I said, my tone a touch combative. Aubrey shouldn't have talked about Augusta and silk and shine. He'd never had silk and shine.

He didn't speak. Then he brought a morning *Telegraph* from inside his coat and unfolded it on his lap. "I don't understand either, Wiley. You should have told me you know the last man's name. You should have told me before Grace Lynn Rose."

Then he read: "Frost, who has recently assumed responsibility for Augusta Crawford's care, says she's told him of a fourth man involved in the alleged 1951 sexual abuse and death of a young California girl. Frost says the man's identity recently surfaced in conversations with Mrs. Crawford whose mental state he describes as 'fragile.'"

Aubrey stopped reading and looked at me.

"Show me some hate, Wiley. I lost a niece and here we are: only you know the last one. Augusta Crawford knew all the time but she connects mind and mouth only during a full moon."

He snapped his eyes back to the newspaper and continued Grace Lynn Rose's story: "Frost says he'll reveal the name to the *Telegraph* if the man—who still lives in Ransom—doesn't publicly confess within 48 hours."

Pulling off his hat and placing it beside him on the bench, Aubrey Winslow made a half-turn toward me. The anger in his face looked almost menacing. Then he started in on me.

"You found the Reverend Mr. Rayner and Augusta Crawford together. You found an old man with his hand in an old woman's pants."

"Yes," I said.

"Where're your killing feelings, Wiley? Remember Augusta on the ground in the pines? It's the same hurt. A man can't be an ice cube and you know you're glad Bobby and Champ Crawford died." He paused, then, "How'd you kill Bobby?"

I didn't answer.

Aubrey flipped his cigarette about three feet away and watched smoke curl up in a thin, wavering stream. He slipped to the edge of the seat, hands grasping at nothing, lips wet, sweat showing through the back of his coat. "Visions and daydreams run me crazy, if you want to know the truth. I see my sister's girl being passed around, man to man. She didn't know whether to cry or spit, didn't understand about dying or why she'd die alone. I wonder if she wanted her mother."

"I'm sorry, Aubrey."

"Get mad, Wiley. Tell me his name."

"No."

Aubrey lit another cigarette and blew smoke straight out in front of him. Puffs and ringlets and twists rose and quickly vanished into the air.   He laughed, wickedly, like he knew something I didn't. "What did you see Augusta Crawford and Phillip Rayner doing, Wiley? Had her naked, I bet. On a bed? On a couch? I can see that poor old woman now: tongue lolling out of her mouth, trying to do what he told her."

"No," I said, loudly, near tears. "Phillip Rayner!"

Aubrey stood and put the hat on his head. "You're too easy, Wiley."

Right.

Chapter 24

Surly and silent, Aubrey Winslow had me drop him at the cab stand on Van Buren Avenue. Before he got out, he offered me a drink from a pint bottle in his coat. But I had no urge for whiskey.

Through the rear-view mirror, I saw Aubrey get into a cab. Gone. Out of sight. Opposite direction. Again, I had surrendered to him. What would he do with this secret?

I drove to J.T.'s Amoco and pulled up next to a pump and rolled down my window. I tried to keep my mind occupied, narrowing my thoughts to the empty gas tank, how many gallons it would take to fill it and the cost. Calculate and recalculate. Stay calm.

J. T. Harrison popped out of the station, wrung off the gas cap, stuck the hose nozzle into the tank and stood there, staring at the figures running up dollars and gallons. Never too friendly, he stopped the pump, screwed on the cap and passed by my open window on the way to the windshield.

"Sixteen dollars," he said.

I gave him a twenty.

He took a final swipe on the windshield, stepped back to the window, took the twenty, stripped off four ones from a wad of bills and handed them to me. "Looks like Widow Crawford cleared up that army cap pretty well," J.T. said, folding his money and not looking at me. "How'd you get it, anyway?"

Placing the four bills in my wallet, I neither answered nor looked at him.

"Nice day," he said.

"Nice," I said, starting the car and pulling into the street, not even ruffled by J.T. Harrison. Next stop: Luck's Food Store, across town. Most of the way, my mind stayed on items for the food order. But I didn't get past whole ham before an avalanche of questions nearly smothered me.

Am I guilty? Of what?

Running an ambulance?

Caring about the sick and hurt?

Loving Augusta?

Knowing how Bobby Crawford died?

Scaring Champ Crawford to death?

Discovering Phillip Rayner and Augusta?

Knowing Aubrey Winslow had a niece named Blithe Tanner?

Finally understanding the sadness of an eye for an eye?

Mumbling, I finally pulled into Luck's parking lot and saw old man Hardy Luck sweeping the front sidewalk. As I passed him, heading for a parking spot, he must have thought I'd spoken to him. So he stopped sweeping and set his mouth to work. I had no idea what he said because I had my windows up.

I collected my list and got out of the car. Hardy Luck stood at the market entrance, leaning on the broom, smiling and looking much like he thought I'd agreed with everything he said.

"Wiley, you can play for a dollar a chance," he said, pointing to a young woman at the first check-out counter. "Just tell that girl how many chances you want, give her the money and you're in."

"In what?" I asked, thinking it might some new promotional stunt for TV dinners or eggplant.

"Pool," he said. "Chance to win money."

"I don't need money," I said.

"Play for fun, Wiley."

"No," I said, moving past him and picking a push basket with a bad wheel.

Hardy Luck followed me into the store.

"Come on Wiley, this is your doing. Buy a few chances."

I looked at him but didn't speak.

"You said you know the fourth man. Write his name down, drop it in that box with your name on it. When we draw day after tomorrow, you'll win easy money."

He pointed to a Tide soap box at the checkout. A sign taped to the side read: "Fourth man pool. Dollar a chance."

I looked at him and silently admitted to myself that putting Phillip Rayner's name in the box appealed to me. After I left, Hardy Luck would tear through the box, find the name and tell everybody. Ransom could stop wondering. Phillip Rayner and I could stop suffering.

"No," I said, walking up the cereal aisle, looking for bran flakes.

After paying at the checkout for cereal and skim milk, I gave the clerk, young Jo Linda MacReady, two hundred ten dollars for Augusta's bill and the order. Thankfully, the girl just took the money, smiled kindly, and didn't ask me if I'd murdered anyone.

I stepped out the door and heard a siren. Intuition boiled into a thought of Aubrey Winslow involved in something, somewhere, because of what I had told him. Would they find him, smoking pistol in hand, the preacher dead as hamburger and blood everywhere?

Of course, I didn't know and didn't much care. Aubrey'd have to be his own problem, not mine.

The ambulance screamed by about the time I opened my car door. Red lights flashed across store windows, windshields and faces of the curious who stood at the curb to watch.

I backed around and headed toward the street, missed the

turnout and thumped over the curb. Knowing people would chuckle and point at Wiley Frost's driving, I didn't look at anybody but kept my eyes straight on the road, trying to keep the ambulance in sight, remembering speed limits.

Of course, at that rate, I arrived at Pettigrew Memorial long after the ambulance stopped at the curb. A crowd trailed into the street. Men, women and children, most whispering, kept eyeing the church door. Cotton Angely stood closest to the church door, surely claiming to have been the first person on the scene.

Two small boys, under school age, hung behind their mothers. An old woman with a cane jabbered at Timmy Payne, the assistant minister, emphasizing with an animated thrust of the cane toward Timmy's face or onto the street blacktop.

I parked a half-block away, put on my straw hat and pulled it down on my forehead. Self-conscious? Yes. Intimidated? Yes. I had to see what had happened but didn't want to answer questions. Thirty seconds after leaving my car, I felt a pull on my sleeve. Rocko Stone, Ransom's only male hairdresser, smiled at me.

"Glass cuts," Rocko said. "He'll get a Band Aid and a bill for two thousand dollars." He laughed like he worked for Blue Cross. I couldn't muster a snicker because not five steps away, Aubrey Winslow stood at the back of the crowd.

Police cars and people transfixed Aubrey Winslow like a five-year-old before a monkey cage. Mouth agape, he stood on tiptoes following the action, especially the movements of Police Chief Toby Pugh whose car wailed to the curb.

"Move back." Pugh spoke through cupped hands. "We can't work here unless you move back." Frankly I hadn't seen anybody work. Officers stood about, grim, leaning over, trying to talk to each other like they shared a common secret. Occasionally a policeman acknowledged someone in the crowd with a nod.

I turned to Rocko Stone.

"Study window broke, glass everywhere," he said, mouth taking a severe droop at both corners. "Everybody's talking about gunshots.”

"Anybody hear a shot?" I asked, keeping my head up, scanning the crowd and keeping an eye on the church door like the others.

"Everybody says it sounded like a shot."

"Anybody see anybody shoot?"

"Nobody saw nobody at all," Rocko said, "Except for the big old fat man in a hat who ran around looking for a phone to call the rescue truck. “

By the time I got that information, Aubrey had disappeared, either left or lost himself in the crowd. So, I walked away from Rocko Stone just as he clasped hands to Pettigrew Memorial's gleaming white spire, offering a silent plea to the Almighty to heal Phillip Rayner's wounds.

I'd edged my way into a space about four yards from the sidewalk, watching rescue people run back and forth for supplies from the ambulance. Suddenly a cloud of cigarette smoke curled around my face and inched mercilessly into my nose and poor sinuses. No doubt, Aubrey Winslow stood behind me.

"Wiley, isn't this something?" He whispered to the back of my head and off to the right. I didn't turn around but did glance to either side to see if anyone noticed him or stood close enough to hear what he said. Aubrey's voice sounded excited, at least as keyed-up as that of a pyromaniac directing fire trucks to flames.

"You should've seen the glass fly. You should've seen that rascal run."

A chill charged through my shoulder blades and out both arms to the tips of my fingers. Aubrey got closer, concentrating on my left ear, deciding I might be deaf in the right. "Seeing him bleed and pick glass out of his hair made me real sympathetic."

Still, I didn't speak, turn or move.

"Damn, Wiley. How deaf are you? Don't worry. Nobody saw me. I've had a fine time, seeing familiar faces in this crowd, people I locked up."

My legs began to tremble.

"Come on, Wiley," he said. I'm no bloodthirsty killer.

Man's living. He's got a good shot of fear and don't know where it's coming from. He's terrified. I want him terrified. Makes me feel better."

At that point, two policemen waded into the crowd, looking over faces, checking a few ID's. I didn't look back at Aubrey or see Phillip Rayner on a stretcher but stepped forward about three feet, eased to my left and trickled through the crowd to my car.

After years of pretense, intrigue, innuendo and inference, pain and only a trace of optimism, one might have expected me to expect the unexpected.

Oh no.

I'd turned left on Castle Road, taken another left on R. J. Reynolds Street and made my way back to Pickett. About two minutes from Augusta's house, my car rolled from one side to another, like a great weight shifting, like loose ballast in an old ship's hold.

Aubrey got up off the rear floor complaining about cramps. He lit a cigarette and draped his arms over the passenger seat. "You could have said something to me. Wiley, you could have acted like you knew me back there."

Furious at Aubrey for sneaking into my car, I checked the rear view mirror, slowed the car and said: "Aubrey, just shut up, take your cigarettes and gun and get out."

He laughed. Loudly.

"For God's sakes, Wiley. I ain't got my gun. I just slung a rock through his window. Like little David."

Chapter 25

By the time I parked at Augusta's back gate, Aubrey had snatched my sanity into his hands, squeezed and crushed and gouged until I felt like joining Augusta in her comfortable world of detachment and denial.

"Preliminaries, Wiley. Priming the subject with fear heightens a killer's creativity. Do you get my point, Wiley?"

I cut the engine and pushed back in my seat, deciding to sit still until Aubrey heard me. How could I maneuver him to more productive channels: Like returning to Reno. I'd buy the ticket.

"My question," Aubrey said, his voice even, tone calm although he'd begun to pontificate, "is why would a man like Phillip Rayner get mixed up with Bobby Crawford and his crowd?

I didn't answer.

Puffing on a cigarette, Aubrey tapped my shoulder. I turned a little in my seat to look at him. "Wiley, you got to work up more heat for vengeance," he said, now looking amused. "It cleanses. Just like a refiner's fire."

Such profundity, coming from him, and so inappropriate to

boot—startled me so I wanted to laugh. I turned back to the wheel to hide my face. Of course, Aubrey didn't shut up. He rambled along, philosophically, like a water colorist or sculptor proposing a pictorial route to creation. "If I had the time, I'd use mail," he said, thumping his cigarette out a window. "Just enough unsigned abuse and threats to make him afraid of dark rooms."

He paused. "How much time we got, anyway?"

I looked at my watch: A little after noon.

"Look Aubrey, I didn't make a binding promise of forty eight hours. I want this man to own up and pay his price. Ransom needs to get rid of unworthy heroes, ghost worship and hurtful, homegrown voodoo."

Aubrey took a deep breath.

"We got a day and more," I said, wishing for the conversation to end. "Think about gambling in Reno."

He laughed.

I just sat there, hung my head. "I give up," I said.

But Aubrey Winslow didn't hear me. He'd left the car and walked to the end of the alley, pitching cinders at flower pots and ivy-covered trellises. A minute more and he turned out of sight, over-sized shoes kicking up thin puffs of dust.

Esther Coleman finished serving Brunswick Stew and cornbread and left Augusta and me at the long dining room table, silently sharing an interlude of peace.

"Let's go to the library," Augusta said.

While I stood there clearing up a few dishes, I smiled — at the pleasure of the moment. Maybe she had my name wrong but she enjoyed my company and I, hers. "Yes, we'll go to the library." I said, hearing contentment in every word.

I headed for the kitchen with the small stack of dishes. Augusta followed, carrying glasses and serving bowls. Esther Coleman greeted us, took the dishes and quickly slid them into soapy water in the sink. A pleasant, round-cheeked woman, Ester Coleman kissed Augusta and told her to rest quietly for a while.

"I am tired, mother," Augusta said.

Ester Coleman smiled and turned back to the dishes. A second later, she glanced out the kitchen window and asked me who might be at the back gate.

Top of a head, she said. Dark-grayish hair. Eyes on the kitchen window. I quickly stepped to the door, opened it and watched for movement. A meter-reader, I thought. Perhaps it could have been a child, self-absorbed, climbing, playing Indians and forts.

Augusta said she'd go on to the library and start the phonograph. That gave me the opportunity to investigate, just for safety's sake. Ester Coleman followed me out on the porch, arms folded, stern and positively fearless.

The gate latch still held in place. I looked back at Mrs. Coleman. "I saw fingers too," she whispered, apprehension in her voice. "Somebody opened the gate. Closed it when they saw me at the window."

Could Toby Pugh's detectives be snooping? Did a friend of Champ Crawford's drop by, intent on disruption? A thief, looking for money?

I flicked up the latch, pushed the door open and stepped into the alley. My shoes crunched on gravel and for an instant, I fooled myself, allowing the sound of my own feet to alarm me into thinking someone approached.

Jittery? I should say.

Ester Coleman cleared her throat. "See any tracks?"

"Just my own, Mrs. Coleman."

"Oh," she said, stepping back inside the kitchen.

Looking left and right, I saw only my car, parked where I'd left it. Nothing human or animal stirred. A few normal sounds prevailed: a distant, whistling parrot, a vacuum cleaner, the grinding of a car's ignition on Pickett Street, the easy crackling of falling leaves.

Not much.

Closing the gate, I snapped the hook into the eyelet and, still listening and watching each side of the yard, walked up the stairs and back into the kitchen. Mrs. Coleman had left the room, presumably to check on Augusta. I liked that. I liked remembering the days when Augusta presided in the Morefield house as the center of everyone's attention.

Voices at the front door interrupted the thought.

Mrs. Coleman's large frame blocked my view so I headed up the hall to see the caller. She stepped aside, turned for the kitchen and I saw young Linwood Lupton, Ransom's worrisome encyclopedia salesman, move quickly into the foyer. He put a leather case on the floor, took off his dark felt and held it in his hand by his side.

Tall and thin with a full head of black hair, Linwood Lupton kept nervous eyes on me like I might not let him stay long enough to say anything. His Adam's apple rippled up and down, and he quivered like a frightened dog.

"Afternoon, Mr. Frost," he said, standing straight, like some poor hazing victim, bracing for upperclassmen, ready to perform any assigned task, as distasteful as it might be.

"Books, Mr. Frost," he said, kneeling to crack open his briefcase. He handed me two colorful brochures. "This one is for Mrs. Crawford and this one's for you," he said. "These books got color pictures now. Why, you can see an African lion that looks so real you can imagine hearing a roar or seeing one running through a house swallowing ornery dogs."

He thought that remark funny and spent a few seconds laughing and clapping his hands, no doubt congratulating himself on his humor.

"We don't need books, Linwood," trying to be patient and remembering Augusta waited for me in the library. "We got enough books here right now."

"Can I come into the living room and sit down with you?" he asked, stepping inside without an invitation. "How's Mrs. Crawford?"

I didn't answer his question but stepped a little more to my right to head off any further entry into the foyer. "Linwood, I wish you'd go find somebody else—maybe down the street a few doors. Mrs. Crawford's trying to get better and this is an interruption."

He thought about that.

"Just look at the brochures," Linwood Lupton said. "Show them to Mrs. Crawford. People told me she likes books and these are new. Help her catch up."

A brief chill shook me. Somehow I didn't want Augusta to catch up. I wanted to slowly tell her those things she needed to know. With Linwood Lupton's books, I'd have to immediately explain war and atrocity, nuclear bombs and poverty not more than a mile from her house.

"Not now, Linwood."

He sympathized: "Mr. Frost, don't worry about me at all. You and Mrs. Crawford look over those brochures and I'll come back in a couple of days and take your order."

I shook my head.

He droned on: "Just to take your order, I'm going to give you a video history of all the Arab-Israeli wars and a weather radio with American Encyclopedia's name written on it."

"No, Linwood," I said, trying to sound gruff and emphatic. "It'll be years before we get encyclopedia." I touched his arm, handed him his case and gently pushed him to the door.

"I can get you a video history of the Korean War. Would Mrs. Crawford like that better?"

"No," I said, edging him out the door and onto the porch, handing him the brochure, reluctantly allowing good manners to slip through my screen of good instincts. Linwood Lupton continued to talk after I closed the door.

"Mr. Frost?" Ester Coleman came up behind me just as I peeked through the curtain of the front window, assuring myself of Linwood Lupton's departure. After I saw him drive away in his brown, post office surplus jeep, I turned about and took a tray bearing two cups of steaming black coffee.

"Decaffeinated," Mrs. Coleman said, smiling. "Miss Augusta can have her coffee and her nap."

I took the tray and short-stepped my way through the living room furnishings, nudged the library door with my foot and stepped inside. Trying to hold the tray with one hand and pull the door closed with the other, I didn't look too closely for Augusta, expecting her to be on the couch against the far wall.

Curiously, I didn't notice her in the armchair behind the door until I'd closed it, gotten to the coffee table to set down the tray and quickly began to grow frantic when the room appeared to be empty.

"Augusta," I called, approaching her chair. "Are you hiding from me?" The question sounded childish but not knowing what I'd be dealing with from minute to minute kept me in a ready state for changing situations.

She sat in the chair, eyes closed, and I decided she'd drifted back there looking for a book, grown weary and decided to rest. Only when I got directly in front of her did I hear her mumble Bobby Crawford's name. She held a long-stemmed red rose with both hands.

It didn't take long to suspect Phillip Rayner had gotten into the house. I called Esther Coleman and asked if she'd heard anything or seen anyone.

"Someone's here or has been here," I said, standing still long enough to watch the dear woman's face transform into a pale mask of fear and disbelief. She started apologizing, like she'd purposely allowed entrance, and I put one finger to my lips, trying to silence apprehension and concentrate on finding the intruder or confirming he'd left the house.

"Call me if she's been hurt," I said as Mrs. Coleman headed for the library to keep watch over Augusta. I began at the front door, walked a direct line to the back door and back to the library door, looking for signs.

I found rose petals—like they'd been pulled from a blossom and left in a trail—stretching from the back door, up the hallway, through the living room, into the library and back to the stairs. He'd walked past Mrs. Coleman, past me twice.

How? Did he hide behind furniture, piece by piece?

At the foot of the stairs I found a cluster of petals, like he'd torn one rose apart, waiting for me to rush from the library after I saw the one he'd given Augusta. How long had he stood? Why didn't he face me when I ran to the kitchen for Mrs. Coleman?

Had he been at the top of the stairs, looking down and laughing? Should I call the police?

Never.

I took each step carefully, wondering if the intruder might suddenly appear and throw me to the bottom of the stairs.

All the way upstairs, I picked up rose petals and grew wary, concerned that someone considered me fool enough to follow rose petals to my doom.

Who watched? Who saw me coming?

At the top of the stairs, I dropped my collection of rose petals into a large ashtray and decided to follow the line wherever it might go and forget about cleanliness and order.

I turned right, stepping quietly on hardwood flooring, trying to get to the bedrooms on that side of the house, throw open some doors and either find someone or consider the whole bizarre matter concluded.

Turning the knob to Mr. Morefield's room, I wondered how long it had been since anyone had entered. Would the lights work? Had the lamp bulbs deteriorated beyond use?

I pushed, reached to the right inside the door, and clicked on the light. Cobwebs. More cobwebs. Spiders. Thick dust on chests of drawers and lampshades, books stacked carefully on the nightstand, tarnished silver and gold bookmarks pinpointing parts the reader never finished.

Closing the door, I moved down the hallway, stopped at the guest room, opened the door. The light didn't work but I scanned the grayness for some minutes, trying to detect movement or sound.

Nothing.

At Mrs. Morefield's room, I hesitated because I found more rose petals—like someone had either recently entered the room or at least stood there like me, wondering if it might be a good place to hide.

Inside, cobwebs. A frightened squirrel exited through a crack in the far windowsill. I noticed dusty, ornate bottles on the dresser, thought of Mrs. Morefield's perfume and stood still a moment, locked into fanciful recollections.

At Augusta's door, I paused long enough to remember our last evening so long ago. She drew the curtains tightly, undressed in the dark and lay beside me. That night and since, I'd never regretted the moment.

"Always," she said.

An hour later, she told me goodbye.

The door squeaked when it opened. Seeing Phillip Rayner sitting on the bed, arranging roses on the pillow like a tender, red fan, didn't surprise or frighten me.

He looked at me, smiling. "Wiley Frost, we'll talk tomorrow," he said, standing. "Cobb's Graveyard, just before dark. You'll be interested in what I have to say."

I nodded but said nothing to avoid confrontation. He might have wanted to stay and argue. Dressed in a light gray suit with a dark blue tie, he stood, walked to the door, turned and faced me. He took a rose he held in his hand, broke the stem and pushed the shortened flower into his left lapel button hole.

"Good afternoon," he said, heading down the stairs to the front door. He nodded to Mrs. Coleman who'd heard him speak and rushed dumbfounded from the kitchen to the foyer. He opened the wooden and screened doors, stepped on the porch, leaving both doors open. Still at the top of the stairs, I heard him on the porch steps and briefly on the walk.

Chapter 26

Through most of the next day I fretted over meeting Phillip Rayner, silently speculating about what he had to say and whether I should be cautious about my well-being.

At 3:45 p. m., after an early lunch and brief nap at Augusta's, I got behind the wheel of my car, touched the .32 pistol in the seat beside me and set off for that sad, forgotten field on old Charlie Cobb's farm.

Personal bravery played no role in this small drama. Realistically, I expected no more aggressiveness from Phillip Rayner than from myself. However, considering his strange, bold intrusion of Augusta's house, I questioned his stability more than my own.

Somewhere during the drive out Carter's Mill Road, Aubrey came to mind, giving me some moments of concern as to where he might be and if he posed a threat of interference.

I kept glancing at the rear view mirror. On one occasion, I even pulled to the shoulder and opened rear doors and trunk to make sure he hadn't stowed away.

As I got closer to the turnoff lane back into the field, I wished

I'd stayed with Augusta. At this point, talking with her, even in her odd state of grace, would make more sense than a confrontation with Phillip Rayner.

I made a left turn and bounced and jolted my way up the lane, cursing Charlie Cobb's neglectful descendants, who paid more attention to the golf course and bar at Ransom Country Club than keeping their farm roads in good repair.

The path snaked around a field of soy beans. Near the end, cemetery monuments came into view but I didn't see Phillip Rayner's old blue Plymouth. Might he be hiding in the brush, shotgun or butcher knife in hand, set on ending my life and taking Augusta? I slowed the car, bumping over ruts and sliding in washouts, took the .32 from the seat, and slipped it into the right pocket of my windbreaker.

Now a trifle more self-confident, I picked up a little speed and shortly stopped at the edge of the graveyard, just down from Spaghetti, a migrant Italian farmhand who died in 1954. Before I brought him to Cobb's Graveyard, Spaghetti became an odd joke in Ransom because nobody knew anything about him, especially his right name. I buried him for free. I didn't mind.

Before turning off the engine, I sat for some minutes, gazing from side to side, looking for signs of life and noting the sun retreating behind treetops, leaving golden edges on headstones, leaves, undergrowth, limbs and grass. Until that minute, I'd never considered Cobb's Graveyard more than a disgrace. But the power of that evening's sunset changed that, giving me a welcomed sense of peace, freeing the faces of those I'd placed there to roam my mind, laughing, smiling, chatting.

Then Phillip Rayner arrived.

I watched through my rear view mirror as the old Plymouth groaned and swayed over the gutted lane. The car kicked up a spiral of dust, not unlike sudden whirlwinds that often spring up on open land, fed by a breeze caught in a complexity of currents.

He didn't park beside me but stopped about fifty yards away, perpendicular to a line of pine trees near the river.

He got out.

I turned off my engine and got out.

He walked toward me.

I walked toward him.

Any observer might have concluded these two old men advancing on each other were getting set to duel. I kept my hand on the pistol and nervously adjusted the brim of my brown felt hat. Rayner fingered the red and white print tie he wore with a navy suit.

He had a red rose in his lapel and his face seemed so resolute, so pale. He kept his hands to his sides except when he reached to an inside pocket for a handkerchief. The movement startled me and I nearly pulled my pistol.

If I'd had more time to study Phillip Rayner that evening, perhaps I could have recognized the intensity of his pain, pledged to recant my promise to Grace Lynn Rose and prevented what happened.

But as we neared each other, my thoughts retreated to the night on the common when I approached Bobby Crawford much the same way. However, the substance of the two encounters struck me as clearly different: With Bobby Crawford, I carried murder in my heart. For Rayner, anger thumped just under my breastbone. Why didn't that simple emotion subside and allow me to tell him to go home and forget about me and Grace Lynn Rose?

He stopped in front of me. I continued a couple of steps because I wanted clear sight of him in the dwindling light.

"I'm glad you came," he said.

I didn't even nod.

He looked to his left, to the headstones, then back to me: "She's here. I remember. Can you show me?"

I pointed—to the far edge of the cemetery.

"That side. Over there," I said, using my left hand to give general direction. With my right hand, I toyed with the butt of the pistol in the windbreaker pocket.

"Take me there," he said.

Silently, I walked the few steps to Blithe Tanner's grave.

Rayner followed me and watched as I leaned to clear the headstone.

"Wiley Frost, you have to understand the power of Bobby Crawford and those other men. You have to understand what happened in the hotel room. You have to believe I stumbled from innocence to moral breakdown and have spent more than forty years trying not to think of it."

I stood and said nothing.

He continued: "Like many others, I found Bobby Crawford heroic, despite the worst of stories. I cared for Augusta Morefield and her family and spent long hours with them, praying for the dying mother and father and asking Heaven for answers, to tell me what would become of Augusta."

He turned and walked toward my car. I walked beside him, cautious and alert.

"After her parents died, I cared so much for Augusta I couldn't control feelings and actions and all my moments seemed filled with anxiety about her. Simply put, I wanted to be her husband. The more I dreamed, the more reason abandoned me. I even considered smothering my poor, sick wife, Jean Ann."

We stopped in front of my car. "What are you going to do?" I asked. "The newspaper wants a name."

"What do you want?" Phillip Rayner rubbed his hands together and looked up at the orange fringe setting into the treetops. On the river, a duck squawked and in the graveyard, a tiny field mouse skittered through high grass.

I wish I'd never answered the question.

"Your public confession," I said, sensing the words carried far less passion than the hell-bent obsession I'd felt for Phillip Rayner's ruination. Had the pallor of his face complemented my own weariness of ache and deception? What might be left for either of us if I forced him further?

He held up a hand, requesting silence. His eyes fixed on mine. "How could you force disaster upon me when you're suspect yourself?"

At that instant, I knew Rayner could end our conversation, go back to Ransom and have nothing more to do the next morning than deny my accusation to Grace Lynn Rose. He'd suddenly reminded me of my own vulnerability and the emptiness of vengeful thinking.

But he kept talking: "Wiley Frost, Augusta Morefield shocked me when she married Bobby Crawford. Such an unworthy partner! Had losing her parents obliterated her common sense?"

At that point, I wanted to interrupt, to tell him I'd felt the same. But Phillip Rayner didn't slow his words long enough for me to find an opening.

"I met Bobby when his train arrived the day of the parade. I planned to leave my wife and the church and devote myself completely to Augusta Morefield. With intellect and reason, I believed I could convince Bobby Crawford to find another woman. He cared for himself, not Augusta. I told myself if he rejected my argument, he'd probably take money. So when he stepped on the station platform, I asked to speak to him. He said for me to come to the hotel later."

He paused and took a deep breath. "After the parade, I got to the hotel as fast as I could. The desk clerk laughed and told me I'd find him in 310. When he opened the door, he wavered on his feet and I realized that until he achieved some sobriety, there'd be no point in making a proposal to him."

"But you didn't leave," I said, trying to get to Blithe Tanner, the heart of the matter.

"No," he said. "Bobby Crawford, his brother and the other man appeared friendly. But whiskey bottles sat on the table and not one of them seemed to be completely dressed. Champ Crawford had no shirt. Waverly Barnhill wore a towel around his middle and Bobby Crawford had on only undershorts."

"So you joined the party," I said.

Phillip Rayner blinked at my obvious skepticism. "I told Bobby Crawford I wanted to speak to him but would return later. Then as a cruel joke, they pulled me into the room, cursed me and took my clothes. I couldn't scream because Champ Crawford had jammed fingers halfway down my throat. When I tried to bite him, they laughed and joked among themselves about a gift for me. Of course, I didn't understand."

With the light nearly gone, Phillip Rayner pushed both hands in to his jacket pockets. By then, I'd forgotten the pistol, touched it and wished it in the glove compartment of my car.

For a moment, he stared at the blackening sky. I asked if he'd like to sit in my car or at least turn on the parking lights. He shook his head.

"These drunken, sweating, stinking men pushed me into another room. I saw the woman, bound, blindfolded, struggling, trying to free herself from the bed. Holding a broken bottle in my face, Bobby Crawford told me what I must do."

"So you did."

"I did."

"They forced you."

"Yes. Each time I tried to break away, they waved the bottle at me, then at the woman, laughed and forced us back together. They demanded cooperation, not resistance."

"You called her cherry lips. Do you expect me to believe you?"

"No," he said.

I paused, trying to gather myself, hoping Grace Lynn Rose hadn't camped on my doorstep and wondering why I'd made that mindless agreement. How could I judge Phillip Rayner and not myself?

We stood in the dark now. Rayner seemed a tall, lean, shadow in front of me and, to him, I must have resembled a dark, oversized watermelon, standing on end in a field.

"Bobby Crawford never allowed me to speak, to make my proposal. Augusta didn't know of my feelings or plans but she knew about Blithe Tanner when police came for Bobby Crawford after the girl died," he said. "Augusta told me she'd seen Bobby on the common the night after the parade. For the first few years of seclusion, that last sight of him occupied her mind. Then she retreated completely."

For a moment, neither of us spoke.

"You liked the young girl, didn't you?"

"Yes," he said. Then he fell silent.

In substance and implication, Phillip Rayner's remarks profoundly angered me. And in my heart, I felt a gathering of pain and rage which left me cold and shaking.

Bobby Crawford.

For so many years, how many prisoners had he held?

My mind jumped ahead, months and years, to examine life with a woman whose mind served a dead man. Would she ever call my name? Should I close her house, put her away and visit on weekends? Should I keep her with Esther Coleman, allowing her freedom of familiar surroundings?

Should I find a psychiatrist, hypnotist, root doctor?

And what of Phillip Rayner, now that he'd spilled his soul at Cobb's Graveyard? Grace Lynn Rose awaited, anxious if not feverish. Blithe Tanner lay in her grave, not fifteen feet away and I stood with a man who bore at least some responsibility for her death.

He stirred, taking his hands from jacket pockets and clasping them in front of him, twisting hand over hand, like someone frantic to be gone. I walked to the driver's side of my car, cracked the door and stood in the light. Phillip Rayner remained at the edge of a dim semicircle, his face only partially visible.

"You'll have your statement tomorrow," he said.

Even in my anger, somewhere inside me I wanted to tell him I'd send Grace Lynn Rose on a chase in another direction. But the words wouldn't come to my mouth.

Then Rayner looked straight into my eyes.

"Just like you, I played Bobby Crawford," he said, suddenly smiling. "For more than 40 years, the demon of my soul owned Augusta. It seemed no worse than taking Blithe Tanner."

His lips moved slightly but he offered nothing more and moved away from me, into the darkness—in the direction of his car. I took the pistol from my jacket and fired over his head until it emptied.

Chapter 27

By the end of my days, the shock of seeing Phillip Rayner's dripping, mud-caked Plymouth car dragged along Richmond Street may subside, but it won't ever go away. Certainly, I'll never forget feeling responsible for something terrible.

Sensations like that come rarely in a barber's chair. Mostly, you relax to the rhythm of scissors and comment only sparingly to the barber's chatter. But on the afternoon after meeting Phillip Rayner, I became suddenly paralyzed, unable to rise from the chair when Ollie Harris and two waiting customers rushed to the window of the Ransom Barber Shop, speculating loudly about what might have happened.

"Hit a ditch," somebody said.

"Did it rain last night?" another asked.

But old Ollie had it right: "Black, black mud," he said. "River bottom mud."

Terrified all would turn to look at me, I sat still in the chair. Surely, my face had turned pale and my eyes looked like dinner plates. I wished for a quick glance in a mirror, just to make sure my tongue had stayed in my mouth.

Ollie Harris moved back from the window and stepped behind me. He started again with scissors and comb.

"You letting your hair grow, Wiley? Not much on the top, of course, it's thick in the back."

"Busy," I said.

"Nature's flattop," Ollie said, chuckling.

He continued snipping, used clippers to clean up the back of my neck, then set upon me again with the scissors.

"How's Mrs. Crawford?"

"Well," I said, hoping he'd change the subject to something like crops or weather or maybe businesses closing on Richmond Street because of new malls.

"I understand you're taking care of her now." he said, pumping up the chair a time or two.

"Yes," I said.

"Fine woman," Ollie said. "I cut her father's hair, even at the house, after he got sick. Why's she stayed by herself all this time?"

"I don't know," I said.

"She crazy?"

"I don't know."

Ollie paused like he might be thinking of another question. I squirmed in the chair and crossed my legs.

"When you going to tell Miss Grace Lynn Rose the name of the other man with Bobby Crawford at the old hotel?" He dabbed at the back of my neck with a towel and continued snipping.

"You finished yet?" I asked, trying hard to show as much impatience as possible.

"No," Ollie Harris said. "You got a nest of wild hairs on the back here, Wiley. You know you want to be beautiful for Mrs. Crawford."

I ignored the remark.

By then, Taylor Bledsoe, the men's clothier, had come from his store next door and announced Phillip Rayner had died in the water in the old blue Plymouth. Ollie continued to work on me, Taylor Bledsoe left and the two men waiting put their heads together and started whispering, glancing at me as they talked.

Ollie and I didn't talk much for the next few minutes. The conversation of the two men seated by the front window seemed to grow into a quiet argument. One flattened out his hand and angled it downward to emphasize an idea that the car raced straight down the steep river bank and into the water. The other fellow did much the same thing but he flipped his hand, showing the palm, indicating he thought the car had turned over in its decent.

To me, it didn't make much difference. Phillip Rayner had taken his life and I'd been the cause. How much disaster can one man cause? Even with study I couldn't find an answer.

Suddenly I felt confined in Ollie Harris' barber chair. My mind raced with visions of Rayner, hands on the wheel, pulling on the lights, finding a clear path in the trees, hurtling himself over small brush and stumps into the water. What had he thought when the water covered his face?

For a second, I trembled. Ollie Harris put a hand on my shoulder, then started dabbing shaving cream around my ears. He slapped his razor on the leather strap attached to the barber chair. Faces of Blithe Tanner and Augusta Crawford paraded through my consciousness. Had justice prevailed? My justice? Aubrey's? the Almighty's?

For a prolonged instant, I felt I'd lose control, leap from the chair and bolt out the door, screaming like a madman. But my senses returned about the time Ollie Harris started on me with his straight razor.

"You know, Wiley. It's a shame a man like Phillip Rayner died like that. He should have been stretched out in his bed at home and breathed his last among family and good friends."

"Yes," I said, but didn't expand my agreement.

"To drown in that river...I just don't know."

Ollie paused, then continued scraping around my ears and down my neck. "I remember a young boy drowned in the river in 1947. When they pulled him out, he had mud in his mouth, all down his throat."

I remembered the incident but said nothing.

Ollie Harris started on the other ear. "Didn't Phillip Rayner take care of Augusta Crawford?"

"Yes," I said.

"Well, you won't have to worry about him anymore," he said in a lifeless, near-whisper.

I didn't respond, fearing the next swipe of his razor might cost me my head.

About the time I stepped onto the sidewalk, a dingy, white City Cab stopped at the curb. The large man who edged out the back door, rear first, reached across the seat and handed the driver folding money.

"Thanks, Alvin," the man said. "I'll call you." The cabby waved but didn't speak. The car roared off in a cloud of blue smoke, leaving the figure before me coughing and wiping at his eyes with a handkerchief.

Then Aubrey saw me. He smiled and laughed lightly. "Wiley," I've got some great news. Let's go talk."

Wary about being seen with Aubrey, I turned and walked toward my car around the corner. "Tired of talking, Aubrey. I want to get down to living in peace. I don't need any more excitement."

He followed.

"But this is news we both been waiting for. I don't know anybody else I can tell but you. Slow down. Come on to the Dixie Grill for pie and coffee. I'll pay. That's a good invitation, Wiley."

Somehow, I didn't agree.

"Toby Pugh goes in there," I said. "And I don't want coffee and pie."

Aubrey pulled up beside me and walked along, dusty, old wing-tip shoes slapping on the sidewalk. "I just don't understand you, Wiley. You wanted to get something back on Phillip Rayner just as bad as I did. Now you act like you're the King of Russia and don't know me."

Right. Anxious to sight the car, I kept my eyes focused ahead, not even looking at Aubrey, not acting in the slightest like I knew him. Like ignoring a fat wooly worm.

That, however, didn't dissuade Aubrey.

"Wiley, I'm sick of this. I've got something to tell you and you need to listen. You can't answer no questions from nobody, especially a policeman, unless you know everything. For sure, you don't know what I've got to tell you."

We reached my car and I walked around to the driver's side, key poised to unlock the door.

Aubrey paused on the other side. His face became downright grim. "Aubrey, if you don't listen to me, I'm going to fall down right here, have a pure fit and attract the whole town. People going to ask you why you'd leave a poor man to shake and tremble and slobber on the sidewalk? How come you couldn't be good enough to put a stick in his mouth?"

Then he smiled.

I pushed the key into the lock. "Get in," I said.

Don't even start the car, I told myself. Sit quietly and listen. Hustle Aubrey away quickly. Get to Augusta's.

"How do you want me to start?" he asked.

At that, I sighed, loudly and long. "Aubrey, this isn't my tale. I don't know where it starts, what's in the middle, what's at the end. How should I know what you're going to say? Get it said."

I felt my temper beginning to boil and heard my voice rise and fall in a mixture of sarcasm and restrained anger. Could anybody see us?

Aubrey thought for a minute and decided: "I'm going to start at the beginning, Wiley, at the part where I followed you out to Cobb's Graveyard."

I couldn't believe it.

Aubrey settled in the seat and lit a cigarette. He rolled down the passenger window to let out the smoke. Of course that made me realize I had no options: If Aubrey didn't talk me to death, he'd smoke me to death or have a public fit.

"Alvin Hooper took me in his taxi. Followed about a

quarter mile behind you all the way. Suspicions, Wiley. I had
suspicions you might be going off to kill Phillip Rayner by yourself
and rob me of another pleasure."

He smiled at that.

I didn't.

"After you turned up old Charley Cobb's lane, I got Alvin
to let me off there and paid him to come back in two hours. Then
I walked through the field, jumped ditches, tore my pants, got my
shoes wet and cockleburrs up my pants legs. I walked around behind
the graveyard, into the pines on the river and sat down on a stump."

He shifted the cigarette to his left hand and draped his right
arm over the window frame. That meant a slight outside breeze blew
a steady stream of smoke right into my nose. "Out the window,
Aubrey. You're going to suffocate me."

Aubrey grunted, put the cigarette in his right hand and held
it outside the car.

But I could still smell it.

Finally, he took a puff and flipped the butt away.

"I saw you but you didn't see me. You had the lights on in
your car and I saw you sitting, looking around, like you expected to
spend your last moments with some swamp creature dragging you
across the tombstones to the river."

Aubrey paused and looked over at me. "You had fear on
your face, Wiley."

"Apprehension," I countered. "I had no business out there
in the dark. Should have been playing Canasta with Augusta."

"Then I saw Rayner's old blue car. He parked right near the
pine woods where I sat. He got out and walked over to you and I just
stayed on my stump. Seemed like a good seat for some action."

I kept my eyes down, fingering the horn ring.

"When you and Mr. Rayner started walking toward the
cemetery, I stood up to watch, just in case you decided to crack his
head with a broken stone. But from what I could see in the dim light,
you didn't get too close to him, Wiley. Afraid of what you'd do,
Wiley? Tell me. Did you show him little Blithe Tanner's grave?"

"I showed him the grave," I mumbled, preferring to leave his first question unanswered.

"Then you walked back to your car and stood there, talking," Aubrey continued. "What did he say to get you so mad? When you pulled your pistol, I got up on my stump, trying to see every detail of you putting a bullet through him. But you missed him, Wiley. You shot all around his head and didn't hit him a single time."

He laughed. "Christ, Wiley, I had shot and leaves and little limbs falling all over me."

"You think I wanted to kill him?"

"Of course, you did, Wiley. Why'd you take a gun with you if you didn't plan on killing him?"

I rested my head on the seatback, feeling the breath slowly slip from me and return, thank God, in even pants, not frantic gulps.

For a few moments, we didn't speak. Then Aubrey crossed his arms. "I want you to know I'm responsible for this—for Phillip Rayner's being dead," he said.

"I don't care, Aubrey."

He ignored me.

"I pushed his car," he said, batting his eyes on and off the ceiling, like a movie star trying to be cool.

I sat up, turned and faced him. "Tell me," I said.

Aubrey squirmed around in the seat and pulled at his open shirt collar, like he imagined a too-tight tie pressuring his throat.

"After you quit shooting and left, Rayner got to his car, opened the door, sat down and closed the door. Get closer, I said to myself.   So like an old Indian scout, I moved from tree to tree, pausing in shadows. Didn't stumble even once."

I glanced out the window and saw Curtis Mayo, the meter-reader coming down the sidewalk. Trying to hide myself a little, I slipped down in the seat, thinking the steering wheel might block his view.

"Hello, Wiley," he said, passing and not even looking my way.

I didn't answer. Then Aubrey started up again: "Phillip Rayner sat there in the dark for ten minutes maybe, then he started his engine and turned on the lights. For a few seconds, I thought it might be a good time to pull him out of the car and choke him."

"So what happened?" I asked, growing impatient.

"Big surprise, Wiley. Big. He just aimed that car between some trees and it took me a second to realize he planned to run in the river. I jumped up and about the time I got to where I could see, he drove over the edge of the bluff and just stopped, taillights up in the air and red just glowing on trees. I even glanced at my hands and they had a red glow. I swear they did."

"How long's this going to take, Aubrey?"

He ignored me.

"Poor fellow just hanging there. Couldn't even kill himself for having hung the car on a stump. I gave him a push," Aubrey said, looking at me and smiling.

He paused, took a cigarette from his shirt pocket and tapped the end on his old Zippo lighter. "You know, Wiley, he saw me. Rolled down his window and waved me on to give him a push, just like I'd stopped to give him a hand on a city street."

He pointed at me with the unlit cigarette.

"River swallowed that whole car," he said. "Just sucked it right up."

Chapter 28

It seemed more like a farewell for some brave, Teutonic prince than for a suicidal old preacher in a little town like Ransom, North Carolina.

Black streamers stretched from balcony railings to either side of the polished mahogany pulpit. Large floor floodlights illuminated the open coffin. Even with that, from the back of the church, I could only see the still, pale nose of Phillip I. Rayner.

Cynthia Allred, the organist, swayed side to side, forward and backward as she played a slow, mournful version of "Rock of Ages." Almost in step with the music, stone-faced men, women and children shuffled down aisles and took seats, whispering apologies to those who rose to let them pass into pews.

"No." The very audible sob came from Winnie Mountcastle, the elementary school principal's wife. That set others—men, women and children—to sniffling.

More than anything else, curiosity propelled me into Pettigrew Memorial four days after Phillip Rayner's car had been taken from the river. And the mere thought of facing so many suspicious people prompted me to prepare for the event. So, early that morning, expecting the worst, I spent an hour before the bathroom mirror, practicing stiffening my jaws with resolution and fearlessness.

Would I be blamed for this death?

The question produced no answers until I began searching for a seat. Quick glances for a vacant spot showed me a throng of eyes, collectively examining each of my movements. People filled empty pews that could have accommodated me. But when I approached, bodies spread, denying me space. That pushed panic and pain into my throat and heart, quickly dissolving any resolution or fearlessness my brain might have generated.

So, I chose exile: An empty pew in the bad light of a back corner.

Arranging myself, funeral program in hand, legs crossed, I saw the children about me slip closer to their mothers, no doubt frightened by the sight of a man pursued by rumors of murder. I heard low tones and the occasional mention of my name or Augusta's. A man's voice complained that my presence insulted the dead.

Be calm, I told myself.

Nobody, except for Aubrey, knew I'd been at the river with Phillip Rayner.

Nobody knew how Bobby Crawford died.

Only Aubrey knew how Champ Crawford died.

But many of those in Pettigrew Church that day took for granted my role in all those events. Regrettably, if I ever engaged in honest argument, I could not deny the validity of their positions.

I sat still against the hard seatback but my mind drifting into the quiet consideration of people who celebrated life and death of a man they only thought they knew. Who would have guessed Phillip Rayner joined Bobby Crawford and the others in the crime against Blithe Tanner? Did anyone care that he'd used sad, confused Augusta as his mistress for over 40 years?

Should I stand in my place and speak in judgement of Phillip Rayner's life? Should I loudly define his moral deceptiveness?

No, I thought. Listen to the music.

Smile.

If you can.

But self-lecture didn't help. Suddenly the church had filled but I still sat alone at the end of a thirty-foot wooden pew. Glancing front and back, I caught no one's eye and certainly received not even a nod of a head.

But just as the music stopped and Deacon Albion Whitehurst stepped to the pulpit, a woman pushed past my knees and eased into the seat beside me.

The Devil had me again.

After Grace Lynn Rose sat down next to me, I spent the next few minutes silently asking the Almighty why he'd made her my seatmate. I recall closing my eyes, bowing my head and silently praying she'd disappear.

But when I opened my eyes, the relentless reporter, pad and pen in hand, had moved closer to me. "Wiley Frost?" Grace Lynn Rose whispered. People who recognized her squirmed and talked softly. I looked down, trying to focus on the laces of my shoes. Grace Lynn Rose patted my arm, as if in pity.

"This is a day of sadness." The Deacon's voice, strong and deep, rose over heads and descended like a spreading octopus, tentacles slithering to every corner of the church, capturing ears, sympathetically caressing brows and cheeks, gathering minds.

"Let us praise Brother Rayner," boomed Albion Whitehurst.

All heads bowed. I looked to the ceiling. While the Deacon prayed, my eyes followed the course of cross-beams and the intricate networks of stained-glass windows. I could only think of Augusta opening her door to Phillip Rayner. That led me to wonder if this fastidious, departed brother could survive eternity with leaf fragments in his hair or river grass up his nose.

I laughed, disguising a snicker as a cough.

But just as the choir started singing, I received another jolt when the considerable bulk of Aubrey Winslow shoved and fretted into the pew. "Move over," he said to Grace Lynn Rose. "I got to sit by Wiley."

The intrusion must have surprised the reporter so much that she quickly moved away from me to allow Aubrey room. And for the next few moments, the three of us must have seemed a true curiosity. Grace Lynn Rose whispered questions to me and tried to lean around Aubrey to hear my answers, should I speak. Finally, she and Aubrey jostled, grunted and pushed until she relented and sat still.

"See Wiley? I'm your interference," Aubrey whispered. I never looked at him, keeping my reply to a silent stare at the Deacon and his white-robed band of singers.

What happened next will always be locked into my memory. Now, recalling the incident, my poor sense of humor takes control, returns me to that day in Pettigrew Church and forces a smile.

I was trying to concentrate on the music, so I didn't see Augusta until she'd fluttered down the far aisle and danced in front of Phillip Rayner's coffin. The shocked deacon and choir watched each pause and toe-point while the words and rhythm of the old hymn twittered into silence.

Aubrey Winslow gave me a quick, hard punch with an elbow, shook his head and whispered. "Look." He said, his voice a low mutter. He nervously fumbled in his coat pockets liked he needed a cigarette.

"What you going to do?" Aubrey asked me. He'd found a cigarette and held it closely in his hand, sitting there, like me, watching a sixty-one-year-old woman ballet dance in a funeral.

"Nothing," I said.

"You got to go get her, take her home."

I kept my eyes on Augusta. "She's wearing the green ballet costume from her dance recital. She wore it the last two days before her high school graduation," I said, my voice subdued, nostalgic, like telling a story.

"For God's sake Wiley, you're as crazy as she is," Aubrey said, puffing like his nerves had overtaken his brain.

Grace Lynn Rose reached around Aubrey and tapped my leg. "What's she doing?" she asked, curling her lips back like she'd just walked past a smelly dumpster.

"Dancing," I said. "She's dancing."

"I got to find a photographer," she said, trying to stand. Aubrey Winslow gently pulled at her arm. She sat down again, abruptly. "Watch now, Miss," he said. "You're seeing some real dancing." He looked at me, eyes wide, jaw wobbly, signaling me with a nudge that I should do something to bring Augusta under control.

And I might have done that had Augusta not taken the next few steps. She centered herself before Phillip Rayner's coffin and bowed deeply and remained in the position for seconds that seemed forever.

Paying tribute, I thought.

Accepting accolades, I thought.

For a moment, I listened to the silence in the church and watched the unbelieving expressions of people around me.

Nothing here, I decided.

So I rose, stepped quietly up the aisle, pushed past the ushers and through the front doors. Outside, on the concrete walk, I stopped in the early afternoon sun to wait for Augusta.

PART V

Chapter 29

By the time Augusta got into the car, I'd blamed television for her performance. Not only that, I silently cursed Esther Coleman for allowing Augusta to see news about Phillip Rayner. Remembering her dance, the wobbling of old legs and flashing of vacant eyes, made me regret I'd ever bought Augusta a TV set.

People will always be amused at recollections of Augusta Morefield Crawford as the faded, stiff old ballerina who thumped, bumped and smiled down the aisle at Phillip Rayner's farewell. I, however, had acquired feelings: Her final bow before the coffin had turned my heart stone cold and scattered my brain into pitiful fragments of memory and anger.

Augusta, however, giggled and tittered about dancing her last recital. I returned silence, suddenly unable to feel love that had consumed nearly all my life. Everyone in Ransom knew about Augusta and me. How could I live with new humiliation?

"Goodbye, goodbye," she called as we passed the church, heading toward Pickett Street. People who followed her from the church had gathered at the curb, some stern, red-faced and angry.

Grace Lynn Rose stood in the street, writing in her notebook. Aubrey Winslow and a few old women, all pressed in the crowd, waved.

"I've never danced so well. Don't you think, Father?"

Instead of answering, I threw a quick glance at the woman beside me, at the ancient ballet dress, the securely-laced, worn-out toe shoes and bare, thin white legs. Air from the open, passenger side window sent the smell of mothballs to my nose.

"Father, am I flushed? Tell me quickly. Are my cheeks fire red?"

"Only a little red," I said, playing one more role. "Just pink."

"You will tell mother how I danced, won't you?"

"Yes," I answered, truly wishing Mrs. Morefield would step from the mists and take her daughter off my hands.

We intersected Pickett Street at Rivenbark and all the way to Augusta's house, my mind churned with thoughts I never beleived would pass through my head.

Yes, I'd go to the bank and arrange a trustee for Augusta. Then I'd take a tour, to the British Isles, Istanbul, Tel Aviv and Bombay. I'd cruise through the Strait of Malacca, stroll Tokyo's Ginza and Hawaii's beaches. Finally, I'd rent a car in San Francisco and drive back to Ransom.

By the time I returned, all would be different. Augusta would be able to speak and act with good sense and we could be friends again, free to walk by the river, to browse the library, to shop for food, all without the stares and whispers of Ransom people. That, at least, is what I told myself.

All the way to the curb in front of her house, Augusta chattered on about her dancing. "The little children had their eyes on me," she said, a laugh in her voice. "They followed my every step. I do wish we had a school in Ransom strictly for ballet dancing."

Then her voice dropped away to a whisper. After I stopped the car, she sat for some minutes, speaking quietly to the reflection of her face in the car window. "You're a fine dancer," she told the face in the window. "Did you see how quietly the audience watched? No talking at all."

For a few more moments, we sat in the car. Augusta spoke to the window as I gripped the wheel like a man trying to squeeze the life out of a garden snake.

Run. My mind kept repeating the word. The rhythm of repetition hammered together the small plan of action I'd considered during the drive to Augusta's house. So it would be: A day to get the trustee, another to pack and fly away.

But then, Augusta sat upright in her seat and spoke, her voice excited. "Oh, father, I must go inside to change," she said, her hands pulling at the door handle. "A young man is coming."

"Who?" I asked, always wondering, always hopeful.

She paused and looked around the car. "I don't know," she said.

About midnight that night, everything changed.

My old Samsonite bag lay half-packed on my bed when I took Esther Coleman's phone call. Only then did I understand a geographical cure would change nothing. And later, in the cold, early morning darkness, walking toward the War Memorial Fountain with Police Chief Toby Pugh, I begged the Almighty for honest strength and peace.

"This is how we found her," said Toby Pugh, swinging his flashlight to the left, catching Augusta's face under the sheet of clear plastic.

"That is Mrs. Crawford, isn't it?"

"Yes," I said.

"Now look over here, Mr. Frost."

I followed Chief Pugh's flashlight beam. When the light struck his face, Crazy Wallis Pender snorted, coughed and rolled over on his left side. Seconds later, his deep, disturbing snore rattled in the night, putting to shame any noisy bird or animal.

"Is this the fine Augusta Morefield?" asked Chief Pugh, pulling up the collar of his windbreaker against the chill.

"No attraction here," I said, my voice emotionless, my feelings blank. "He's as insane as she is. That makes him good company."

Toby Pugh didn't answer. He stepped over to Augusta and touched her shoulder. She opened her eyes. "What's wrong, Father? My husband and I are sleeping under the stars, by the wild Atlantic Ocean. Smell the air, Father. Can you smell the salt? Can you taste it?"

I could smell the paper plant upriver and taste my frozen spaghetti dinner.

"Come on, Augusta," I said, trying the gentle tone I remembered Mr. Morefield often used with her. She sat up, rubbed her face with both hands and tried to smooth her hair. She still wore the green ballet dress and toe shoes.

She leaned over Wallis Pender, pulled back the plastic sheeting and kissed his cheek. "We can go home now," she said, tugging easily at his shirt.

I took two steps forward and with knees snapping and popping, knelt just beside her. "He'll stay here, Augusta. He must be in his office by eight," I said, knowing that when light came, Wallis Pender would be up, pushing his rusty grocery cart all over Ransom, rummaging through garbage cans for scraps and discarded wine bottles that held one last swallow.

"Up here, Miss Augusta," Toby Pugh said. He firmly clutched one arm and helped to her feet. "I'll take you home." Wallis Pender farted and turned onto his stomach.

Frankly, I didn't pay much attention. If Chief Pugh got her home and safely in the care of Esther Coleman, fine. If he didn't, I'd be gone tomorrow. Anyone I could find to be legally responsible would have the worry.

I just didn't care anymore.

"Mr. Frost?"

The voice startled me into a fit of shivers that seemed more cold than fear. For a few seconds, I didn't look behind me, wondering if dear Mrs. Morefield had granted my wish and come for Augusta.

"I saw the police cars, Mr. Frost. What happened here

tonight?"

I turned to find Grace Lynn Rose.

"Nothing," I said, calming myself with quick mental recitations of bank account numbers and naming the seven wonders of the world.

Dressed in sweatpants, sneakers and hooded shirt, she seemed a bit more human than the critical, sharp-tongued reporter I'd encountered so many times. We stood staring, each trying to read the other's faces in scant light from a flickering street lamp. The wind from across the river picked up, intensifying the cold. I rubbed my hands together, clapped several times and stamped my feet.

"Come home with me, Mr. Frost," said Grace Lynn Rose.

I said nothing. But when she turned and walked off across the common toward Northwoods Apartments, I walked to the street, locked my car and headed in the direction she'd taken.

Chapter 30

With each step toward the small mountain of concrete and light where Grace Lynn Rose lived, I felt disaster striding with me. But when a man needs peace, he's likely to go anywhere, even to an enemy.

"Here, Mr. Frost." Lights glowed on every apartment door, illuminated concrete walks and even encircled the swimming pool, unused now and covered by canvas. "Second floor, Mr. Frost." I looked up and found her just above me, leaning over a steel railing, looking down, smiling like she'd captured a prize pig.

She checked her watch. "One twenty-five," she said, turning toward the closed door behind her and motioning to me at the same time. "Stairs are just ahead of you. We'll have to be quiet, you know."

For a moment, I felt like a surprised schoolboy, unexpectedly invited to the home of a disreputable woman. "What do you want?" I called, a tremble in my voice. How ridiculous did I sound?

"Come up here, Mr. Frost," she called, her voice light and easy.

I didn't answer right away, pretending I had no interest in finding the stairs or her. The cold pushed through my jacket, grabbed at my skin and made me wish for warmth and a kind voice.

"I'm looking for the stairs," I said, speaking up to the shadow form fiddling with keys at the door. How could it hurt to talk to her?

"Two steps forward, three steps to the right," she said.

Curiosity pushed me to the bottom of a short, turning flight of stairs. I took each step carefully, watching closely where each foot landed. Certainly, I didn't need to be dead of a broken neck at the foot of stairs leading to Grace Lynn Rose's apartment.

At the top, I stood for a second, looking over the broad courtyard, marveling at children's slides, monkey bars and see-saws. The instant brought memories of childhood: zipping down an otter slide into the river, climbing tall trees and hanging upside down on limbs until my mother screamed so loudly I had to come down.

The wind whipped at my face and I bowed my head against it. "Where are you?" I called down a long concrete walkway with a multitude of doors.

"Here." A few feet away, Grace Lynn Rose stepped out of a lighted, open doorway and waved me ahead with one hand. She still smiled and I saw nothing evil or conniving in her eyes. So I walked on, ever wary, decidedly careful.

If I'd been told beforehand an aggressive female reporter could behave like a gracious hostess, reaction from me would have amounted to either laughter or hoots of disagreement. The surprise of how kindly she took my hand and led me into her small apartment swept over me, soothing a rumbling stomach and even easing the chill in my bones.

"Oh," I said, scanning the walls which held pictures of wild geese flying in V-formation, John Lennon, and Jerry Falwell shouting to a spellbound congregation.

Still dressed in sweat clothes, Grace Lynn Rose edged me along toward a steady-burning gas fireplace. "Sit here," she said, motioning to the thick, upholstered armchair by the fire.

For a second, I resisted. "Why did you ask me here?"

She laughed lightly—a true giggle, I suppose. "Why did you come here, Mr. Frost?"

"Cold," I said.

"Oh," she said. "Then let's get you warm." She ran one arm around my back and touched an elbow with the other, again guiding me toward the chair.

"No," I mumbled, purposely avoiding her touch. I walked to the chair without her support, sat and leaned over, trying to get my frozen hands close to the flames. I didn't even look back to see what Grace Lynn Rose might be doing.

Then I heard a thump.

At the sound, I looked to my right. The woman had dropped to her knees beside the chair. Her face, pleasantly expressive, loomed at me and she seemed to be squirming closer on her knees. I could neither imagine what her thinking might be nor understand her closeness. In fact, in all our other conversations, we sat apart, reacting to each other like veteran sparring partners who keep distances, look for openings, and try to avoid smashes to the jaw.

She'd pulled back the sweatshirt hood. Electricity from the cloth had made the end of her ponytail look like the back of an aroused porcupine. Her hair, usually bushy and neat beyond the rubber band, had dispersed in all directions, leaving wild strands to hang in limp, fuzzy confusion.

"Are you warm enough?" she asked, patting my arm. "Let me help you with your coat. This fireplace warms in a hurry."

I unzipped my jacket. "I'll get it," I said, pulling and twisting and tugging until I finally got it off.

"I'll get a hanger," she said, rising to her feet.

"No, no," I protested. "I'll just put it here on the chair arm."

"Oh," she said.

Silence.

She looked at me and I looked at her.

"Coffee, Mr. Frost?" she asked, suddenly standing and moving off to the kitchen adjoining the living room. I glanced to my left and saw a bedroom: Deep red carpet, navy bedspread, navy curtains, a poster from a Grateful Dead Concert and a large, framed photograph of George Jones performing onstage.

"Yes," I said. Keeping my eyes on the yellow-blue flames, wondering if it wouldn't make real sense to get up, put on my jacket and leave. But the girl had become almost likeable. In the warmth and quiet, I thought of attentive fathers and daughters.

From my seat, I caught the scent of fresh ground coffee and could hear the scoop gently swishing as she filled the coffee maker basket. I even heard Grace Lynn Rose humming but the tune didn't register with me.

"That was Augusta Crawford out there on the Common tonight. Right, Mr. Frost?"

For a moment, I didn't answer, irritated that she'd broken the peace and retreated to her customary abrasiveness. "Let's try another subject," I said, my voice rough, almost a growl.

"If it wasn't Augusta Crawford, what brought you to the Common, Mr. Frost? Surely you didn't come to watch Crazy Wallis Pender sleep."

I stood, picked up my jacket and rammed one arm into a sleeve. She dropped a spoon and almost dashed around the end of the kitchen counter. She waved both hands, much like a traffic policeman trying to stop an antsy line of drivers.

"I'm sorry," she said, appearing close to tears. "It's my compulsion to ask questions. And sometimes I make ridiculous comments."

I fumbled for the other sleeve.

"Don't go," she said. "I've just started the coffee. You can stay for the coffee, can't you?"

Thinking of the cold, the fire, my present distance from Augusta and the coffee made me change my mind. But I said nothing, just pulled off the jacket, held it in my arms and rearranged myself back in the chair.

For maybe five minutes, I sat like that, leaning forward, watching the flames, rubbing my hands, enjoying warmth on my face. Suddenly, hearing no sound except the gurgling of the coffee maker, I became curious about her. Had I spoken harshly enough to make her cry? Had she hidden herself to shed private tears?

I didn't know. But a second later, when I glanced left, my eyes stopped at the doorway to the bedroom. Grace Lynn Rose stood at the foot of her bed, naked in a pile of sweat clothes. "Beautiful," I mumbled to myself.

Chapter 31

At the time, I considered it a mistake. Perhaps she'd forgotten to close the door or decided nothing could distract me from the chair and fire. But she continued to stand there, staring straight at me. I stared back, trying to concentrate on her eyes.

We might have remained like that for hours had I not coughed, breaking the strange spell that had suddenly mesmerized me, an old man with a weak heart. With the sound of my rasping, Grace Lynn Rose smiled, took one step forward and closed the door.

I turned back to the fire.

A few seconds later, the bedroom door opened. "Mr. Frost, coffee's done. Black? Cream? Sugar?"

"Black," I said, not daring to turn toward the kitchen. "Maybe one teaspoon of sugar." Sweat had dampened my forehead so I pushed the big chair back a few inches from the fireplace.

"Whisky, Mr. Frost? It'll go well with coffee."

"No," I said, wondering what Aubrey would do in a situation like this. Could a little whisky hurt? Who cared?

"Well, why not," I said.

Suddenly Grace Lynn Rose, wearing socks and a thick green robe zippered to the neck, stood beside me. I looked up at yet another smile and took the steaming mug she held out to me. I sipped and watched her as she stepped back to the kitchen counter and got her own cup and a half-glass of whisky.

She looked at me and laughed as she moved to the small, brown vinyl couch across the room. "I don't know what you must be thinking of me now, Mr. Frost. Here I am a single woman, having coffee and whisky in the early morning hours with a gentleman caller."

Nonsense, I thought. Small talk, I decided.

She put her coffee cup on the table in front of her and picked up the glass of whisky. "Cheers, Mr. Frost. To better days for you," she said, seriousness in her expression.

Without reply, I watched her drink the whisky.

Grace Lynn Rose put the empty glass on a table in front of her and propped both legs, crossed at the ankles, beside it. "My father taught me how to drink like this, Mr. Frost. He didn't like watered whisky. He said I should drink like a man."

She smiled. I managed a half laugh.

"I'm warm now," she said, pointing first to the fire and then to the whisky glass. Then she unzipped her robe about six inches. "Let me get you another whisky."

"My God," I muttered.

"No more? Okay. You've been on the Common at night, haven't you, Mr. Frost?" She tilted her head slightly, trying to behave like a curious, cute puppy, I suppose. "People say Bobby Crawford's spirit walks the common, looking for vengeance."

"Bobby Crawford never had sense enough to be a spirit," I said.

She smiled and pulled the zipper down about six more inches, drew her feet back from the table and suddenly sat primly, bare skin showing at her chest. "I want to know what you know."

"Nobody's business," I said, beginning to sweat.

"Whole town's been in an uproar for months now, Mr. Frost. It's everybody's business. Do you think Augusta Crawford cares? She's spent forty years mourning Bobby Crawford, Mr. Frost. Now she's sleeping in the dirt with Crazy Wallis Pender."

Anger, sadness, regret, guilt. I wanted to wipe it all clean. I didn't want to think anymore. Not anymore.

Grace Lynn Rose leaned forward. Breasts tumbled around under the robe. "Tell me about that night in 1951," she said. "Augusta Crawford's free of it. Now free yourself."

I understood what she meant.

"I've got no honor, Mr. Frost."

I understood that, too.

"Whisky," I said.

After two drinks, my tongue engaged and wouldn't stop. Even watching Grace Lynn Rose, her robe nearly open, taking notes on a yellow pad, didn't slow my words. I wanted to be done with it. Forever.

So I began: "You've never seen such a rain," I said. "Thunder and lightning started about eight o'clock. Windows rattled in the funeral home office and my desk lamp went on and off a half-dozen times. With four dead bodies in the next room, all that flash and noise might have frightened anybody else. I remember being annoyed because I couldn't finish bookwork in the dark and wondered if Augusta had gotten home before the storm."

Right then, I drank a little more whisky from the Barney Rubble glass Grace Lynn Rose had given me. The whisky burned down my throat and into my stomach. More words tumbled from my mouth.

"Of course, I didn't care a thing about Bobby Crawford. He could have been seared to death by lightning in my parking lot and liability would have been my only concern."

I paused and pointed a finger at the reporter.

"I want you to understand Bobby stood much taller than me and had a terrible mean streak, especially when he'd had a drink. But fear didn't play a part in my decision to lock up and go look for Augusta. It didn't matter to me that he might be waiting in the parking lot with a baseball bat. Finding Augusta seemed urgent. Besides, fear would have left me the second I took a pistol from my desk and put it in my pants pocket."

She looked up from her pad and nodded, like she agreed.

"So I turned off the lights and cracked open the back door. The wind blew like a hurricane, rain swept in through the door and quickly formed a small puddle in a low place on the concrete floor. I felt for the pistol, stepped outside, kept my eyes half-shut to keep the rain out, and locked the door. When I turned around, I glanced from side to side, checking for Bobby Crawford. Frankly, if he'd been in the parking lot, I doubt I'd have seen him because of the increasing darkness and the strength of the rain and wind."

"Could you have shot him?"

"Yes," I said.

She put down her pad, stood up, walked to the kitchen and returned with the whisky bottle. She came to me first, leaned over and poured my glass about three-quarters full. I kept my eyes on the glass as she poured.

"Had Bobby Crawford left?" Grace Lynn Rose shuffled back to the couch, sat down and gave herself a half-glass. She put the bottle down on top of some magazines, picked up her pad and pen and looked at me.

"Well, I didn't see him. He might have been under the ambulance. All I had on my mind was getting to my car and on the road to Augusta's house. Dangerous night. Trees swayed. Limbs broke off and fell. Some power lines down. Water flowed in torrents down street gutters. Traffic lights out. Nobody on the sidewalks. Remember all that. Bad enough to be driving in that mess. Suppose you had to look for somebody?"

"Did you find her right away?"

"No," I said. "Drove all the way to her house, got no answer at the door and headed back downtown again. Didn't see her until I got on Ricochet Road, a spur off Pickett, maybe six or eight blocks from the Common. Walking in the rain, all by herself. Clothes wet and sticking to her. Hair drenched, water pouring off her face. I slowed, tapped my horn and motioned for her to get in the car. She kept walking, mouth tight, arms swinging, unseeing, unhearing."

I blew the horn again, got no response so I pulled over to the curb and got out. Had to run to catch her. 'Augusta,' I asked, 'have you been home?' She kept walking but glanced at me and nodded. 'Why didn't you stay there?'"

The reporter stopped note-taking long enough to sip whisky and coffee. "Hard-headed soul," she mumbled.

I looked at her but didn't comment.

"Finally, I grabbed Augusta's arm and pulled her to a stop. The rain and blowing made it hard to speak and to hear but I told her we had to get out of the rain. We could get sick and die. No time for walking in weather like this. I promised her tomorrow would be dry and she could walk tomorrow—downtown, anywhere she wanted to go."

"What did she say?"

"Nothing very nice," I continued. "She told me to get out of her way. She wanted to find her husband and kill him."

Chapter 32

Kill him.

The reporter squirmed like she wanted to leap from the couch, crash through the closed apartment door, and sprint to *The Telegraph* office.

"Augusta Crawford said that?"

"Yes," I said, amused but not surprised that she interrupted her scribbling to take whisky. "It pleased me. If ever a woman had reason to kill her husband, Augusta did. Finally, she'd awakened to find Bobby Crawford more cruel predator than hero. It made me want to help her. After all, I had a pistol. She didn't even have an umbrella."

Grace Lynn Rose's eyes grew wide. She stopped writing, scratched at her right cheek and looked at me, straight and hard. "You confessing now?"

I ignored her. "Right away, I realized good sense had no place in Augusta's thoughts or intentions. She pulled away from me and I let her go. Before she'd taken too many steps, she became a blur in the rain and wind."

"Then you helped her kill him."

"Be quiet and listen," I said, my voice testy, nearly un-bridled, certainly unkind. "In this situation, killing or dying didn't amount to a major consideration. Good souls, Augusta and Blithe Tanner bore pain and scars from Bobby Crawford. So if you write a story about this, don't concentrate on revenge. Give value to justice, consider human condition and survival instincts."

"Lecturing, Mr. Frost. Continue."

Arrogance. I didn't like it but didn't comment.

"Obviously, Augusta didn't have a chance of killing Bobby Crawford by herself. I truly believed I could help her—just like taking her arm to cross a street or picking up dry cleaning or finding flowers she liked. To me, killing him meant no more than stepping on a cockroach. I wouldn't have had a thing on my conscience."

At that point, whisky and exhaustion nearly took my breath away and I stopped talking. My head ached, my back ached, my face and hands felt scorched beyond redemption and my tongue hurt from chattering.

"Go on, Mr. Frost. What's the matter?"

"Tired," I said, resting my head on the back of the chair.

"Close your eyes," she said.

So I did. Seconds later, fingertips began pushing and knead-ing my temples. Soothing sounds of easy breathing and feminine scents descended, floated into my senses and remained. I could have been a weary child again, content for a mother's touch, more than willing to have my poor mind numbed, ready for peaceful sleep.

Then it stopped. Abruptly.

"No more time for this, Mr. Frost. Keep going. Sun'll be up in a few hours."

Eyelids and mind struggled with consciousness. "What then?" I asked, my voice dulled by weary confusion and not really caring about an answer. Slipping back, I dreamed—of Grace Lynn Rose and an old woman, both nude, on a bench on the Common. I walked to them. The dream ended with an unblushing Grace Lynn Rose introducing a shameless Augusta Crawford.

"Mr. Frost?"

Frightened, undone by the dream, I opened my eyes and saw the woman in the green robe sitting on the brown couch with the yellow pad in her lap.

"Yes. What?"

"Tell the story, Mr. Frost."

I stood and, for a minute or so, walked around the room, trying to make my brain understand sleep couldn't interrupt. "Coffee," I said, taking my mug off the small table beside the chair and motioning to Grace Lynn Rose to fill it.

A moment later, she placed the hot cup in my hands and I sat down again and began to talk. "I stood there in the rain, then decided to leave my car and follow Augusta on foot. I'd be clever. Just like Boston Blackie, I'd stay far enough behind not to be noticed but still near enough to Augusta."

"Her path took us through the older section of downtown, the part that hadn't changed in a hundred years. Some storefront windows held old, dusty display items of another time—old timey baby carriages, tiny fingernail scissors, high-top shoes, shaving mugs and brushes. The wrecking ball got all those old places. Parking lots now."

A sip of coffee burned my mouth and I hesitated. Grace Lynn Rose said nothing but waved me on with a half-circle motion of her pen hand.

"The rain began to ease but that didn't help visibility or the cold, clammy feeling of being wet to the skin," I said. "I kept my distance from Augusta, staying about a half block behind her. Blinded as she was by anger and rain, she never once paused or acknowledged me. Surely if she'd encountered Harry Truman on the sidewalk, she wouldn't have paid attention to him either. I felt thankful for that thought."

Slowly, my mind settled. Details kept coming to mind and I worked hard to put the pictures into words, hoping Grace Lynn Rose could taste the rain on her lips and experience the pounding heart and racing mind that accompanied each of my steps that night.

"Augusta continued down Ricochet Road until she reached the dead traffic light at Raleigh Avenue. When she turned right on

Raleigh, I lost sight of her. So I ran the last few steps to the corner. From there, I saw her standing about the middle of the block, at the door of Willie Harvey's poolroom."

"Poolroom, you said."

"Good place to find him. Bobby's favorite place. He and Champ and their unholy friends convened there evenings. They shot pool and drank beer. And in the summer, when the front door stayed open, they yelled at pretty girls."

Since the rain continued heavy enough to be   concealing, I crossed Raleigh and walked down the opposite sidewalk, stopping directly across from Willie's place."

"And?"

"Augusta knocked. A small, balding man appeared with a flashlight. He held open a screened door—just enough to talk to her. I recognized Willie Harvey right away and stood there in the cold and damp, wondering exactly what they might be saying."

"When Willie Harvey pointed toward the Common, it didn't take a genius to figure that he'd told her where she could find her husband. Augusta turned sharply and headed toward the Common. On the sidewalk across from her, I moved slowly, keeping my eyes on her. But I did notice as I passed in front of the poolroom that men inside had put candles on tables so they could keep playing."

At that point, Grace Lynn Rose left me for the bathroom. In the silence of her absence, I wondered what Augusta might be doing and considered calling Esther Coleman for a report. But automatically now, I decided any news would be bad. Perhaps she had run away again. Visions came to me of Augusta with Bobby Crawford, dancing for Phillip Rayner and sleeping under the plastic with Crazy Wallis Pender.

Why not me?

The bathroom door opened. "Where do we pick up?"

"I don't know," I said, my mind wandering momentarily. "She'd nearly reached the Common, hadn't she?"

Grace Lynn Rose finished off her whisky and resumed her position with pad and pen. She glanced at the Budweiser clock in the kitchen. "It's three-forty five, Mr. Frost. Let's get going. Let's get her to the Common."

What if I wouldn't tell? What then?

I looked down at the gas fire, points of flame in line, no flaring, no crackling, no smell of wood smoke. "Since all the street lights had gone out, darkness covered everything, just like some heavy, black blanket had been thrown over the world. Dark, yes. Impossible, no. In the rain, wind and occasional lightning, I could see Augusta had picked up her pace and I had to trot to maintain sight and direction."

"She stepped on the Common about a minute before I did. We both stopped. She surveyed the landscape, head turning slowly. Abruptly, she started running toward the short pier by the boat ramp. I moved ahead, too, but not as fast. If events unfolded the way I wished, I wanted distance to see. I wanted to see Augusta throw off the spell of Bobby Crawford."

"What happened?"

"Augusta had nearly reached the pier when Bobby Crawford, still a little drunk and wobbly, climbed out of the river and onto the pier. He walked to the edge of the grass, shaking his head like a wet dog. Fool had been swimming in the storm. Only had on under-shorts."

"Then?"

"Lightning flashed everywhere. In the intermittent light, I saw Augusta literally leap up around his chest, kicking and gouging, both hands around his neck. If she'd been strong enough, she would have choked him to death."

Chapter 33

"Bitter, ugly struggle," I said, taking a pull on my whisky. "You've never heard so much screaming, cursing and flesh pounding flesh."

Grace Lynn Rose put down her pen and looked at me. I wondered if my story had prompted a vision in her mind. Could she see that poor girl's hands tearing at Bobby Crawford's face? Could she feel the blows he threw to her stomach and ribs?

"Hungry, Mr. Frost?"

"No," I said.

She rose, walked quickly to the kitchen and returned to the couch with a box of grape-flavored pop tarts. She extracted one, ripped off the covering, took a bite and sat munching while I tried to decide on words to describe the most ghastly moments of my life.

"You hear them say anything?"

"He called her a whore. She called him a son of a bitch."

"Oh." Grace Lynn Rose pushed the last bite of pop tart into her mouth and chewed. When she finished, she spoke again: "That's pretty standard stuff for angry people."

I nodded. I agreed.

"But put yourself where I stood. I'd known Augusta since childhood and never seen her violent. Ever. For a minute or more, I watched, hardly able to accept what I saw. She clawed his bare chest and raked her teeth across one shoulder. In the constant lightning, I saw a little blood on him. It didn't last long in the rain."

"What did you do, Mr. Frost? You haven't said a word about your part in all this. As much as you loved Augusta, surely you got in it. Had the pistol, didn't you?"

Of course I remembered. "Every option raced through my head. Should I step up and shoot Bobby Crawford? Would Augusta break away from him long enough for me to do that? I naively thought of going to them and demanding they stop. If they stepped back from each other, then I could get a clear shot at him."

Memory of thunder, lightning, rain and terror flooded my mind as it had so many times over the years. Smell of blood, smell of death. Even enough rain to float Noah's Ark couldn't have diluted the certainty that Hell itself had descended to the Ransom Town Common. For a minute or more, I sat without speaking, trying to keep emotions under control. I wanted to weep — but not in the presence of a woman eating a grape pop tart.

"Finally Bobby Crawford pried Augusta from around his neck and hit her in the face with his fist. She fell backward, landing on her back. Stretched out flat and breathing hard, she kept her eyes closed and sobbed steadily. He stood looking down on her, smiling, like he'd just decked Joe Louis. With a hand, he wiped blood off his neck and told her he'd kill her if she jumped him again."

By that time, I'd concealed myself behind a large Crepe Myrtle. Anger ate at me, dug at me, formed into searing rage inside me, then disintegrated, reformed and jammed my brain, leaving me to frantic speculation about what I should do. Augusta rolled over, face-down, whimpering like a beaten child. At that moment, fear flowed from me like the streams of water running off the Common and into the river."

"They didn't see you?"

"No. Focused on each other."

"Did you think about Augusta, about protecting her? Did you think about Blithe Tanner? Why didn't you do something?"

Silence. "All my thoughts concentrated on one thing," I said. "Killing Bobby Crawford. I meant to do that. Augusta could just stand aside and I'd do the job. Then she and I could be together again."

"The sky-ripping strokes of lightning shot all round like rockets, suddenly dropping to earth, popping, crackling, illuminating, giving trees ghostly forms. They seemed like risen skeletons, stalking across the Common, looking for me."

"Of course, if all that lightning had converged on Bobby Crawford and reduced him to cinder, quite possibly there would have been no pain for Augusta and me, not to mention justice served for poor Blithe Tanner. The three of us paid terrible prices because of him. Naturally, it didn't work that way."

Grace Lynn Rose smiled at me. "Try hard not to get caught up in all that," she said. "Keep on with the story. This is terrific. Terrific."

I'll never understand how so much agony — more than forty years worth — could be 'terrific.' But I knew what terrific meant to her: Ransom people coming up their walks, morning *Telegraph* stretched between hands, shaking heads in wonder at Grace Lynn Rose's front page headline. How long before I'd see Toby Pugh?

"Before I stepped from behind the Crepe Myrtle, lightning showed me Bobby Crawford standing maybe two feet from Augusta. She stayed on the ground, her left cheek resting in wet grass and red mud. Her breathing had eased. But I could still hear quick gulps for air, sounds which reminded me of final agonies of people who'd died before my eyes.

"Bobby Crawford had lost his breath, too. 'What's the matter with you?' he asked, staggering a little and gasping a lot. 'What you trying to do to me? You know who I am?'

Augusta said nothing.

He laughed. 'Get married, you said. Follow me around, you

said. Anywhere. Cook for me, wash my clothes. Have babies.'

Augusta sat up and tried to wipe her eyes with her hands. 'Death do us part,' she mumbled, her voice breaking in sobs for breath.

'What's that mean?' Bobby Crawford took a step forward. Lightning crashed into the woods on the other side of the river and I saw his face, drawn and menacing, teeth bared, gold-capped tooth catching light, blood seeping from fingernail scratches on his cheeks.

'I'm killing you,' Augusta said suddenly. 'Can't you see I'm killing you?'

'What for?'

'For that girl and me,' she said."

I pushed around in the chair, trying to find a new position to keep some of the heat away and I remembered how that remark shocked me. Watching Augusta tear into Bobby Crawford, I'd honestly doubted her motives amounted to much more than wild jealously. And certainly jealously had it's place in that strange, violent scene on the Common. But I hadn't realized poor Blithe Tanner had touched somebody's heart besides mine.

"Then Bobby turned on the charm. He took the few steps to Augusta and stood silently by her, looking down like the master of the universe. 'She don't matter. Girl like that, do anything for a smile. You don't know any better either. Come on now, I'm going to take you back home. I got to see some people.'"

"She told him no. He told her to come on. She said no. So he grabbed her hair and dragged her toward the street."

Grace Lynn Rose got excited: "Did you do anything? Tell me what you did."

I stood, sidestepped a little to the right and sat on the arm of the big chair. Honesty and a little drunkenness made me want to face her. "I'm not sure what got hold of me. I stepped away from that tree and called his name. 'I'll take her home,' I shouted. That stopped him. He turned and watched me walk toward him. I swear I didn't feel one speck of fear. He started walking toward me, Augusta still in his harsh grip. When we got about ten feet apart, I reached for the pistol and the hammer hung in my pocket."

Anticipation turned Grace Lynn Rose's face beet red.

"A few seconds later, Bobby Crawford dropped Augusta, charged and hit me in the face three or four times. He put me in a headlock so tight I felt my eyes might pop out on the ground. Dazed and choking, I remember how he cursed and dragged me toward the pier. Suddenly, he stopped, stood me up and hit me again. I tumbled backward, hit the ground hard and lay prostrate. The pistol slipped from my pocket. Next thing I knew, he'd pulled me to the end of the pier and pitched me overboard. River water struck my face so hard it made me sick.

Chapter 34

"If it hadn't been for my compulsive fear of swallowing raw sewage and for the War Memorial Fountain, God knows what might have happened to Augusta and me that night."

"In those days, every hamlet and town along the river used it to carry away sewage. Swimming in that stuff may have meant nothing to Bobby Crawford but my heart nearly stopped when I felt water close over my head. Panic jolted me to the surface, brought me to my senses, engaged my pitiful dog paddle and despite the quick current, propelled me toward a cluster of old pilings about twenty feet from the pier."

Grace Lynn Rose wrinkled her nose and shook her head. "Hell of a place to be," she said, taking the point of the pen and jabbing lightly into her hair, scalp-scratching. "How did it smell?"

"How do you think?" I shot back. Jesus, lady.

I finished off my whisky and declined the three-quarters empty bottle when she held it toward me. "Shy, shy. That's what you are, Mr. Frost," she said, laughing lightly.

A little drunk. That's what you are, Miss Rose. The silent thought spread a smile across my lips.

Mix a lot of pain and a little whisky and even old Wiley Frost can smile. But not for long.

She glanced at her notes. "In the river. At the pilings. Head definitely above water."

"Yes," I said, emphasizing with raised tone and an easy, flat-handed slap on the chair's arm. "The lightning went on, crashing all over the sky, illuminating everything. Rain fell in billowing sheets, whipped by a river wind. It took maybe two minutes—from the time I landed in the water—to reach the pilings. Thick slime on the first piling kept me from getting a grip and I slipped off. Kicking and paddling like a wild man, I finally locked both arms around another."

"Did you think you'd drown?"

"Yes," I said. "But I decided very quickly that if I had a choice of being beaten to death by Bobby Crawford or drowning in that river, I'd take the beating."

She looked at me blankly, like the choice could have been too difficult, had she been in my place. She poured a swallow of whisky in her glass and focused attention back on the yellow pad. "What else did you think?"

"Wallowing in that foul water, I thought strategy. First, I had to get out of the water. So, I paddled about five feet from the pilings to a concrete retaining wall directly in front of me. Since the water ran higher than normal, I had no trouble getting my hands on the top of the wall. I edged myself along, hand over hand, creeping down the wall to the opening for the boat ramp, also concrete. Seemed easy enough to just walk up the ramp and onto the Common. But the slime got me again. I spent at least another full minute slipping, scrambling and clawing for traction. Finally, I struck a clear spot with one foot, pushed myself up on the ramp. From there, I got as far as the grass and collapsed."

At that point, she stood, stretched and interrupted: "Back on the Common now. What did you expect to find?"

"Bobby Crawford dragging Augusta around by the hair."

"Then what?"

"Find the pistol. I'd kill him."

She sat down.

❖

Crawl. That's what I did. "Sprawled on soggy ground, blood flowing from a broken nose and lacerated gums, I breathlessly congratulated myself on surviving the river. I lifted my head, trying to catch sight of Augusta or Bobby Crawford. Rain and darkness made visibility almost nonexistent. I could see maybe ten feet. How could I get the pistol to protect Augusta from her husband? Locate the pier, I decided. Keep my eyes and head to the ground, pray he'd not picked it up."

Realizing conclusion had nearly arrived, Grace Lynn Rose nervously pulled at her hair, twisting strands together and gently tugging. Her attention repeatedly shifted between me and the note pad on her lap. "Feeling my way along the retaining wall, I found the pier within a couple of minutes. The pistol had to be in the grass, three or so feet away from the pier. On hands and knees, moving left, moving right, patting the soggy ground, I finally found it. As soon as I got my hand on the grip, I stood, pointed the barrel in front of me, hoping Bobby Crawford might suddenly step where I could see him."

"Determined to shoot."

"Yes," I said.

She pressed: "Convinced you could do it."

"Every bullet in his belly. Pitch him in the river. He'd end up in Pamlico Sound if he didn't hang on a snag."

She smiled. Like she thought I might lack the courage.

"I started walking toward the street, taking each step carefully, trying to see as far ahead as possible, wary of running into a bench or Bobby Crawford. Near the War Memorial Fountain, I saw the two of them, shadow figures moving in a darkness my eyesight could slightly penetrate. He pulled her by one arm, not by her hair. Through the din of the storm, I faintly heard Augusta's cries. She fought him by offering no resistance. So he had to pull dead weight on the ground, slowly and laboriously, like a hundred pound sack of onions."

Grace Lynn Rose slipped to the edge of her seat. I crossed my legs and folded my hands in my lap. "He stopped, leaned down and slapped her on the back of the head. Augusta snatched her arm away from him, sank to the mud, using both hands to cover her head. He kicked at her with a bare foot, saying words I could neither hear nor understand."

"Where'd you have the pistol?"

"In my hand."

"Would it fire wet?"

At the time, I doubted it.

"He hadn't seen me. At about eight feet, he might as well have been sitting on the end of my gun barrel. I eased to one knee, fired two of my six bullets and missed both times. He looked straight at me, then jumped behind a mound of dirt next to an open trench where town crews had installed the fountain's water pipes."

"Augusta?"

"I guess she thought Bobby had a gun so she stayed on the ground, crawling toward me. Through the mud on her face and arms, I could see trickles of blood and swelling around her eyes. Her nose looked a little crooked and surely she'd broken all her fingernails.

"Hand over hand. Pushing ahead with mud-covered bare feet. Not crying exactly. Whimpering, maybe. Groaning a little. From what I could see of her eyes, they seemed fixed in a way that looked like pure determination to me. Survival instinct, no doubt."

"She crawled to you. You comforted her, then carried her in your arms to your car and drove her home. Great stuff!" Grace Lynn Rose's voice broke. I saw tears on her cheeks.

Are histrionics a compliment to good story-telling?

"No. I didn't do that," I said. "There's more. But I'll never forget Augusta scratching toward me. She called my name, you know. Over and over."

Chapter 35

Death.

Many a night, I've laid sleepless in my bed, hearing thumps and grunts and human cries that got lost in the downpour on the Common that night. Painful recollections of what I saw and did have hounded me like a demon's curse come true. Now, sitting across from Grace Lynn Rose, fear caused trembling hands, shaking legs and a dry mouth. The time had come to reveal the most haunting memory of all.

I rose from my chair, stepped forward and got the bottle off the table. My empty glass had turned over by the armchair, so I picked it up and poured three fingers of whisky. "This last part is hard to tell," I said, sipping and speaking in a voice that sounded much like a whine. "I've never told it before. I don't know what to say. I don't know how it'll come out."

Grace Lynn Rose looked at the kitchen clock. Three fifty-five. She mumbled something about a very late makeover for the morning edition, or at least an 'extra.' Not paying much attention, I sat down.

"Go on, Mr. Frost," she urged. "Time. Time. Look at the time."

I swallowed about half the whisky and enjoyed the heat travelling to my stomach. "Street lights came on," I said. Visibility improved but rain put a dull, halo effect around each lamp, leaving images a blur. Lightning had stopped. Augusta crawled. Bobby Crawford bobbed around behind the mound of dirt, trying to decide which way to escape, I thought. His head shifted left and right, up and down, like a silly kid playing hide and seek. Since I had the pistol, I had no idea he'd charge me."

"Son of a bitch," Grace Lynn Rose whispered.

I kept talking: "Still holding the pistol, I'd moved toward her on hands and knees. Bobby Crawford had been carrying a gun. I wanted to catch her hand and pull her behind a tree so she'd have cover if he started shooting. My weary mind demanded I think of everything. Or at least try."

"But I made a mistake. Augusta got close enough to hold out a mud-covered hand. Taking my eyes off Bobby Crawford's roost behind the dirt pile, I pushed the pistol into my right front pants pocket, crawled forward and grasped her wrist. An instant later, he fell on me, slashing my head and face with fists, elbowing my back, spitting and cursing. He even bit the back of my left leg. But when he swung down on my neck with a forearm, my brains became mush. Voices and movements around me seemed distant, hollow-sounding, unintelligible. Any second, I expected a final blow that would send me to oblivion. But it didn't come and I opened my eyes enough to see Augusta Crawford, dangling head down over her husband's shoulder, screaming for me and clawing at his bare back."

Perhaps five minutes passed before brain and body reengaged. My eyelids fluttered involuntarily and strange, cramping spasms ripped up and down my left leg, the one with the bite. Did that make any difference to Grace Lynn Rose? For getting myself in a mess like that, could anyone offer sympathy?

"When I finally came to my senses," I continued, "I didn't see anybody and assumed Bobby Crawford had hauled her home. God knows what would happen to her when he got her there. So I got to my feet and took a few steps to the left. Since I felt only a little pain from the blows, I took more steps and finally found the nerve to walk. On the sidewalk, I looked back at the rain still falling on the Common and cursed myself for failing so miserably."

"How did you fail?"

Such a stupid question.

"Well," I began slowly. "I failed because I didn't intervene soon enough when Augusta and Bobby fought down by the pier. I failed because I got thrown in the river. I failed because I shot at him and missed. I failed because I let him beat me up again and take Augusta."

I paused. "Anything else?"

She continued taking notes, never offering a comment. But she did nod, signaling me to go on.

"Then I saw them — at the War Memorial Fountain — just to my right, maybe twenty feet away, right at the edge of a streetlight's reach. With so much mud on them, at first I could hardly tell one from the other. Finally I recognized Augusta's form. She sat with her back to the mound of dirt. Bobby, crosslegged beside the open trench, faced her. He talked, she listened. He wiped some of the mud away from around his eyes and laughed. Augusta didn't smile, didn't frown, didn't move. Then all Hell broke loose again."

My last remark made the reporter so nervous she stood, paced a little between the sofa and the coffee table, then sat again. "Now somebody dies," she whispered.

"Now somebody dies," I repeated. "I stepped off the sidewalk, dropped to the ground and scooted on hands and knees as near to them as I could, trying to stay out of any fragments of light on the grass. Well-shadowed, I crawled within twelve feet or so and stopped to watch them."

"He had his eyes on her but he kept inching forward. Finally, he got close enough to reach her. He took her by the shoulders and pulled her toward him. She resisted, pushed back at him, threw him off balance so he had to catch himself with one arm to keep from falling backwards. That's when I took the pistol from my pocket."

The picture came back to me as vividly as any memorable cinematic death scene: The Japanese sniper's bullet that killed John Wayne's character in "Sands of Iwo Jima." The bloody finale of "Duel in the Sun" with Jennifer Jones.

"I knew I had four bullets left and figured two might shoot him down. I'd use the other two to finish him if he still had breath. Suddenly, Bobby stood and waved his arms, cursed Augusta and put his foot in her chest, pushing her back against the dirt pile. I fired the pistol, clipped his left ear and enjoyed every second of his squealing and hollering. The second shot headed for his belly but he twisted, like a football running back, and disappeared into the trench. Two seconds later, he lurched halfway out of the hole, grabbed Augusta's ankle and pulled her in with him."

Grace Lynn Rose wiped her forehead with a Kleenex.

"For maybe two minutes, I didn't move. I suppose I expected him to come up shooting, charge me again or throw Augusta's dead body out of the trench. I crawled forward, determined to end the horror with gun blazing. I'd reach in the hole, yank Augusta out of the way and shoot that bastard between the eyes. The power of that vision brought me to my feet and sent me hurtling toward the trench. I reached the edge, stopped and pointed the gun barrel straight down and snapped back the hammer.

"What did you see?"

"Augusta on her back. Bobby Crawford squirming around on top of her. He was clutching her throat with one hand to hold her down. With the other, he was trying his best to pull her legs apart."

"She's struggling."

"Yes," I said.

"What did you think?"

I paused and finished my whisky. "My mind told me the obvious: If I let loose with the pistol, I'd likely hit Augusta. The pistol shook in my hand. I aimed and re-aimed, cried and cursed, sank to my knees and begged deliverance."

❖

Grace Lynn Rose looked at the clock. "How much more?"
I stared at her, exasperated.

"Go on. Quickly."

"I heard them shouting. Parrot voices above the sound of the rain. "I kept the pistol pointed into the trench, trying to get a fix on Bobby Crawford's head. Augusta pushed and shoved while he struck blows to her knees and tried to get one leg between hers. Suddenly, the whole scene changed: Augusta threw one foot against the side of the trench, pushed hard and twisted Bobby on his back. She beat at his face with both fists but I finally had a clear shot. The gun never fired, though, because the trench wall caved in and sent me down into the hole with them. Gun in hand, I found myself struggling for breath under a small avalanche of mud."

"My God," she said, eyes nearly bursting from their sockets, voice shrill and impatient.

"At first, I thought my life had ended. Quite frankly, after what I'd seen, I felt no frustration about not living out a full life. But the old instincts kicked in, those feelings about protecting Augusta that had gotten me a mouthful of muck and a cold, cold blackness. I held my breath, pushed hard with both hands and broke through the mud that covered my head. Lying on my back, I wiggled my feet and kicked as hard as I could. In a few seconds, I freed both legs and wobbled to my knees."

"Why didn't Augusta die there?"

"I dug her out with my hands. She was nearly unconscious when I pulled her up on the grass and moved her maybe five feet away from the trench. It took her a few seconds to clear her head and understand what had happened. By the time I got back to the edge of the trench, one hand had emerged from the mud and I saw another scratching for clearance. Bobby Crawford lived. He just wouldn't go away."

"About that time, Augusta came up and stood beside me. When she saw his hands, she jumped back into the trench, grasped the one to her left and pulled. 'Wiley. Get down here and help me,' she screamed. Slowly, I eased into the layer of mud covering Bobby Crawford and took the other hand. We pulled. Half his face

appeared.   Mouth, nose, eyes. He saw us. He laughed.   First a
sputtering. Then a cackle. Then heavy laughter — accented by a half-
scream, hard, deep breaths and a lot of spitting. He shook his head,
trying to throw mud from his eyes."

"'You whore,' he said, looking squarely at Augusta and
opening wide to show his gold-edged front tooth. She dropped his
hand, lurched to the right, clawed at grass and tree roots until she
pushed herself over the remaining trench wall and onto the grass."

"That left me in the mud with Bobby Crawford. His left
hand firmly gripped my left hand. I told him to let go my hand. If
he let go, would I get him out? Sure, I said. Just let go. He did. I
climbed up on the grass. Ten seconds later, the rest of the trench
caved in and swallowed him."

Chapter 36

Bobby Crawford lost his life.

Augusta lost her mind.

Over the years, I've come to understand that mad night on the Common — in terms as stark, emphatic and unbelievable as death itself. That horrible conflict left me believing experience alone is enough to make the cup of insensibility tempting.

As soon as the dirt stopped falling, self-esteem, and even downright arrogance surged through me like wild water against delicate shoreline. No longer did I feel intimidated. Wiley Frost found himself to be an instant, self-made, self-proclaimed knight who had rescued a tender damsel from more than a little distress. I had never been so proud.

Grace Lynn Rose looked at me, a blank, shocked expression on her face. "After all that hell, you spent over forty years waiting for this woman. You waited for a chance at a normal life with her— home, contentment, old age?"

"Yes," I said, glaring back at her. "But I'm done now."

"You sure?"

I nodded. "Not much time left. Augusta's waiting for Bobby Crawford, now and forever. Just taking a little time out for men like Wallis Pender." My words carried a bitter edge I didn't try to suppress.

We sat in silence for a minute. "Finish," she said.

"My interlude of glory didn't last long. Doing all that mental breast-beating caused me not to think about Augusta or particularly care where or how she might be. I knew Bobby Crawford lay buried under the mud, dead of a crushed chest, if not suffocation. But I didn't understand about Augusta until I became aware of a presence on my right. Never have I seen such a bedraggled human being. Shredded blouse. Holding her skirt with both hands to keep it from falling around her ankles. By then, the rain had washed her face clear of mud and blood but in the street lamp glow I could see deep scratches and dark bruises forming on her cheeks, neck, and under her eyes."

"How about you?"

"Worse shape, I expect. My nose had stopped bleeding, teeth ached, neck throbbed. The bite on my leg stung. As a parting gesture, I thought Bobby Crawford might have given me rabies."

Forcing a laugh, she shot a quick glance at the clock.

I turned my head and looked into the fire. "Every event of that night has played through my mind incessantly in the last forty years. But only one recollection tells me the sum total of human folly: Augusta and me, there on the Common, gazing at a long stretch of loose earth that should have ended the turmoil."

"How did she react? What did she say?"

"Nothing. Not a tear. Eyes sightless, fixed ahead, occasionally blinking," I said. "Her attention didn't waver from the cave-in. She made no sound or movement. For some inexplicable, ungodly reason, dear Augusta had battled Bobby Crawford for her soul and won. But her heart and mind lay buried with him."

Grace Lynn blinked several times, glanced at the white, plastered ceiling then back at me. "Tell me the rest."

"Rain slowed to a drizzle. Fog settled across the Common. Everything appeared perfectly dreary—just like Augusta and me. When I realized what had happened to her, my high opinion of

Wiley Frost suddenly didn't seem so important. Of course, I'd hoped she'd be proud of me, perhaps even a little awed that I'd rid her life of Bobby Crawford. She might have thanked me. She might have kissed my cheek. We might have walked away from the Common, arm in arm like lovers, never looking back."

"You got her home."

"Yes. I still had the pistol in my hand. I put that back in my pocket, carried and dragged her the first few blocks. We stayed in shadows to avoid anybody who might be wandering around that late. By the time we reached Pickett Street, she was steadier, didn't stumble as much. I took her arm and guided her along. Like leading a blind woman.

"We made it to my parked car. I opened the door and shoved the pistol under the driver's seat. Five minutes later, we'd reached the foot of her front porch steps. I knew she kept a key in a concrete flower pot. Fumbling around in the pot, I tried to decide what to do. Call the police? Call a doctor for Augusta? Finally, I got my hand on the key, got her up the steps. The second I stuck the key in the lock, I knew Bobby Crawford's fate would be my secret to keep. Forever, if I chose. Certainly, I had nothing to fear from the only witness who stood a foot away from me, gazing into space."

The newspaper reporter nodded in agreement.

"I led her up the stairs and to the large bathroom just down from her room. Standing next to the shower, I stripped away what remained of her clothing and mine. I maneuvered her into the shower, bathed her, washed her hair and did the same for myself. Dirt clogged the drain several times. I worked one foot across the drain's grill, forcing mud through tiny holes. We stepped onto the bath mat and she shivered as I dried her with a towel. When I helped her on with a nightgown, she smiled, slightly. But her eyes never focused on me. She looked past me, into some dimension I couldn't possibly enter or understand."

"You left."

"Yes," I said. "I took her to her room, put her in bed, pulled covers up around her neck, kissed her and told her good night. She didn't say a word. I turned out the light but left her door cracked and a hall light burning."

To finish the story and to relieve my aching back, I stood, walked to the kitchen counter and leaned against it, still facing Grace Lynn Rose.

"The rest is fairly simple," I explained. "I cleaned the bathroom, rolled up her clothes and mine, grabbed Mr. Morefield's huge, old overcoat from a closet and left by the back door. I walked barefoot through the alley and around to my car, drove to a town trash can in front of April's Drug Store, dumped the clothes and went back to the Common."

Her eyes widened, mouth dropped open a little.

"I searched all over and finally found Bobby Crawford's pistol and uniform on the grass off to one side of the pier. Threw the pistol in the river."

Then I lied to her: "I tied the uniform up around a big rock. Threw that overboard, too."

"The Army cap?"

"On the bottom," I said, voice still firm. Surely God would get me for so many lies.

Grace Lynn Rose stopped writing.

Silence.

"That's the story?"

"Yes."

"Nothing more?"

"No," I said.

"Champ Crawford?"

"Pity."

"Phillip Rayner?"

"Another pity."

"Regrets?"

I turned away toward the fire.

Grace Lynn Rose stood, tucked her yellow pad under her arm as she walked toward me. She stopped, looked me in the eye. For several seconds, neither of us spoke.

"Good night, Mr. Frost," she whispered, zipping her robe. An instant later, she stepped away from me, into her bedroom, and closed the door.

"Good night," I said to no one. Then I walked back to the chair, sat, took a deep breath and again watched flames dance before my eyes.

"Wiley? Wiley Frost?" The voice cracked my consciousness. Fireplace heat and the unmerciful doorbell rattled my groggy brain, leaving me to assume I'd awakened in a fiery dungeon.

"Come open this door, Wiley. Quick! Can't you hear me? How much trouble you in now? What if she gets pregnant? How's an old man like you going to explain a thing like that?"

Aubrey Winslow's last sentences snapped me wide awake, my eyes opening like those of a pop-eyed frog. It took me maybe a half-minute to clear my thinking. Strange surroundings, all right. But I knew nothing about anybody being pregnant.

I got to my feet. Empty whisky bottle on the table. Wall pictures of John Lennon, Jerry Falwell, and even the wild geese seemed alive, all eyes on me. At that moment, it didn't matter which being in which picture had judged me foul, worthy of the Devil's attention. I had to stop the doorbell and Aubrey's shouting.

The bolt popped back and I opened the door. There he stood, in his pretend detective's felt hat and trenchcoat, mouth half-open, grinding away on the few teeth he had left. I recognized Alvin Hooper, a City Cab driver, standing just behind him. He never looked at me but glanced side to side, like a lookout for a bank robbery.

Aubrey stepped inside and half-turned to Alvin: "Go on back to the cab. I'll get him straight and we'll be there in a minute."

Then he pushed the door shut, looked around the living room, and started on me.

"For God's sake, Wiley. What you doing here? Ain't you got no sense at all? This woman is dangerous and here you're carousing with her."

"You don't know anything," I said.

He pointed. "Just look here, then. Whisky's gone and the

couch's got pieces of paper wrappers all over it. Looks like confetti. There's been a mighty frenzy here."

I felt my face redden, kept silent, and quickly staggered to the bathroom. When the first slap of cold water hit my face, my brain finally engaged and I realized Grace Lynn Rose must have left the apartment. Without speaking to Aubrey, I grabbed a towel from a rack by the sink, patted my face dry and stepped around to the bedroom's open doorway. Bed still made. Robe on the floor. Of course, she'd gone to the newspaper. Soon enough, reaction from her story would dog my heels, maybe even turn me into a convict!

"How'd you find me?" I folded the towel and put it back on the rack.

"Solid detective work," Aubrey said. "Found your car. Followed tracks up here."

I shook my head in disbelief.

Aubrey gave me one of his know-it-all looks. "You walk heavy on your heels," he said. Then he fixed his eyes on mine, pushed his chin out a little, daring me to disagree.

"Where's my jacket?"

"On the floor by the big chair," Aubrey said.

I took three steps, scooped up the jacket with one hand, stuck my arms through the sleeves, pulled up the zipper and faced him. "I told her everything. She knows about Bobby Crawford's dying. When she's through, I won't have anything to keep to myself."

"Wiley, I swear, that's the craziest thing I ever heard you say. How many times have I told you don't ever admit to nothing. Besides, you didn't tell me first."

"What do you want to know?"

With one hand, Aubrey snatched off his hat, dabbed at his forehead with a handkerchief and put a cigarette in his mouth. He whipped the Zippo from his trenchcoat pocket. He toyed with the lighter, running his fingers over it, opening and shutting the top. When he finally lit the cigarette, I thought I'd choke.

"No time for telling stories," Aubrey said, his mouth drawn down in a frown. His look made me feel neglectful that I hadn't told him first.

"I got to go to Augusta's house."

"You're going to Reno, Nevada," he said. "Don't even try to argue with me."

In the back seat of the cab, as we wound through downtown, I told Aubrey I didn't disagree with running away from Ransom, but needed to see Augusta. He heard the first part and smiled. He listened no further. Neither did Alvin Hooper. Both kept quiet all the way past the Methodist Church and onto Pine View Valley Avenue.

I pleaded: "Understand me, Aubrey. I don't like hiding. But if I have to, I'll go to Reno. But I need time. Need to stay here long enough to know if the newspaper's going to save me or put me in jail. Just me. Augusta doesn't need saving."

"Ain't no time left, Wiley." Aubrey, sitting beside me, growled and rolled down the window to spit. Alvin nodded his head like he agreed.

"Take me to Augusta's," I said, using the most emphatic tone I could muster. "At least let me see her, try to explain what I said to the newspaper. Even say goodbye. Maybe she'll understand some of it. If she doesn't, I'll still know I tried to do the right thing."

For a minute or so, Aubrey didn't speak. He fiddled with his shirt pocket, got out another cigarette, lit it and blew smoke all over the cab. Both my eyes filled with tears and poor Alvin Hooper coughed like he'd just sucked in a full load of diesel smoke.

Aubrey took off his hat, rolled down the window to let smoke escape and turned to me. "Wiley, if I take you to Augusta's you're going to miss the plane to Reno," he said softly. He paused, dropped his chin slightly. "If I let you do that, I'd be doing you wrong."

"I don't want to go to Reno now Aubrey."

Alvin twisted around to look at Aubrey then turned back to the wheel. "I can't do this all day," he muttered, just loud enough for the two of us in the back seat to hear.

"Turn off on the Raleigh Road," Aubrey said, pushing with

his big feet to sit up straight in his seat.

"No," I said, calmly. "Get me a paper."

"Raleigh road," he said to Alvin. "I'll give you fifty dollars to make the airport in exactly ninety minutes."

I ignored Aubrey, handed Alvin two fifties and motioned for him to stop at the Jiffy Market ahead on the right.

Out of the car and fumbling for change at the newspaper machine, I heard pathetic exasperation in Aubrey's voice. "Alvin, Alvin, Alvin!" Silently, I exulted in being the kind of masterful businessman Alvin Cooper understood.

"War Hero Lost in Accident," bellowed the heavy, black streamer across the top. A subhead elaborated: "Ransom's Wiley Frost Saved Augusta Crawford from Death in Cave-In." Quickly scanning, I realized Grace Lynn Rose had again twisted nearly everything I told her. According to her, Augusta and Bobby Crawford had stumbled into the trench, trying to get home in the rain. She wrote that Wiley Frost said he happened along and saved Augusta Crawford but could not rescue her husband. "Frost told *The Telegraph* he never explained Bobby Crawford's death to authorities for fear his well-known, long-time friendship with Mrs. Crawford might trigger misunderstanding and scandal."

Alvin Hooper started the car. Aubrey took a last puff on his cigarette and flipped it out the window. He rolled up the window slowly. When he had the glass in place, he rummaged in the side pocket of his coat, extracted a hundred dollar bill, a ten and two ones. He handed them across the seat to Alvin Hooper. "Raleigh Road," he mumbled.

I opened my wallet, got a hundred dollar bill, two twenties and a ten. Alvin Hooper accepted the money in silence. "Pickett Street," I said.

"Shit. I got no more money," Aubrey lamented. He stared straight ahead, most of the color out of his face.

"It doesn't matter, Aubrey."

A few minutes later, the dingy cab stopped before Augusta's

house. Aubrey kept looking forward, his eyes almost fixed.

Nothing left to say. So I got out of the cab; walked up the sidewalk. At the door, I rang the bell. Augusta, in a charcoal sweater, long, gray skirt, rolled-over white socks and black and white oxfords, opened the door. A bright, white ribbon adorned her graying hair.

We stood in silence. Then I half-turned and waved to Aubrey. I saw him look my way through the coating of grime on the window glass, raise his hand and smile tentatively. An instant later, the cab rattled away down Pickett Street.

I turned to Augusta.

Her tone so low and soft I could barely hear, she said, "I had no idea you'd be coming to see me today. Please, come in. Robert Lee'll get some lemon punch. I'll show you a new painting Father brought from Charlotte."

Then she moved closer, eyes suddenly wide and focused, face turned up to mine, and whispered, "That is you, Wiley -- isn't it?"

"Yes," I said, a quiver in my voice. Then I stepped inside and followed Augusta toward the hall and into the long, gray shadows of her solitude.